C000302586

Bouch
Through my Eyes

Bouch
Through my Eyes

Mark Boucher

with Neil Manthorp

Jonathan Ball Publishers
Johannesburg & Cape Town

All rights reserved.

No part of this publication may be reproduced or transmitted, in any form or by any means, without prior permission from the publisher or copyright holders.

© in text: Mark Boucher and Neil Manthorp, 2013
© in photographs: as credited

First published in 2013 by
JONATHAN BALL PUBLISHERS
a division of Media24 Limited
PO Box 33977
Jeppestown
2043

ISBN 978-1-86842-590-7
Also available as an ebook
ISBN 978-1-86842-591-4

Design and typesetting by Triple M Design, Johannesburg
Cover by Michiel Botha
Cover photo by Morne van Zyl
Statistical profile compiled by Andrew Samson
Set in 10,75/15pt Utopia Std
Printed and bound by Paarl Media

Twitter: www.twitter.com/JonathanBallPub
Facebook: www.facebook.com/pages/Jonathan-Ball-Publishers/298034457992
Blog: http://jonathanball.bookslive.co.za/

Contents

Foreword by Johann Rupert

My love for sport is there for all to see. My first love, cricket, as well as golf, rugby – and many others. I am a supporter, a participant and, of course, a sponsor, so it should be no surprise that I have formed close associations and friendships with many great sportsmen over the years. Mark Verdon Boucher is most certainly among the greatest of them.

He began his career as a very young man and I watched him develop as a cricketer and a person over many years. It was from a distance at first, before we came to know each other. Real bonding occurred late one night in the West Indies when I took the blame for being the host of a late-night party!

As he admits with such honesty in this reflection on his life, it can be difficult for young international sportsmen to stay in touch with the real world while they are travelling and living in the largely artificial one that is created for them. Bridging the gap between the worlds and developing interests outside the sports environment is not only important for the individuals, but it also makes them better sportsmen. Almost all the best and most enduring sportsmen are those with the most balanced perspective on life and the most rounded personalities. There are some exceptions, but they simply prove the rule. Mark is so aware of all of this now, and admits that he was not early on his career. Most importantly, he would like to assist and advise other young sportsmen to learn from his own experiences. It is a genuine and generous objective.

Mark throws himself into everything he does with complete commitment. Not only is he willing to learn, but he has the humility to ask questions and the aptitude to absorb information. I believe he may even have a head for business in a couple of years' time!

I allowed him to 'steal' a membership from me to Leopard Creek. It would have been too cruel to give Jacques membership there and not Mark. It would have been a lifetime of torture for him. But the main reason I wanted Mark to be there is because of the intensity with which he plays the game and competes. There is no greater pleasure in the game than beating someone as determined as Mark. And why would I want to deny myself that pleasure?

Johann Rupert
Chairman, Richemont and Remgro

Foreword by Jaques Kallis

Mark Boucher is my best friend, but that wasn't always the case. I hadn't had a great Cape Schools season in 1993, and then Wynberg came up against Selborne. I'd heard a bit about this Boucher kid – then I nicked my first ball to him. As I walked off I heard him saying: 'Jacques who? Kallis who? Thought this guy could play!' Then I saw my dad's car driving away. I thought: 'And now ...?' I played the rest of the game, but when it finished Pops wasn't there. I was given the message: 'Your father said that if you're going to play a kak shot like that, then you can find your own way home.' It's a long walk from Wynberg to Lakeside. I had to find my own way home. It was a decent ball but, as Dad said, you need to make a plan to a decent ball.

The next time I came across Bouch was at the National Academy. We didn't click – we didn't spend much time together. He was always out partying. I thought he was an idiot!

The next time was at Newlands when Border played Province. He scored two 50s against us and played really well. I think it was the first time that people started noticing him. I still wasn't sure about him, but I could see he could play. You couldn't help admiring his guts against the Western Province pace attack on a green wicket.

Then he came to Pakistan to take over from Dave Richardson and we became roommates. I wasn't sure what to expect. A day after he arrived I was admitted to hospital for an appendix operation. He couldn't have been more caring when the guys came to visit. He was the new kid, and he was respectful, but he didn't hold back in his support. We certainly clicked from then on.

My sister Janine stayed with Mark's folks when she was posted to East London for her physiotherapy community service after Dad died. She stayed in Bouchy's room. He wasn't there, obviously, but he likes to tease me that my sister has slept in his bed. When she had her own place it was just down the road, so she still spent every Thursday evening with Mark's family. So we both became close to the Boucher family.

We were in Bangalore when Hansie approached us, not that we realised what was happening. We laughed it off as one of Hansie's jokes. Mark realised the potential seriousness of it later and explained why we had to mention it at the King Commission.

It was a surprise to some people outside the team when he was appointed as Polly's vice-captain, but it made sense to the players. He was the sort of character people followed and even the senior players respected his opinion. And he has very strong opinions. In 18 years he's never admitted to me that he was wrong about anything, let alone apologised for it. He will always find a way to be a little bit right! What you see is what you get. He is upfront, straightforward and honest. I enjoy people like that, but there are others who don't. Of course he overstepped occasionally and pissed people off, but don't we all? The clever guys learnt to walk away from a discussion with a smile on their faces once they'd proved him wrong – because he would never admit it!

To be a successful coach, captain or leader you have to realise that you can't treat everybody the same. It takes different things to make different people tick. Mark used to have a 'one size fits all' view and approach, but there is no doubt that he learnt to change as his career progressed. He was always honest, but he learnt to be softer as the years went by.

He was incredibly valuable to the bowlers – and he had the most knowledgeable hands in the world. He could tell what sort of mood you were in by the way the ball landed in his hands. He'd catch a couple and then say: 'OK, what's wrong?' He could pick the away-swinger from the in-swinger before we were even in our delivery stride. He'd say: 'If I can see it, the batsmen certainly will. You've got to hide it better.' We were in awe of those eyes.

He still insists that the fastest spell he ever kept to was bowled by me. I'm pretty sure that's 'mate talk'! It was against Sri Lanka in the 1999 World Cup. There's no doubt I 'clicked' that day. I was given the new ball and we bowled them out for 110 defending 199. There were no speed guns in those days and I always tended to hit the keeper's gloves harder than expected, so maybe he was caught off guard. We were still pretty new to each other back then. Or maybe he was just standing too close. We'll never know, because once he's said something he sticks by it. He was still saying it was the fastest spell he kept to after he retired! And I love him for it.

He was so full of energy during the Switzerland camp before the 2012 England tour. He had overcome the desperate disappointment of missing the 2011 World Cup and had been completely reinvigorated and reenergised. I imagined it was like a marathon runner entering the stadium to complete the final lap. He had a smile on his face at every stage; he was happy and at peace with the fact that the tour of England was going to be his final lap. My heart skipped a few beats when I saw him so fit and enthusiastic. I had absolutely no doubt whatsoever that he was going to leave the game as he deserved to, as a champion.

It's true that I instinctively wanted to accompany him back to Cape Town once we realised the true extent and seriousness of the injury. The tour suddenly didn't seem so important any more. He was grateful for the gesture but then gave me quite a talking-to about not being stupid. 'We came here to become world Test champions, and you're going to make sure we do,' he said. He then explained that his parents and girlfriend, Carmen, would be able to take care of him.

It's good to think that you have a friend to turn to, for any reason or at any time, but I never really needed to turn to Mark – because he was already there. He knew when he was needed and there was nothing, literally, he wouldn't do for a friend. It was a bit awkward when he spoke up for me, after I was left out of the Proteas' T20 side, and was then fined and given a severe reprimand. I asked him, please, to keep his mouth closed next time. But that would go against his instincts. Sometimes he would urge me to speak my mind, get things off my chest. I would tell him not to be so spontaneous and instinctive, to think about things and calm down before he spoke. Although there are some fairly obvious shared interests, as personalities we are quite different. We enjoyed learning from each other – and there was a lot of laughter.

For some people, a friendship is defined by always having something to talk about. For us, it is about being just as comfortable when there is nothing to talk about. We never got into each other's space when we roomed together on tour and never felt the need to make small talk.

We have various business interests together, including our wine label – The Innings – but I have a sense there will be a few more once I've joined Mark among the ranks of the retired. I hope to accompany him on many more rhino expeditions in the future and to take his money, again, on many more golf courses around the world. In return, I already have a few coaching tasks lined up for him at my Scholarship Foundation.

Thanks for everything, Bouch. It's been a fantastic journey together, but it's just the beginning.

Jacques Kallis

Introduction

There are many historical and statistical accounts of my career, so I see no need to add to them here. It has been said of me that I tell a good story, and there is no doubt I have a few to tell from a 15-year career in international cricket.

My sense of history and of the 'relevance' of the cricket that took place during my career is naturally subjective. I have welcomed the opportunity for all of those involved in my career, from a playing, administrative and personal capacity, to have their say in this book. But, for me, it is simply an opportunity to recount some of the stories and events that occurred.

It feels peculiar to write a book about my life at the age of just 36. I have lived a fabulous life, but in many ways I am aware that it is just beginning.

Nothing gives me greater pleasure than having a braai with friends and chatting about the ways of the world and the direction our lives are taking. So pull up a chair, pour yourselves a drink and join me for a chat about who I am, where I came from, and what I have seen and learnt about cricket and life in the last 20 years.

We start from my earliest days as a sports-mad youngster, so it's longer than 20 years! And we end, of course, with the injury that cost me most of the sight in my left eye and ended my career shortly before I had intended to retire anyway.

Do I have a message? Is there something I would like you to take away from reading this book? No. But if there is some knowledge that we may share, or a lesson or two that may be of interest (usually learnt the hard way by me), then that would be a happy bonus.

I hope you enjoy the read. I've certainly enjoyed the journey.

But it is not the end. It is just the beginning

Mark Boucher
October 2013

9 July 2012

The days of trying to make warm-up games competitive were long gone. We were strongly focused on getting what we needed out of the two-day game against Somerset. The bowlers wanted to bowl a certain number of overs and the batsmen wanted an hour or two at the crease.

Taunton is a pretty ground, like many of the smaller venues in England. The town is also a perfect, low-key place to start an important, high-profile tour. It was to be, effectively, the World Championship of Test cricket. After 15 years of touring the world as a professional, I was more 'ready' and excited for this tour than any other. I'd made peace with the fact that it was going to be my last series before I retired from international cricket.

The real world could wait a bit longer, though. Instead of making plans for the future, I had thrown myself into training and preparation like never before. Coach Gary Kirsten had given me his complete support and had enough respect to plan my exit strategy with me. I was happier than I had been for several years. This was a tour I was going to experience to the fullest. There had been too many times when I hadn't appreciated or savoured the moments and memories enough. Not just 'big' moments or victories, but just walking out to play Test cricket in front of 20 000 people. Nothing was going to escape me this time.

The game started uneventfully in the morning session, although it was clear that we were a bit rusty. But we reminded ourselves that it was about finding rhythm rather than statistics.

After lunch we were back in the field. The overcast skies darkened a bit more and it started to rain lightly. I had glasses on so I took them off and quickly signalled to the change room that I wanted a helmet. Imran Tahir came on and bowled a googly to one of the tail-enders (Gemaal Hussain) and it went through his defence.

I felt an immediate and immense pain in my eye. I pulled my gloves off and lay on the ground, covering my face. I'll never forget turning around to see who was there and trying to gauge how serious it was. I saw Jacques out of the corner of my eye – my good eye. I couldn't tell how he was reacting. He never gives much away ...

I tried to open my other eye and I couldn't; everything was just black. I stood up and felt a bit wobbly. I looked down at my glove, my white inner glove, expecting to see blood. When it came away without any red I tried to figure out what had happened. It didn't make any sense.

I saw some clear mucus on the glove, but I couldn't work out where it came from. I couldn't see anything out of the eye. The first sense of panic started, but it was from the fear of the unknown. When you are injured the first things you want to know are diagnosis and prognosis. I wanted our physiotherapist Brandon Jackson or Doc Moose (Dr Mohammed Moosajee) to run out and say, 'It's a cut, you'll need stitches, but you'll be OK.'

Something serious had happened, and I was scared and confused. My world was shrinking – I could only see half of it. AB de Villiers was fielding at cover and he came rushing over to help. When he looked at me his face changed dramatically and he turned away with an instinctive 'oooh'. It was my first confirmation that something was badly wrong. Many weeks later, AB told me he thought he had seen a black pupil running down my cheek. I didn't know about that at the time. Fortunately.

Brandon ran onto the field and, putting my arm around his shoulder, started helping me off. I was walking fine although I was beginning to shut down mentally. The shock was setting in. Suddenly it was like my legs had been cut off and I'd been shot by a sniper at the same time. I could feel nothing below my waist, let alone in my feet. I dropped to the ground like a brick.

I was carried off. They took me upstairs, removed my pads and put shoes on me. My eyes were closed the whole time. They put me into a wheelchair and took me to the hospital. I still didn't open my eyes. I was too scared and didn't know what to expect. I was in bad shock. I didn't want to think – or couldn't.

In the last few moments before I left the ground, I'd heard a couple of people in the crowd say 'Hope you get well soon, Mark.' It didn't sink in straightaway, but, as I lay on my back, in the hours before the surgery, I knew it was all over. There had been something in the tone of those voices. It was done. I knew there were major issues ahead. Although I clung to an outside hope that it might not be as bad as I feared, I knew deep down that it was finished – the tour, at the very least. But if the tour was over, what else was there? My dream for the coming six months had been to finish international cricket on my terms and then to make a contribution for the Cape Cobras. Everything was over. I didn't know for sure, but I *knew*.

Jacques Kallis

He always had either glasses or a helmet on – sometimes both – when keeping to the spinners. But it was overcast and the game was drifting. It was a meaningless game anyway.

When he went down I thought: 'Jeez, Bouch, I know it's a warm-up game and you want to get off the field, but get up now; it's been long enough.' But he stayed down longer than normal and I knew that there was something wrong. He took his hand off his face to check for blood, but there was just some white stuff on it, and something black. I knew it was trouble. I turned away and thought I might faint. I'm very weak like that. I walked away and tried to breathe. When I saw him collapse a second time I knew it was extremely serious.

5

I was not out at the end of the day, but I told Gary I wouldn't be playing the second day of the game. I spent as much time at the hospital as I could that night and then spent the following day with him.

I arrived at the hospital and was given a sedative. I was numb with shock and fear. Bizarrely, the doctor, Jonathan Rossiter, turned out to be from East London. He was calm, reassuring and professional. If only we hadn't been chatting in those circumstances.

He explained that it was a serious situation. 'We are going to operate,' he said, 'but we can't do it yet because you have just had lunch, so we need six hours for that to settle. We are going to go in and see what we can do.' Then he said: 'You must understand it is very serious. I have to be honest with you … I don't think you are ever going to see out of the eye again.'

It was almost a relief to hear the words. All those fears were present in my thoughts. To hear them confirmed was a weight off my mind. I signed the papers I needed to sign and he said they would fix me up as best they could and send me back to Cape Town to see what the specialists there would say.

When he left, I was truly on my own for the first time, and I was broken. I was crying. For the first half an hour I didn't know what to think; it was like I was staring at myself through tunnel vision. Where do I go from here? Everything I had known in my adult life was gone.

Doc Moosajee was outside going through the logistics and signing a mass of forms for me, as I couldn't do it. It helped a lot that he was there, but it didn't change the feeling of helplessness. Wayne Bentley and Riaan Müller were outside, too. They are great men – real unsung, backroom heroes. But there was nothing they could do for me.

I lay very still for around half an hour, eyes still closed but with tears pouring down my cheeks. This cannot be happening to me, I thought. Yes, it can. It *has* happened. How would it affect my life? Mountain biking … would that still be possible? Would it be dangerous? Golf is another burning passion of mine. Would I be any good? Would I be able to hit the ball? Bugger that. What about driving? Would I need a driver? I've lost an eye. But I still have another one. Other people have lost eyes and they cope. My body was still but my mind was flying – so many thoughts and questions. If I felt any self-pity in the time between the ball hitting my eye and the publication of this book, it came during that half-hour.

About an hour later, all the long chats and endless hours of listening to explorer Mike Horn in the Swiss Alps the previous week came back to me. I genuinely believed that 'fate' had been involved; I'd always been the last one to leave the room each night, and I had tapped Mike for as much of his experiences of adversity, pain and the 'ultimate' challenge as I could. In retrospect, it felt very much as though I had been preparing myself for this ordeal by seeking out and absorbing ways to deal with pain and confusion.

The strength from those memories came at once. It wasn't just the loneliness that disappeared, but also the fear. His description of how he stared death in the face without blinking was a reminder that I wasn't dying and that I would recover and cope, even if it was with one eye.

I was facing a huge challenge – no doubt about that. I kept thinking about a story Mike had told about snakes. Maybe it's because of my fear of snakes. He had lain on the floor of the Amazon jungle for three days, unable to move and thinking he was going to die from a snakebite. I was lying in a comfortable hospital bed, a very long way from death – albeit with only one eye.

I also kept thinking about a letter that Bertha Cronjé received after Hansie died. Whenever you think you're in a bad situation, when things can't seem to get worse, there is always, *always* someone in a far worse position.

I started to feel determined and surprisingly calm. My resolve felt strong; I was going to get through the next hour or two – the operation – then the night, the next day … I would take it step by step but I would get through it, and I certainly wasn't going to complain or feel sorry for myself. I knew it was going to be painful, but the process of healing had already started and I hadn't even gone into the operating theatre.

When I look back, the speed with which I recovered emotionally and regained my composure was amazing. I had changed as a person during the Switzerland trip, grown up a little bit more. I was at a point of my life where I was contemplating the next stage and was therefore paying more attention to things outside cricket, but I was also pretty convinced that some element of this whole ordeal was preordained. I refused to let myself get down, although there were many depressing days to come.

I was wheeled in for the operation. It was just to stitch me up as best they could and to stop the bleeding. I was heavily sedated afterwards but I was able to talk to Jacques, Graeme and AB. Apparently the rest of the side were outside as well, but I wasn't aware of it at the time. The guys were cracking jokes about me abusing the nurses. I knew then that I was going back to Cape Town.

Dr Jonathan Rossiter

I remember the day quite vividly. Taunton is normally a sleepy county town and our eye department does not see much ocular trauma. As a keen follower of international Test cricket, I was well aware that South Africa was playing Somerset, prior to the Test series with England. Mark Boucher, of course, still holds the record for the most Test dismissals by a wicket-keeper, and was due to complete his 150th Test.

I was contacted by my colleague, who simply said to me: 'Jon, I have got a really nasty eye injury for you; it's Mark Boucher.' I was dumbstruck. On arrival on the ward I recall meeting the team manager, Dr Mohammed Moosajee. He was a medical practitioner, and, interestingly, was previously the team doctor. He is an impressive character and was extremely supportive of Mark.

My first meeting with Mark was in the examination room. He was wearing a protective shield over his injured left eye. He was very quiet and obviously in a deep state of shock. I was quite starstruck meeting him, actually, but had to remember to be very professional. My first thought was how I wished

I could have met him in different circumstances. I examined the eye, after removing the protective shield, and could tell immediately that, unfortunately, this was a career-ending injury. The eye was obviously severely traumatised.

I covered the eye back up and explained to Mark that the eye was very seriously injured. I emphasised that it was very difficult to predict what, if any, sight he would get back in this eye. I recall Mark's response quite clearly. He stared me in the eye with his good eye and said: 'Doc, I want to see out of this eye again.' I explained that I would do my best, but that the aim of the operation was simply to restore the integrity of the eye and to lower the risk of serious infection. Clearly, Mark was going to require further surgery in the coming months.

I changed into my theatre clothes. While waiting for Mark to be anaesthetised I browsed the BBC website. One of the main headlines was of course Mark's injury and his imminent emergency surgery. It was quite surreal, knowing that I was going to be the person doing the surgery!

I remember looking at Mark on the operating table, just prior to preparing him for surgery. The normal elevation of the eyelid from the eye was gone. He had evidently lost a significant amount of the eye contents. After preparation, I carefully inspected the extent of the injury. It was much worse than I feared. Clearly the entire iris and lens were absent. Much of the anterior segment was filled with haemorrhage. There was a significant corneal/scleral rupture, extending near half of the length of the eye on the medial side (the side closest to the nose). The rupture extended backwards, and I had to disinsert the medial rectus eye muscle in order to see the full extent of the rupture. There was prolapse of the vitreous gel through the rupture and, as a result, I suspected that the retina, which was not visible, must have been damaged. I would say that that this was the worst ocular trauma case that I have had to deal with.

9

I then began the meticulous process of suturing the rupture. This was an extremely delicate and quite difficult procedure. I had expected the operation to take perhaps 90 minutes when I first assessed Mark, but in fact it took four and a half hours. I had to reinsert the medial rectus eye muscle at the end. I was aware that my sutures were quite tight and causing some corneal distortion. There was no alternative. At the end of the procedure I was quite pleased with the result.

I returned to the ward to let Dr Moosajee know how the procedure had gone. I was immediately struck by the fact that the whole of the South African cricket team and coaching staff were on the ward to offer Mark their support. This speaks volumes of Mark as a man. Again, I was a little starstruck seeing the likes of Jacques Kallis, Graeme Smith and their colleagues on the ward. They were all extremely concerned for Mark.

The next morning, Mark was still quiet and in shock. Before removing the protective eye shield and pad, I was very careful to warn Mark that he might not see anything out of the eye. I had suspected that the retina had been injured and that it could even have become detached. I then projected light into the eye and was astounded to find that Mark could clearly see it – not only that, but he could very accurately locate the light when I shone it into different parts of the visual field. This was a very positive finding, and meant that the retina was still in place. However, I have seen enough ocular trauma to know that, with this type of injury, there is a real risk of the retina going on to detach due to vitreous gel incarceration to the wound. I explained to Mark and Mohammed that, without doubt, Mark was going to require further surgery. Clearly it was in Mark's best interest to have this nearer home and with the support of loved ones. We agreed that it would be wise for him to be transferred back to Cape Town.

I have watched the video of the incident on many occasions. I am still astounded that such a severe injury occurred. Clearly this was a freak accident, a one in a million. If you had asked me whether such an injury was possible, I would have said 'No'. One can only surmise that the bail was accelerated into the eye by the ball and that it must have struck the eye in an oblique fashion, causing the eye to rupture. I can't remember who told me, but I understand that Mark had left his helmet off during a rain delay and was going to retrieve it at the end of the over. This is a terrible irony.

Once I got back to my hotel room in Taunton I was hit by another sledge-hammer of reality. Jacques, Paddy and Graeme packed my kit and personal things, trying not to make a complete mess of it. They desperately wanted to do and say the right things. They said: 'You're in a bad way; what do you think about making the big decision immediately, put an end to the speculation before it even begins?' They asked me what I wanted to do and never put me under any pressure. It was clearly my decision. They asked me what I would like them to do and say. Even though it was obvious, it was largely down to them that I was able to make the decision to retire. When your best mates look you in the eye (literally, in my case) and say, 'You're never going to play cricket again,' you tend to take their word for it.

I said: 'Yes, it's the right time.' We were all quite calm as we drew up a press release, but when they left I broke down again, sat on the bed and just cried. It was the sight of all my kit and the Proteas badge, knowing I would never wear it again. It was also the realisation that, as soon as they walked out of the room, they were going to make the announcement. That was it. Not even an outside chance of making a comeback sometime in the future.

It wasn't the way I wanted to finish. So much passion, energy and determination had gone into playing this one final series. I wanted to be a part of something special, something to remember for the rest of my life. I was convinced we would win the series and become the best Test team in the world. Absolutely certain. And I was equally certain that I was in the right frame of mind and body to do myself justice and to make a contribution. But that wasn't going to happen. The tears didn't help, but I couldn't stop them. I didn't even try.

I never lived or played for statistics. A lot of players say that but have more of an interest than they will admit. But so much had been said and written about the fact that the Lord's Test (16-20 August) would have been my 150th, and I was excited about that. Mind you, I was the first person to remind the media, friends and team-mates that you never take anything for granted in this game. I could have broken a finger in the first Test and finished with 148 caps. But that wasn't what was upsetting me. It was purely the fact that I was no longer, and would never again be, a part of the family, the brotherhood of Test cricket.

Jacques returned a little later by himself. He said that there were bigger and more important things in life than cricket, and that, because I was his best mate, he didn't want me to go through this ordeal alone. He said it was bad enough that it had happened anyway, but completely wrong that I should be leaving on my own. I wasn't immediately sure of what he was saying, but then I realised he was talking about leaving the tour as well and coming back to Cape Town. I would have been shocked – but I was already in shock.

I explained that I wasn't going to be alone and that there would be plenty of time – many, many years hopefully – when we could chat about this over a beer at our leisure. I told him it would be a waste of time for him to come back now anyway because I was mostly going to be in bed asleep. I planned to give my body as much time as possible to recover, and that required rest and relaxation. Besides, my mother and father had already made arrangements to move to Cape Town for my recovery period and my girlfriend, Carmen, would be around to look after me. It was kind of him, but I explained that there were people better qualified than him to look after me!

All of that was important, of course, but it wasn't the main issue. The most important thing I could think of was Jacques playing his best cricket and helping to make all my dreams come true. I asked him to go out there and play for the team, play for both of us, and make sure we got to number one. I said that the best thing he could give me as a friend would be the pleasure of watching him play at his best while I got myself sorted out. I left the decision to him, of course. The last thing you want to do with Jacques is tell him what to do. He'll do the opposite. Maybe I'm a bit like that, too. I said: 'I can't change your mind or make the decision for you, but I would prefer it if you stayed here and got the job done rather than be hanging around in Cape Town with me, doing bugger all.'

I cannot say enough good words about Doc Moosajee. I will never forget the way he treated me and conducted himself. Honesty was so important during the initial trauma, and he was the rock of certainty around which I built my recovery. He supported me at every stage and was in contact with my family and girlfriend the whole time.

I saw an old friend, Ian Smith, at Heathrow Airport before the flight back to Cape Town. My injury had been all over the media and, amusingly in a way, it was still a feature on the Sky Sports news channel while I was in the business-class lounge. People were staring and pointing. I had grown used to that over the years, but this was different. They weren't asking for autographs this time. It was more ... I'm not sure. Pity? Curiosity? Sympathy? I was still partially sedated, but Ian came over and gave me his very bests. He looked at me straight – I was already beginning to feel conscious of how people avoided my gaze – and said 'Vasbyt, bud. You'll get through this.' I'm not sure how I responded. But it was good to see him there.

I was heavily sedated on the flight to Cape Town, but Doc looked after me every minute of the way. Every hour or two – I'm not sure how often – he needed to wake me up for injections and pills to ease the swelling. The flight passed quickly for me because I was so drugged up.

What a way to go.

Chapter 1

Early years

I was a feisty little character at school, especially on the squash court. My dad often used to come and watch me play on match days and I must admit there were times when I lost my temper and my racquet paid the ultimate price. It wasn't difficult to break a racquet because they were all wooden in those days.

One day, during an important league match, I broke my racquet against the wall after losing a contentious point. I tried to avoid my father's gaze but I could feel it burning down on me. I was very fortunate to have a sponsor, even in those early days, so at least he wouldn't have to buy me another one. It was a very quiet drive home that night. I'm sure he took a longer route than normal. He hardly said a word. It would have been easier if he had yelled and told me what he thought of me and my behaviour.

When we got home he took every single one of my racquets, old and new, and locked them away in a cupboard. The following day, when I wanted to go and practise, he said: 'No. You will never play squash again until you learn to control your temper.'

That lasted about ten days. Perhaps it was less, but it felt like months. I was convinced that he would back down and let me carry on playing. Then, one day, I realised he was deadly serious. It was a shock. Another couple of days passed while I worked on my strategy. There was no strategy. Eventually I broke down and begged him, tearfully, to let me have my racquets back. I told him I had learnt my lesson.

We discussed what had happened and he explained to me that sport was about performing to the best of your ability and that you can only do that consistently by maintaining discipline and keeping your emotions, particularly anger, under control. He explained that there was nothing wrong with anger, it was a natural part of competition, but that I needed to learn what to do with it.

It was a life lesson I never forgot, and it came back to me at a number of crucial times in my cricket career. Whenever I felt my temper beginning to fray, I would say to myself: 'Get a grip, Bouch; just now you'll get your squash racquets locked away.' Having no experience of parenting I can't say what works and what doesn't, but, from my experience of being a kid, I could take a belt to the backside or a good yelling, but taking away the things I loved most – that really hurt.

Many of my fondest sporting memories from childhood are centred on the squash court. Squash was the first sport at which I made a sustained impression, although my very first game of cricket, for Selborne Primary in East London, raised a few eyebrows. It was the great Eastern Cape rivalry: Selborne against Dale Primary. I was an opening bowler and I took 8-7 as we bowled them out for 19. It was a promising start to a career that didn't last long. The reason, I believe, was wine gums.

Every time we took a wicket our teacher, who was actually the standing umpire, gave us a wine gum. I reckon I had the whole packet in that first innings. That's how dogs are trained these days – do something good, get a reward – and it worked for me. I reckon that as soon as I realised you didn't always get given wine gums for taking wickets I lost interest in bowling.

But the story doesn't end there. I top-scored in the run chase with 7, but we still lost. We couldn't chase down 19 runs. I remember that game as clearly as some international matches. I wasn't sure just how embarrassing it was to lose a match needing 20 to win, but I had a fair idea that our teacher was expecting something a bit better from us, having shelled out the wine gums. I thought about that game almost 30 years later when Australia were 21-9 in a Test match at Newlands. I thought: 'It would have been good enough for Selborne Primary.'

My mates from school still tease me about my obsession with sport and the way I'd do anything to hit, kick or throw a ball. It was all I really wanted to do. I even joined the Scholar Patrol purely on the basis that they let you leave school 20 minutes early in order to prepare. I *did* prepare – for sport.

I wasn't academic. I wasn't the worst by any means, but the classroom wasn't my strength. I was on the sports field playing cricket every minute I can remember, with a dustbin for wickets and batting whenever I could. And I was never, ever out – I always had an excuse to carry on batting. I used to say that the guy had bowled a no ball, or he'd bowled from the side and I wasn't ready. The other boys used to get quite cross with me for never being out and never letting anyone else have a turn. 'Let someone else have a go, Boucher!' was something I heard a lot. If I had to give the bat to somebody else, then I'd insist on bowling. If I couldn't do that, then I'd stand behind the dustbin and be the wicket-keeper. Looking back, I can see that I was probably always heading in the direction of wicket-keeping. Not only did I enjoy it, even behind a bin with no gloves, but also I just couldn't stand in the outfield and relax; I was always too impatient and fidgety. I needed to be involved all the time; I craved the action. There's probably a medical term for it, but this craving served me well in later life.

My squash career was important for me on several levels. I loved the competition and the fact that I was competitive from an early age. But squash also taught me many valuable lessons about what drives us, what makes us want to win, and the differences in individual personalities.

I was always touring somewhere – not just school matches but inter-provincial tournaments and even overseas competitions. When I was seven, I went on my first tour, to Cape Town, for the inter-provincial tournament. I did really well, especially for a little guy playing in the under-12s.

I was always the youngest member of a team, often by many years, so

I had to hide my doubts and insecurities. People would say, 'Doesn't he cope well?', but I was often nervous and even a bit scared inside. But I was selected on merit and the pride of that made me hide my fears.

By the time I was 15 I regarded myself as a 'veteran' of the touring life. Having played with, and against, men for many years, I guess I'd already started to develop a bit of a thick skin. One of the highlights of this period was being selected for an under-19 tour to Europe. We went to Germany, Switzerland, Sweden, Denmark and England and we played relentlessly. It was the first time I had seen other cultures and experienced a different way of life. It was also the first time I had been removed from my familiar comforts for such a long time – the tour lasted about six weeks – and it provided me with many lessons about 'survival' on the road.

I played in the world under-19 boys' tournaments and took a small amount of consolation from the fact that I was knocked out by the guy who won the title. But it wasn't much consolation at the time. He was an English boy, and he beat me 3-1. He was three years older than me, and that wasn't any consolation either! I was like one of those little dogs with a big-dog complex. As far as I was concerned, we were all equal once we stepped on the court. The most valuable lesson I learnt was the amount of dedication required to succeed at the highest level. For the first time I saw men training until the point of exhaustion. At least, it looked like exhaustion to me. They would have a drink, rest for five minutes, and then go again. It was something I often tried to emulate. When you think you can't do any more, that's when you learn the most. Do another few minutes. It'll be worth it.

Heather Boucher

Mark was raised among avid sportsmen and -women; his family were all involved in rugby, golf, cricket, squash and/ or tennis. Even his grandparents were regular bowlers. Many hours of his childhood were spent at the club on the fields, playing some kind of sport with the other children. There was no option for my children; we were constantly involved in sport – playing it, enjoying it, having post-mortem discussions that verged on arguments, competing against each other, supporting each other, winning together, losing together, feeling the emotions together, disappointments, victories. Sport was our lives, and all of my children participated out of choice – their own choice. It was only when Mark went to high school that we made him choose three sports, insisting that one of them had to be a team sport. He would not have been able to pay attention to his schoolwork if he'd continued to play the seven or eight sports he had played in primary school.

When Mark was three, I remember one evening he came home with his father after rugby practice. His uncle, Peter Saffy (a rugby club selector), had spent three hours teaching Mark how to throw the rugby ball while diving and then to fall on his belly. Mark thought it was so great and demonstrated to us in the lounge, throwing the ball and landing flat on his stomach on the carpet. I was horrified, but he thought it was funny, and that he was so good! I guess that was where his tough and rough training started. Many years later, when Mark was in Standard 9, Peter Saffy said to me one night at a family braai that he had watched Mark playing cricket and predicted that he was going to be one of the best cricket players in the world one day – emphasising 'not only in South Africa, he's going to be world class!' We just laughed, never dreaming what truth lay in those words.

Mark was always a high achiever. Midway through high school I became worried that he wasn't spending enough time studying, but he was still achieving reasonably good results. I contacted his teacher and asked him why it was that Mark's sister Mandy spent hours behind closed doors with her books, but Mark spent, at the most, half an hour before any exam. The teacher explained that Mark had a very high concentration level, and was able to listen and absorb what was being said in the classroom and didn't need to study as hard – hence his fair to good achievements at the end of each year. That level of concentration later proved very valuable in his squash games and in his cricket.

I believe that Mark's grandparents were also instrumental in developing his talent. From as young as two he used to stay with them while we, his parents, were at work. They were very sporty people and used to throw a tennis ball to him and Mandy all day long. They had little tennis raquets and would hit the ball back and forth for hours. This later progressed to hitting against the garage wall and then became a competition to see who could continue the marathon without missing the ball. I'm sure it was an excellent development base for ball skills, patience, endurance and competitiveness – and for building big-match temperament!

Early morning

School days would often start at 4:00 am, with Dad driving me to the squash courts at Hamilton Sports Club in East London. We had to drive because we lived a little way out of town. I would start with court sprints to warm up – short, sharp take-offs concentrating on acceleration and leg strength. Then I would hit balls and go through all my rally routines, hoping someone would turn up for a game.

After a couple of hours of that, followed by a shower, I'd walk to Selborne College, which was close by. I endured the entire school day waiting to get back to my sports schedule. School really got in the way. As soon as classes were finished, I would head to the tennis courts for practice and a couple of games. From there I would move on to the Old Selbornian Club, where we had squash training. After that I returned to school for rugby or cricket practice, depending on the season.

Team sports were followed by cross-country or athletics, and then I went to the pool for an hour of training with the swimming team. By then it was dark, or getting dark, and it was time to walk back to Hamilton to play my league squash match. Then it was time to go home. If I'd won my match, we would stop for a hot dog at a place called Eskimo Hut. The hot dog was often my supper, because there wasn't enough time to have a proper meal at home. I still needed to do homework for an hour, which was about as long as I could keep my eyes open. Then I'd go to bed. Or just fall asleep on my books.

I'm aware of the 'driven parent' phenomenon, as Andre Agassi describes in his autobiography, *Open*. But it couldn't have been more different in my case. I never, ever felt pushed. I loved it, every minute of it. If I had chosen, or asked, to give up something, it wouldn't have been a problem. The only thing Dad insisted on was that if I committed to something I did it properly – and behaved properly. Mom did worry that my academic work was taking second place, and she was right. But – and this is very important – I did what I had to do, and I took it seriously. And so did Dad.

I recall my parents talking about my schedule. They may even have argued about it. Mom said I was smart and that schoolwork should be encouraged. Dad said: 'Just look at him. Can't you see our son isn't going to be an academic? He's got sport in his blood. If he doesn't play it for a living then he'll be involved in sport somehow. That's just him.'

The message reached home with Dad, though. He had always been strict, but after that he never let me miss any schoolwork. If I'd fallen asleep before my hour was up the night before, he'd wake me up even earlier than 4:00 am so I could catch up on my 'book time'. He knew I'd just go straight back to sleep if I tried to work in bed, so he used to get me up at 3:30, or whatever, make me some tea or hot chocolate, and move me to the lounge. It wasn't ideal for studying, but I made myself do it for the reward – not for the grades, but the chance to carry on playing as much sport as I wanted.

Dad pushed hard with my homework, but he pushed me harder with my sport, with one crucial difference: I didn't have a choice with the books. I loved him pushing me and challenging me to be the best

I could at whatever sport I was playing at the time. He loved watching me play, and always wanted me to be the best I could be, but squash was his favourite. I admired him hugely, not just as my father but also as a sportsman in his own right. Rugby and gymnastics were his main events, with a bit of social cricket in the summer. He had been a national gymnast and played rugby for Border. When he talked, I listened.

My parents made some sacrifices in those early years to keep me competitive. It was one thing being selected to play in the inter-provincials or national trials, but you still had to pay to get there. I travelled by train whenever possible, but places like Cape Town required an expensive flight.

When I was nine I was ranked sixth in South Africa at under-12 level. That made my parents very proud, especially Dad. I don't think he ever considered the financial perspective of professional sport, certainly not at junior level.

I reached number 1 in the under-12s, and I kept that ranking at under-14 and under-16 level. I was number 2 in the under-19 category when I was 18. I was determined to win the division the following year, but I broke my arm not too long before the inter-provincials and struggled throughout the tournament. I probably shouldn't have played. The doctor said I shouldn't, but I could hit the ball and there was nothing wrong with my legs, so I couldn't see why not. I had a couple of pins holding the fracture together, so he was mainly worried about the effect of a heavy collision.

I played a guy called Alain Nestel in the final, and it went to a fifth and deciding game, just as the semifinal had against Greg LeMood, who was one of the best in the country. I beat him through sheer determination, but it left me pretty tired. I hadn't told anyone about the injury because I didn't want any opponent to know that I was in pain. Besides, my arm was starting to feel really sore. Maybe I was denying it as much to myself as I was to everyone else. I'd lost a lot of power by the time of the final and wasn't hitting the ball as hard as I could.

I pushed myself harder than ever, driving myself to keep making the effort. It was what I called 'self-talk'. I didn't need anyone else to push me. It had been a long semi in the morning and the final was that after-noon. I was buggered but I just kept thinking back to all the 4:00 am starts, the cold mornings doing court sprints in the dark without anyone else around. Running, up and down, cold sweat pouring down my face. I wasn't going to give up without a fight.

The match was tense and it resulted in Nestel pushing me around quite a bit and becoming overly physical – and shouting at the referee. Dad didn't enjoy his behaviour and he shouted at me to respond. I felt I could wear Nestel down. Every time I felt exhausted, I looked at him and could see the same. Maybe more. I reminded myself that he would be feeling at least as tired as me. I bet he didn't do hours of early morn-ing training.

I hung in there for the first couple of games, but I had to change tac-tics. I couldn't trade big power rallies with him, so I just tried to run him off his feet. It almost worked. He beat me 9-7 in the final game to win the tournament. It was a bitter pill to swallow because I'd trained hard and I wasn't sure how much longer my squash career would carry on. I was determined to finish the age-group era as number 1, as I had been all along. There was nothing wrong with my aerobic fitness, but every time I tried to hit the ball hard I felt the 'bite' followed by the numbing pain.

What made it worse was that it was all my fault. It took me years before I had the courage to tell Dad about how I broke my arm. I told him I had landed badly while taking a diving catch at fielding practice. Thank goodness the X-ray and the doctor's opinion confirmed that as a likely scenario. Apparently a bit of weak bone on the elbow had chipped off – just the sort of thing that could have happened after landing on hard ground. And I did land on hard ground. At my friend's house. I was doing an impression of Axl Rose from Guns N' Roses and jumped off the roof of his house, unaware that there was a washing line below. I broke my arm on the pole. I think I was about 25 by the time the truth came out. That was when I knew I was strong enough to hold my own with Dad – or at least quick enough to run away.

After the game I decided I didn't want to play league squash any more. Dad decided that I needed to tread my own path from then on and asked the excellent Graham Beebe to take over as my coach.

Skill vs strength

By this time, I was pretty entrenched in my self-talk routines and habits, but that didn't stop Graham pushing me as hard as he could. I think he wanted to hear me say 'enough'. He also trained Craig van der Wath, who was South Africa's number 1 squash player for many years. Graham was hard on me, but he also knew that I was hard on myself, so he didn't need to go over the top.

Seeing as we didn't need to work too hard on my fitness, we concentrated on skills. I had the shot-making ability but not necessarily the trickery of other players, so we had to work on tactics and other ways to be smart on the court. I worked hard at recognising my opponent's game plan as quickly as possible and then thinking quickly of the best way to disrupt his plans and rhythm. Sometimes I would play into his hands for a few points to let him relax and think I didn't know what was going on. Then I would try to change things as quickly as possible to catch him cold.

If my opponent was hitting the ball hard, I would take the pace off it and play drop shots and lobs, and if he was playing slowly I would speed the game up. It was always my aim not to be 'labelled' as a certain sort of player. I didn't want my opponents to think of me as a player with strengths and weaknesses. Strange as it may sound, playing squash helped me a lot in later years when it came to 'reading' a batsman or bowler.

The skills routines were relentless, but I didn't mind. I would do them for hours. How many times could I hit the red line on a backhand? I used to draw a little circle on the wall and hit a hundred serves to see how many I could land in the circle. I would see how many times I could boast, run, retrieve and lob – then hit down the wall and boast again. It wasn't bad for fitness, either! How many? I can't recall ... about 30 or 40.

But I was only a little guy at school, so it didn't take much for me to get around the squash court.

Mandy Carr (sister)

We all played together in the backyard as children. My sister Che and I had many a cricket session where we would humour Mark, while he used us to perfect his aim and accuracy for bowling and batting. At times, I think we were the 'dustbin' he aimed at. We also had tennis and squash competitions against the garage wall and used to block up the drainpipe with balls of all sizes. We never had coaches; we were very old school and would practise, practise, practise!

During our squash era, Mark and I went on many South African camps and inter-provincial competitions together, and our mom would sometimes join us as manageress. So it was always a family affair. I clearly remember one inter-provincial when Mark won the tournament using a Super C wooden racquet and was interviewed by Derek Watts. Mark was so little and had such big knees, with stick-like legs. I thought he would need some help to answer the big man's questions! Little did I know that he would end up being interviewed and in the spotlight for many years and would be just fine.

I also recall us going to Queenstown for a tennis tournament. On the way back Mark got carsick and vomited all over my feet. I asked him if he was OK and he said yes, but, minutes later, was sick again. I will never forget this because it was so typical of Mark never complaining, even if he wasn't OK. When the eye accident happened, I knew he would be fine eventually. He has always had the ability to persevere during a tough time and come out stronger.

His words to me when we trained for squash together were: 'Don't listen to your body when you are tired; listen to your mind. Your mind is stronger than your body.'

My father

My father and I have an unusual but very strong relationship. He was strict with me, but I always felt he had a good understanding of where the line needed to be drawn. He would let me go right up to the line, the tipping point, and then he would act. Like most boys, I always wanted to see if I could push the boundaries, and he would let me know in no uncertain terms that I could not! The greatest debt of gratitude I owe him is that he knew I was going to be a sportsman and he encouraged that. He was a sportsman himself. He didn't see the point in wasting times 'exploring options'. It was that obvious that sport would be my career.

He was hard, and I knew that. Harder than the average father. He had been a physical training instructor in the army. He used to really go to town on a couple of guys there, even those ranked higher than him. One of his friends told me a story about how he would ask the cooks for a meal 'after hours' because he was hungry and needed food. Once or twice they refused, but they paid for it the next day on the drill ground! So they respected him and used to open up whenever he was hungry. I could just see my dad doing that! That story always makes me smile.

Once he realised that I could earn my own living and that I wasn't going to be dependent on him any more, he softened up like you can't believe. I think I went from boy to man in about ten minutes for Dad.

His father, my grandfather, was exactly the same with Dad, but I never saw that because he had already mellowed by the time I came along. Again, I heard stories about my grandfather, but, unlike with Dad, I could never imagine him being so hard on his son. He had five sons and two daughters, and all five boys talked for years about how they lived in fear of him. Half a dozen Boucher men ... you would need a lot of discipline to keep that situation under control.

My father told me a story about how he got into a fight at his school, George Randell High in East London. A boy had hit him from behind and my father had tried to fight back, but two other boys had jumped on him while he was down. He arrived home with a split lip and covered in bruises. My grandfather asked him what had happened and Dad said he had no chance but to fight back. So my grandfather phoned the parents of the boy who had hit him from behind and told them: 'Your son is meeting my son at the back of George Randell, now! We will have a fair fight.' The boy arrived with his father and, sure enough, my dad gave the boy a proper klap. When they got home my dad was probably feeling quite proud of himself. And my grandfather gave him the hiding of his life. He said: 'I have told you before, don't fight at school! I understand that you were hit from behind, so you needed a fair fight to sort your own little battle out, but I have told you before – you don't fight at school.' Those were the older days – times have changed now. But that is how he was brought up, and it did me no harm. I benefited from having a disciplinarian for a father.

Chapter 2

Academy days

After matric I was contemplating whether to go to Kingswood College in Grahamstown to do a bridging year, when I was unexpectedly offered the opportunity to go to either the cricket academy at the University of Port Elizabeth (now the Nelson Mandela Metropolitan University) or the Kepler Wessels Cricket Academy. As usual, there was a divergence of parental opinion, with Mum opting for the Kingswood option to give me a better education and Dad suggesting that it was a golden opportunity to play cricket – and study a bit.

We opted for the UPE Cricket Academy. Academically it was not a challenge – even for me. We really had only two subjects, and for the first two weeks of the term I didn't even know where to find one of them. Every time I looked for the lecture room for Human Movement Science I ended up walking straight past it. My knowledge of Afrikaans had never really progressed much beyond the level of communication about fielding positions and batsmen's weaknesses, so the sign on the door that read '*Menslikebewegingskunde*' was never likely to grab my attention. I asked loads of people where the lecture room was, and they all told me the same thing. And there I stood, time and time again, looking at the same sign, which I couldn't come close to pronouncing, never mind understanding.

In fairness, I was a bit 'lost' from day one. I had no idea where to go to register. You would have thought I could just 'follow the crowd', but it didn't work for me. I didn't have a clue. You were supposed to do a minimum of four subjects but everything was in Afrikaans, which was confusing. My heart just wasn't in it. I don't want to be disrespectful, but I was there to play cricket and squash, not to find my way around a campus.

My cricket, fortunately, was progressing well, and I was involved in South Africa under-19 tours, although these were not much indication of the way my career would unfold. During the under-19 tour to England in 1995, I was one of six keepers in the squad, and always a fair way down the pecking order, as I never wore my gloves once! The others included Bruce Hughes, Ahmed Omar and Linda Zondi. I opened the batting and pretty soon I'd pestered enough people into letting me bowl. Neil McKenzie and I bowled a few lengthy spells in tandem.

We were hammered by the England under-19s. Absolutely belted. Marcus Trescothick and Anthony McGrath had an average opening partnership of about 300 ('only' 154.50 if you combine Test and ODI matches). Bowling aside, though, I scored runs regularly enough to make me realise that I could play this game of cricket.

To be brutally honest, I didn't learn much at UPE – at least, not academically. But I learnt plenty about cricket, quite a lot about life and I had a very good time. I was awarded a squash bursary, too, which helped a lot. In my first year I represented UPE in the Intervarsity squash league. One of the early matches was against Rhodes, in Grahamstown. For about two weeks beforehand everyone had been talking about what a huge party the Intervarsity was and that there were usually a few beers going around. More than a few.

I was staying in K-flat in a Unitas Res at UPE. We had a bit of a fines meeting the night before we left, which involved having a few drinks. More than a few. The timing wasn't great, but we were young. In the morning, we set off to drive to Grahamstown a little bit later than we should have done and I was due on court for my first game at 4:00 pm. The guy I was scheduled to play against had been my opponent a couple of weeks earlier in a league match. (Graham Beebe had soon persuaded me to continue playing league.) He took two points off me in that match, which ended 9-0, 9-0, 9-2. And the only reason he got those two points was because Graham had told me: 'Never try to humiliate anyone on the squash court. If it looks like being 9-0, then let him win a couple of points towards the end.' It was a powerful message and a lesson to me. But it only really applied to squash; in team sports I was only too happy to beat another team as heavily as possible. But I never did win a 'clean-sweep' match, and never wanted to.

We stopped about ten minutes before Grahamstown and had another impromptu fines meeting with the K-flat group. I can't recall exactly what they made me drink as punishment, but it included shots of vodka. It wasn't pretty.

When I stepped onto the court I was drunk. Ugly drunk. I hit my head on the walls a couple of times early on, and it became obvious that I wasn't in the best condition. After a while the joke wore off. But I still had to finish the match. I made a fool of myself on the court and ended up winning two points off the guy. I'm not sure whether he let me win them or not, but it was a decent payback for what had happened in our previous encounter.

The next few days were spent partying in Grahamstown. It was quite a jol. The following week, when I got back to UPE, the Rector called me in. He reminded me that I was there on a squash bursary, and asked me how I felt about my behaviour. I felt terrible. I was extremely lucky that the Rector was the father of a good friend of mine, so I escaped serious punishment. I explained that I wasn't aware of the seriousness of Intervarsity and that I was just 'in the spirit of the occasion' and having fun. I really didn't get it, at that stage. I didn't know it was that serious. But I felt suitably crap about it.

A little while later, I began to understand what was going on. I had come from a happy, secure family upbringing, with strict but fair parents who believed in the basic rights and wrongs of life. Varsity was my opportunity to spread my wings and behave in ways I would never have been allowed to get away with at home. But my parents were right – not just because of their values, but because they knew me. But this was my time to experience life on my terms, to break the boundaries and barriers of my childhood, and to experience the consequences. And pay for them.

On the cricket field, meanwhile, a couple of decent performances at the right times, in front of the right people, led to my selection for the Border 'B' team back in East London. Once I was there, a couple of decent games led quite quickly to selection for the 'A' team. My first game was against Western Province in the 1995-1996 season.

But it was a match a year later, against the same opposition at Newlands, that stands out as my 'real' introduction to first-class cricket. HD Ackerman and Sven Koenig were hardly senior players themselves, but they'd played a few seasons of first-class cricket and felt it was OK to laugh at me from the slips while I fought for my life against Brett Schultz, who was on a mission to knock my head off. Believe it or not, Peter Kirsten was batting at the other end. The age difference was 21 years. Not for the first time in his career, Schultz wanted blood – my blood, not Kirsey's. (He had respect for Peter.) So he bowled 150kph bouncers at me and followed up with plenty of verbal ones. I couldn't help wondering what I'd done to upset him so much. But it was just the sight of a 'soft' target that excited him.

In between overs, Kirsey walked over for a chat: 'Bouch, listen here, I think you're doing a terrific job down there. You're playing him nicely, and I know the guys at the back are abusing you and that you're only a youngster, but they wouldn't be doing it if they thought you couldn't play. So just relax and ... keep going.' Relax?

I ended up facing about 90 per cent of Schultz while Kirsey smiled approvingly from the non-striker's end. I managed to make 50 in both innings, which was great, but not as impressive as surviving in one piece until the end of the match. The Province boys came through to our change room after the match for a cold beer. I got a few pats on the back, which I enjoyed, but the real highlight was watching them take the piss out of Kirsey for making such a low score in his first game facing Brett Schultz in his prime. Many of them were former team-mates of Peter's, so they didn't hold back; they gave him heaps about being too old and 'past it'. Someone said that his treatment of me amounted to child abuse. Peter just leant back on his bench and lapped it all up. It was water off a duck's back. Eventually he looked at me with a straight face, and then the smile started to appear, followed by a chuckle, and then full-on laughter. Then it all began to dawn on me. The whole time we had batted together, it had never occurred to me – not once – that Peter was manipulating the strike. I thought he was turning down singles because he was, after all, over 40 years old. There was a spinner bowling at the other end and it was amazing how many twos Kirsey hit off him – and fours. Or perhaps that was in another match! And there was never, ever a single off the last couple of balls of every over. I will always smile at how naive I was.

National Academy

After a couple of seasons, mostly with Border 'B', I was drafted into the National Academy. I think it's fair to say I felt distinctly inferior to many of the other people around me – Jacques Kallis for starters. I regarded Nic Pothas, too, as far superior to me; HD and Sven were also there. They had all played for South Africa 'A' already whereas I had barely started compiling my cricket CV.

I had just returned from an under-19 tour of India, playing on low, slow pitches against a battery of spinners. The first net session at the Academy provided another lesson I wouldn't forget. Clive Rice told me to pad up and bat. We were using the indoor nets, which were comfortably the quickest in the country. It was like batting on an airport runway. The fast bowlers loved it – it was a huge ego boost for them. Even the medium pacers could bowl decent bouncers.

Cedric English bounced me with a good one, which just missed my head but hit an advertising board behind the net. It sounded like a sonic boom. I didn't play the ball well, but I didn't need everyone's attention on me just because it sounded like an earthquake. Ricey glorified the whole situation (and tripled my embarrassment) by clapping his hands together and stopping the entire session. 'OK guys, where is his weakness?' All the bowlers said, gleefully, that I couldn't play the short ball. Needless to say, Clive encouraged all the quicks to bounce me for the next half-hour. I was hit four or five times, maybe six. It was a little brutal, but Ricey was clearly not going to pull me out of there until I had shown the willingness to accept the challenge – and demonstrated some improvement in my technique.

It was a big lesson for me. If you have a weakness in your career, or in your life, people will expose it. Later in life I would learn that the higher you climb up the ladder of life, business or sport, the more ruthlessly are those weaknesses exposed.

Thanks to Ricey and Hylton Ackerman, I developed a technique very quickly – not just effective, but quite good. In a short time I became able to dominate bowlers who tried the bouncer attack against me. I moved on quickly from 'B'-level cricket to first-class and then to international cricket. Take the pain, all of it. And then take the gain.

Dave Emslie

My first exposure to Bouch was when he came to the Academy in PE in the early 1990s. His reputation as a top sportsman had preceded him, and it was well known, for instance, that he had played under-13 cricket when he was still under 11. His academic career was less than spectacular, but he soon made his mark in the Academy, not because of his talent but because of that hard-to-find character trait in a sportsman that says to you: 'This one will make it.' It's not just about talent; it's about intense will and the blind commitment to be the best – a take-no-prisoners type of attitude.

It was not long before Bouch found himself where he belonged, in the cut and thrust of professional cricket. After a short stint with the Warriors, he moved to Cape Town to join the Cobras, only to return to the Warriors a few years later.

This is when I got to know him better, particularly when I managed the Warriors over two successive Champions Leagues.

Bouch's sometimes gruff exterior belied a certain softness and thoughtfulness towards his team-mates. Not one to have a lot of close friends in the team, he seemed to prefer his own company, but he surprised me with the things he did for team-mates – often under the radar.

Having spent time with him, I sometimes wished there could have been more of what I call 'sunshine'. Bouch with more sunshine and less grit, or Bouch with less sunshine and more grit – it's a no-brainer. Give me the gritty Bouch any day. Perhaps in retirement he might reflect that a bit more sunshine would have helped his cause from time to time.

A cricketer earns the respect of his team-mates by getting into the trenches, against the odds, and fighting to the end. Mark Boucher more than earned the respect of his team-mates.

I was once playing a casual game of golf at Humewood Links with Bouch and Andrew Birch. We were on the 17th, two down with two to play, and Andrew was off the green for a must-make putt. Bouch exhorted and willed his partner, who responded by sinking the putt and eventually halving the match. For me, the luckless opponent, it was a valuable insight into why Mark deserves his reputation.

Out of sight, out of mind

Many things have changed in the game, but the fact remains that talented players will struggle for due recognition if they play their cricket in a small or unfashionable centre. Everyone I ever played with at Border, and everyone I have spoken to from other small towns, had no doubt that they would have to perform far better than players from the bigger, more fashionable cities and provinces.

It all stems from media exposure. It's as simple as 'out of sight, out of mind'. People don't talk about players if they don't see them very often, and when the smaller teams play against the bigger ones the matches are invariably given less space in the newspapers than a match between two major teams. Border against Western Province was never the same as Transvaal against Western Province, and even if we did cause an upset and win, the attitude was more 'so what, it's only Border'. At least, that's how we felt.

Steve Palframan did especially well to make the national team in 1996, because the team wasn't particularly successful at that time, though we were certainly on the rise. Every one of the younger players was given a huge boost by Palfers' success and it gave us a new belief and determination. Perhaps there was an element of coincidence about it, but I'm convinced that the four or five 'golden' years we had at Border after his selection were partly as a result of it.

Vasbert Drakes also had a lot to do with it. To be able to attract a top West Indian bowler to East London was a huge coup for the province. Once again, it gave all of us a huge boost in confidence, and that was reflected in our results and also in the selections for the National Academy – Makhaya Ntini, Pieter Strydom and me. We had good, solid cricketers, maybe not technically perfect, but they more than made up for that in attitude. Guys like Brad White, Wayne Wiblin, Dion Taljard – all aggressive cricketers who weren't scared of taking on Western Province or Transvaal, especially if we were playing at Newlands or the Wanderers.

There is a natural bias among journalists, too. If a Border batsman scores a hundred at Newlands then the story is more likely to be about how poor the WP bowling was. But if a Province batsman scores a hundred you can guarantee the headlines.

As for the bowlers, a similar bias exists. If a Border bowler is taking wickets in domestic cricket, he is somehow perceived to be less valuable simply because the wickets are not being taken by a well-known name. Brenden Fourie suffered from that; he had one or two great seasons for Border but never got to move on. When a fast-bowling place became available in the national squad, the selectors immediately looked at Cape Town, Durban and Johannesburg.

In many ways, I never lost my small-town 'grudge' – even after I moved to Cape Town. It was with me throughout my squash days and always made me more determined than ever to beat the 'fancy boys' from the big cities. I felt strongly, throughout the age-group tournaments, that I wanted to be number 1 for Border as much as for Boucher.

There were times when our Border team weren't even playing 'A' division, so I had to play 'B' division team games while I was the number-1-ranked player in the country. I could only contribute one point, but I made sure I did. In the individual tournament it felt as though I'd achieved a little bit more than other players by winning because the depth of players in the Border region wasn't as great as it was in Western Province, Natal or Transvaal.

Even if you make it to the national squad from a small town, the provincial bias doesn't go away because journalists inevitably 'write up' the players from their city and barely notice the 'unknown' guy from the country. If it sounds like I have a chip on my shoulder, it's probably because I do – or did during my playing career. It's gone now. Mostly. Unless you come from a small town, it's a difficult thing to understand. Most of the bias is subconscious, but that doesn't make it less real.

Geoff Love

When I think of Mark, I immediately think of his toughness, determination, competitiveness and never-say-die attitude. I first had a taste of his competitiveness at the beginning of our Standard 3 year at Selborne Primary: he tripped me while we were all rushing out of the class to get to the bin first to decide the batting order for the ever-important break-time Test match. We soon found out that, unless we all stuck together and didn't let him get to the bin first, none of us got much of a chance to bat! On the rare occasions when he did get out, there were always a mountain of reasons why he was not out, ranging from 'We've cut the cake so that guy is not playing' to 'I was not ready'. Everyone who has watched or played alongside Mark would agree that he has never been short of a word or two!

He was always the leader of the pack, whether he was playing squash, cricket, rugby or athletics. This spilled over into off-field antics, too. He'd been on a few international squash tours, so he was well experienced by the time the Selborne College UK cricket tour came around in 1993. On our first night in London, he led the rest of us 17-year-olds to a choice establishment where we were charged £5 to get in, which was to include two pints of lager and a dance show of sorts. After an hour we were yet to taste a lager or see any dancing, so Bouch said we should leave. However, he first had to talk his way past two Terminator lookalikes demanding £1 100 to settle our bill. Eventually cash changed hands. His only comment on the issue: 'Don't worry, boys; we're here for another three weeks yet.'

What has changed over the years? In short, nothing much, other than the fact that he has learnt to play within the rules a bit more. He is without a doubt the eternal optimist, and the only man I know who seems to think it is still possible to win a golf game when you are 3 down and only 2 to play.

Having played a lot of cricket with Bouch in the Border 'B' years, the one stand-out lesson I learnt from him, which has been true to his character over the years, is always to enjoy the challenge of competition and the pressure situations they present. It is easier said than done, but he is someone who has successfully implemented this approach, not only on the cricket field but also in life. It is this unique character that sets him apart from the rest.

Chapter 3

Dreaming of international cricket

I wasn't in the country during the Barbados Test match in 1992, which signalled South Africa's return to international cricket – I was overseas on a squash tour. But I distinctly recall the sense of disbelief that it was happening. Test cricket was an alien concept to me. We'd had the 'rebel' tours when I was a little kid, but I'm not sure anybody really took them very seriously.

My memories of the 1992 World Cup (held in Australia and New Zealand) are very clear, even though I was only 15 at the time. Daniel Steven was a good friend of mine, and we often thought along similar lines. I'm not sure whether it was my idea or his, but we both thought it was a good idea to try and bunk a couple of classes at Selborne in order to watch the matches as they finished in the morning.

On one occasion, we were sitting in the media-communication room watching the TV with the sound on very low. The class we were missing just happened to be Religious Instruction. The master in charge of the matric students, Mr Midlane, walked in to collect a folder and spotted us immediately. 'What are you two doing here?' he asked us. Daniel was pretty quick off the mark, but there's a time and a place to be a smartarse. He said: 'Oh, we don't do RI any more, sir, because we don't believe in God.'

Mr Midlane smiled and replied: 'Guys, you have been busted. You're watching the cricket.' For a moment we wondered whether our patriotic faith might make up for us bunking the other faith, but Mr Midlane's smile didn't mean anything. We were sent to the headmaster's study, where we got three lashes each and a couple of days' detention. But it was all worth it.

Jonty Rhodes became my personal hero during the tournament. It was just me and him – and millions of other kids in South Africa and around the world. I'd love to say that I dreamt of playing alongside him one day, but such a scenario was so far beyond my imagination that it never even occurred to me. I was just a kid and he was a World Cup hero. I wasn't even dreaming of being a cricketer, never mind playing internationally.

I couldn't believe it when people criticised him in the years after the tournament for being able to score only on the leg side and for being a bit 'bottom-handed'; they were all missing the point as far as I was concerned. Jonty changed the way I looked at cricket. He was doing in the field what I tried to do playing in the schoolyard; he was so active in the field I couldn't take my eyes off him. In the years after that tournament, Shaun Pollock would bowl deliveries to certain batsmen who were poor runners so that they could hit them to backward point. If they risked a single, we knew Jonty would run them out. It didn't always work, but when it did it was a special feeling.

He almost invariably did his job with the bat; he was one of the most consistent one-dayers South Africa has ever had. It's not reflected in averages or 50s, but his team-mates and coaches always knew what he had done for the team. Sometimes, if the openers had bogged down and the run rate was climbing too high, he would come in and make a run-a-ball 30 to get the innings back on track. If he had to sweep the first ball he faced, he would. He was the most unselfish, team-oriented cricketer I ever played with. And he was equally unselfish and team-oriented as a person, too.

I found his attitude and approach to cricket continually humbling. If he was dismissed for nought he would come back to the change room and ask the other batsmen if he could throw balls to them, or make them a cup of tea. He kept the change room tidy at all times and never sulked. And he was the same if he scored a hundred. I always tried to emulate him; I didn't always manage it, especially if I was dismissed cheaply, but I can say that I always played for the team and put its needs before my own.

By the time of the 1996 World Cup (held in India, Pakistan and Sri Lanka) I was out of school and playing for Border. I was certainly dreaming of playing cricket as a career by then. I was particularly sad for Dave Richardson when he broke a finger shortly before the tournament, not just because he would miss what was obviously going to be his last chance to play in the World Cup but because it was the only finger he ever broke! He had such great hands, and always took the ball cleanly and softly. He had become such a fixture in the side and it felt like a devastating blow to the national team.

Something I was to see and understand many times in the years to come, however, was that one man's loss is another's gain. And it was particularly exciting for us at Border because the man chosen to replace Dave was our very own Steve Palframan. I can't emphasise enough how important it is to the 'smaller' towns and regions when someone from their ranks earns national colours. The ripple effect lasts for years. Having played and trained with Palfers made me realise, and believe, that people in power – selectors and administrators – did look in our direction sometimes.

We watched a number of games at O'Hagan's pub in East London. We cheered every run Palfers scored and felt very proud just to see him wear the national shirt. Despite Steve's success, however, I never thought in my wildest dreams that I might be able to emulate him. All I could think about was that I was playing for Border only because he was playing for South Africa – and what would happen when he came back!

His success had an effect on many of the Border players. We had a terrific team at that time and enjoyed more success than most other teams from the region. There were some younger players being advised to move to a bigger province in order to further their careers, and some senior players who were also enjoying excellent form in domestic cricket thinking: 'I'll never get selected because I'm 30 years old, and I'm too old and settled to move.' I suppose it's the way of life and sport – the major centres will attract the budding talent and the youngsters with big dreams will be told they need to move in order to be noticed.

Proteas debut

One day in October 1997, I was training in the Health & Racquet Club gym when our Border Bears CEO, Reunert Bauser, called me on my cell-phone. My first thought was: 'What have I done wrong?' But he said: 'Dr Bacher is trying to get hold of you. Can you please call him?' My next thought was: 'Oh shit, I must have *really* done something wrong now.'

I was bloody nervous when I dialled his number. People like Dr Ali Bacher don't call Mark Boucher to say 'hi' and chat about the weather. I had to be in trouble.

His voice came on the line: 'Hello, Mark. How would you feel about playing for South Africa?'

'Jeez, Doc,' I replied, 'I'd love to play for South Africa one day! Of course I would; that's my dream.'

'Well, that's good,' Doc said, 'because you have just been selected to go and replace Dave Richardson in Pakistan. You leave tomorrow. Good luck.'

There was no shock, initially, because the first thing that came to mind was that it must be a prank. But I did know Dr Bacher's voice; I had spoken to him a couple of times before, and I knew he wasn't the sort of person to play a 'Whackhead'-type joke on me. So I didn't say anything much. He continued: 'Dave Richardson's got problems with his calf and you are going as standby for him, but there is a good possibility that you might actually play.'

So I said: 'When did you say this is happening?'

'Well, you leave for Pakistan tomorrow but you will need to get to Johannesburg tonight.'

That was when the shock started. The rest of the day was a bit of a blur. I raced home to pack a few personal things, but I had no idea what I needed and what would be supplied. I said my goodbyes in a hurry, which was probably a good thing – I'm not sure I would have made much sense discussing in detail what had happened. Dad was very proud of me, but he didn't know how to express it because of the rush.

It wasn't until I was on the plane out of East London that I had time to think. It was hard to keep the doubts out of my head. Am I good enough? Am I ready for this? Am I going to make a fool out of myself? The thought of seeing all my heroes, of being in the change room with them ... and then of playing with them!

You can prepare yourself for many things in sport and life, but, as a youngster who'd only played a couple of seasons of first-class cricket, there was no way on earth I could have prepared for this. Older, more experienced players who know their games struggle to adapt to international cricket, but I was still learning so many aspects of my game – and of the game in general.

My attention quickly turned to all the other contenders, the guys who most people – including me – had assumed were well ahead in the queue to take over from Dave Richardson. Top of the list, I believed, was Nic Pothas, who was a good friend of mine at that stage. Surely this should have been his time? Wasn't he the man for the job at this stage? It was intimidating.

I was collected at Johannesburg airport and taken to the United Cricket Board offices at the Wanderers, where I was presented with my kit. Blazers, shirts, ties, playing kit ... wow. I had two full extra bags.

I barely recall anything of the journey to Lahore, except that it was long and I was alone. I flew business class, watched a couple of movies and, surprisingly, managed to sleep pretty well. When I landed in Pakistan I had a two-hour wait at the airport in Islamabad. I had dutifully followed instructions and changed into my 'number ones', with my brand-new green Proteas blazer. I was an obvious curiosity, and several cricket fans

41

circled me trying to work out who I was. Eventually they asked me, but I was too embarrassed to say my name. I told them I helped out with the video analysis. I should have told them I was the team mascot; that would have been more believable.

Finally the travelling was over and I was in the team environment. I looked quickly for the familiar faces and tried not to get in the way of the senior players. I knew Jacques Kallis from schools cricket, and both Shaun Pollock and Lance Klusener were also very good to me. Soon enough I was able to tuck in behind them and become part of the 'junior set'. Only then was I able to start dealing with the worries I had about Nic and Palfers and about my suitability for the job.

I told myself that I had been given an opportunity that was probably way ahead of my time but that it wasn't my fault. The selectors had seen something in me, and they were experienced men who knew a lot more about cricket than I did. So I decided to give my absolute best.

When I started training I was relaxed because Dave Richardson was still training and I was sure he was going to play. But about ten minutes before the team was announced, coach Bob Woolmer came over to me with Hansie Cronje and said: 'Listen here, Dave hasn't passed his fitness test and you will be playing.' I went cold inside and got goose bumps and shivers all down my back. I think I had a mild panic attack. I was seriously worried.

Pat Symcox produced one of his famous 'ice-breaking' moments a little while later. He walked into the change room, looked at me and smiled. 'You nervous?' he asked. I replied: 'Yes, Mr Symcox, I am pretty nervous.' He smiled again and said: 'Well, good, you should be, because if you cock up we are going to lose the Test match.' Everyone burst out laughing, but I had no idea whether he was being serious or not. Everyone else knew he was just being Symmo and trying to calm me down, and, in a strange way, it did exactly that. I may have been the butt of the joke but simply being included in the humour made me feel part of the team. I thought: 'If they feel confident enough to laugh at me then maybe they're not that worried about having me in the team.'

Hansie awarded me my cap and 'full' blazer at a team meeting the night before the Test. As I stood up to receive them, I could feel butterflies in my stomach. After the meeting I walked back to my room carrying my new items of clothing as though they were precious, fragile ornaments. I had a strong urge to put on my Test match kit, with the cap and blazer, all of it, just to see myself in the mirror and to confirm it was really happening. And I would have done, too, if I hadn't had a roommate.

The private capping ceremony is special because it's just you, the captain and the team. The captain makes a 'welcome to the family' speech and explains that, although you will be nervous, you must remember at all times that you are there for a good reason – because you are good enough. He said all ten other players would play for me and they expected me to play for them. (I received my cap again, on the outfield, shortly before the match began, for the benefit of the crowd and the cameras.)

The Test was the first ever to be played at a new stadium in Sheikhupura, about an hour and half from Lahore. There was nothing wrong with the ground, but there were no hotels nearby deemed suitable for us to stay in, so we had to drive there and back each day with a police escort. The start of play was something like 9:30 am, which meant a wake-up call of 6:00 am in order to have time for breakfast, to drive to the ground and to warm up. Most of the guys skipped breakfast and took a couple of pillows on the bus.

My head may have been on a pillow but my eyes were wide open. The traffic was chaos. So were the butterflies in my stomach and the thoughts in my head.

Shortly before the start of play, Symmo looked at me and said: 'You'll be fine ... just remember: if you cock up, we lose.' This time I smiled back.

The ball was reverse swinging by the time I went in to bat. I'd heard about the phenomenon but had never faced it before. In the years ahead I always told young players to try and appreciate their debuts, even if they couldn't enjoy them, to try and take in the little details and look at what was happening around them – because I couldn't remember a thing about mine afterwards. If someone had pinched me at any stage I'm sure I wouldn't have felt a thing.

The best thing possible happened after that: 'Swinger' regained his fitness and I was able to spend some top-quality time just working on my game with him and Bob and the rest of the players and coaching staff. I appreciated every minute I spent with Dave and soaked up every word he spoke to me. If Jonty was my hero, Dave was my idol. He'd been the only wicket-keeper South Africa had had in the post-isolation era, apart from Palfers, and I still found it hard to believe that I might be the one to take over from him.

I was a different player by the time we returned to South Africa. Better technically, no doubt, but a lot wiser, too.

That first tour of Pakistan was eventful in many ways, not least because my roommate, Jacques Kallis, had to have his appendix removed following the first Test. This meant that I moved rooms to share with Shaun Pollock.

Jacques and I were perfectly suited roomies. We enjoyed watching movies and relaxing in the room, we ate the same sort of food and at similar times, we didn't seem to annoy each other, and, crucially in the subcontinent, we had exactly the same policy with regard to the air conditioning: 'on' and 'max'. We lived in an igloo. I had the utmost respect for Polly and considered him to be a good friend, but I knew that rooming with him was probably not going to be straightforward – especially when it came to the air con.

Although he'd been playing international cricket for only two years, Shaun was very much a senior player in my eyes, so I wasn't about to raise the subject of the room temperature. He hated the air con and was convinced it would make him sick. So I lay awake on the first night and just tried to rest. Polly used to shake his leg a little bit before he went to sleep – and sometimes while he was asleep. It scared me a little at first; I wondered if there was something wrong, or if it was just a nervous tic. The twitching leg fascinated me over the next couple of nights, but I was also exhausted because I wasn't getting any sleep.

One night, once I was convinced that the leg had stopped twitching and he was asleep, I crept over to the air con and managed to turn it on without waking Shaun. This was a major triumph and I went back to my bed and fell asleep in a few minutes.

Halfway through the night I woke up feeling hot and sweaty. The hum of the air con was gone. I realised Polly must have woken up and turned it off. So I lay very still and tried to sleep, feeling a little frustrated.

The following morning he asked: 'Did you turn the air con on during the night?' I panicked a bit. What the hell had I done? Disrupting the sleeping patterns of our opening bowler! I was so irresponsible! So I denied it: 'No, no, definitely not,' I replied. 'Maybe it's on a timer or something.'

When Polly went downstairs for breakfast I was still hot and tired, so I thought I'd try and catch a few more minutes of sleep while he was out. I switched the air conditioner back on and was quickly asleep.

When he came back from breakfast and walked into the room he said: 'Jeez, it's like a fridge in here. What's going on with this air con?' At that point I had to admit that it was me and that I was very sorry but I just wanted to get a bit of sleep. Then Polly asked me if I had turned it on during the night, too. I couldn't lie to him again. I admitted that I had.

To my surprise and relief, Shaun thought that was hilarious and we ended up having a good chuckle about it. It wasn't anything to do with the room temperature, but the fact that, as an international teammate of his, I was too nervous to discuss something as basic as the air conditioning.

It's a silly story, but it was important at the time because it taught me a valuable lesson. Guys like Polly might be heroes of mine, but they were still people who were open to communication. I didn't need to feel intimidated by them. That helped me to relax a lot.

Ali Bacher

There was a clear distinction to be made between Nic Pothas and Mark Boucher, although most people thought it was a straight decision for Pothas. He was the senior player and the obvious choice. I was credited with choosing Mark but the credit actually belongs entirely to the late, great Denis Lindsay. I spoke to Peter Pollock, then convenor of selectors, about a replacement for Dave Richardson when his career was obviously coming to an end and Peter spoke to Denis. He was quite categorical: 'You must go with this young kid. He has all the qualities you need. He will grow into the role and be there for many years.' I saw Mark's personality before and during the King Commission and had no doubt that it had been the right decision. He showed responsibility above and beyond his years.

Jonty Rhodes

He didn't seem to miss a beat when he arrived in Pakistan, and he took to international cricket like a duck to water. At least, that is my recollection, even if it isn't his. He might have looked like he was 15 years old, but he acted like a man. The fact that he had his great mate Jacques on tour obviously helped him. It was particularly good for me, too, because it was the first time I had ever seen anybody with a worse cover drive than mine. Everything went through the leg side and it continued to do for the next 15 years.

It was a massive job to take over from Dave Richardson, and we were all concerned about life after 'Swinger', but it soon became obvious that the selectors and Ali Bacher had spotted something very special and unusual about Bouch.

Did I think he would go on to break all those records? No. I just saw a young guy with an incredible desire to succeed and a work ethic that meant I was no longer the last one to finish training.

His journey from youngster to senior player was very quick, and less strong characters might have struggled to cope. He was totally uncompromising – but in the best possible way.

The likes of Allan Donald, Pat Symcox, Daryll Cullinan and Fanie de Villiers had been uncompromising with him and he had seen that approach work. He adopted a similar approach with junior players throughout his career. You cannot afford to have prima donnas in a professional sports team, and Mark applied a very simple principle to himself and to everyone else: 'Fit in or f*** off.'

You can't afford to pussyfoot around if there is a clash of ideas or personalities; you have to sort it out and move on. We are talking about grown men with big egos who are still boys at heart. It can be an explosive environment, and it needs people like Mark for a semblance of order. To me, he never came across as a guy needing help or guidance, even in the very early days. He didn't need any mothering! He may have felt more vulnerable than he showed, but he disguised it well.

Gary Kirsten

Before he arrived in Pakistan in 1997, nobody else in the squad could recall meeting him. We were told to expect a youngster who was confident and cocky, a street fighter who stood up for his team-mates and could be a bit abrasive. And that is pretty much what we got! Fortunately, I had started out with a few rough edges, too. I recognised a number of characteristics that I had shared at his age, so he resonated with me and I liked him immediately.

The real Kallis

Jacques Kallis has been the backbone of the South African batting order for almost his entire career, and he has batted with more responsibility than any other player I have ever seen. After the briefest period of acclimatisation to international cricket, he was the man around whom coaches and captains built their batting strategy. He was always told to 'bat through the innings'.

Barry Richards, one of the greatest batsmen of all time, recognised Jacques as a 'great batsman' but suggested that he needed to improve his strike rate in order to take the step up to the highest level. I respect Barry, and I know he has stayed in touch with the modern game, but I couldn't help asking myself how different things were in the past. The 'consequences' of failure in years gone by weren't quite the same as they are today. Despite all the talented batsmen around him, Jacques was made to feel that the team depended on him being there. He showed in the last couple of years what he was capable of. With Graeme Smith, Hashim Amla and AB de Villiers in the top order, he made the three fastest centuries of his career.

Criticism doesn't get to Jacques much. He has a thick skin. He follows team instructions, which is what cricketers should do. He takes comfort from knowing that he has played for the team, no matter what other people say. Once or twice he has been affected, even really upset, but he gets over it – often quicker and better than his team-mates.

Jacques played under five or six coaches, and when they needed stability, when they needed someone to anchor a first innings or a run chase around, they never looked anywhere else. Gary Kirsten was that man in the early days of Jacques's career but there were several more in the later stages, most notably Graeme, whose record in pressure run-chase situations is the greatest in the history of the game. Nobody has scored more runs in successful fourth-innings run chases than Graeme. If anybody needed a batsman to score 50 in difficult conditions, with their lives at stake, it would be a hard choice between the two of them.

In one-day cricket, Jacques's career strike rate compares to most of the great players of his era, like Ricky Ponting. For most of their careers a strike of between 70 and 75 was exactly what was required – that was match-winning stuff. It's only in the last few years that strike rates of 90 have become more normal, but they had played so much ODI cricket that it was impossible to change their career stats. But both of them were able to adapt and score more quickly as the game changed. Comparing their scoring rate in the first three years of their career to the last three years would prove that:

Kallis *1996-98*: 69.28; *2010-12*: 83.57
Ponting *1995-97*: 66.79; *2009-11*: 81.32

I get quite irritated when people criticise Jacques, suggesting that he has batted too slowly in his career. Maybe I shouldn't get angry, but I can't help it. I know how good he is, and I know how much responsibility he has shouldered throughout his career.

Like most cricketers, I don't enjoy comparing generations. It becomes even harder when a cricketer's career spans a couple of generations, like that of Jacques. But, for what it's worth, I don't believe a finer cricketer has ever existed – in any generation. But then I would say that. I don't believe he has ever received the credit he is due, although it finally started to catch up towards the end of his career. Perhaps that was due to his personality. He was never a 'media baby', never flashy or outspoken. He never sought the spotlight or attention. In fact, he often went out of his way to avoid it. But he always did his duty, never missed an interview or a sponsor's function. If he had had Shane Warne's personality, perhaps, then people wouldn't even debate who was the best all-round cricketer in history. But, then, he wouldn't be Jacques Kallis.

The main reason people don't know the 'real' Kallis is because he doesn't necessarily want them to. In order to remain who he is, and true to himself, he keeps to his own private space. There isn't much opportunity to be private when you're Jacques Kallis. So he cherishes and protects what private time he does get. His friends know him extremely well, however. He keeps nothing back from those he knows and trusts.

He loves the few days he gets to live in his own house, to light a fire, have a braai and just be 'normal'. That's when he's in his element. He has absolutely no airs or graces. He doesn't think he's special. He believes he's lucky to have the talent he has, and he has respected that. He's more of a closed book than some people, but there's nothing wrong with that.

Sometimes I wonder why we have got on so well, for so long, because in many ways we are completely different. But I have learnt from him over the years. The biggest lesson has been not opening my mouth straightaway, taking a bit of time to think about what I am going to say and the possible consequences. Unfortunately I'm a slow learner, but I'm getting there. When I instinctively speak my mind, Jacques will say: 'OK, good, so you've expressed yourself and got your feelings off your chest. But, maybe you could have done it a little differently ...'

It has worked both ways, though. There have been times when Jacques has been burning up about an issue but has kept quiet. I have encouraged him to speak up because that is the only way people will understand how he feels. You can't rely on other people to express your opinions and feelings for you. Once or twice he has done exactly that, opened up about how he feels inside, and he has felt better afterwards.

Jacques's life is public; that's a fact he accepted many years ago. People know that his mother died when he was very young and his father, Henry, raised him and Janine on his own until he passed away in 2003. Those are facts. How Jacques and his sister coped is private. But I'm sure everybody can assume that it wasn't easy for them.

I'm proud of the way the Boucher family has been able to act as a bit of a surrogate family. Janine called herself 'Janine Boucher' for years. She stayed with us when she was doing her physiotherapy practical years in East London and was virtually adopted. We all recognise the struggles the Kallises have had, and there is nothing we wouldn't do for them. They are, in all but name, family.

Chapter 4

First tours

The Pakistan tour was followed immediately by a tour of Australia in December 1997 and January 1998. It was during this time that Makhaya Ntini and I made our one day international (ODI) debuts together, during the triangular series, which also involved New Zealand. It was in Perth, against New Zealand.

Perth was still the quickest wicket in Australia back then – it has changed characteristics significantly since then. Makhaya ran in and bowled superbly for a guy on debut. Outwardly he showed no signs of nerves whatsoever but I knew Makkie better than anyone else in the squad, and I knew that inside he was a whole lot less calm. But he handled the nerves well. His first wicket was the Black Caps' captain, Stephen Fleming – caught by me. It was a special moment for both of us, and for Border.

It might have been a long journey for both of us, but there's no doubt about whose was the harder. I don't read many books, but his is one I look forward to seeing. As a young teenager he came back to my house on a couple of occasions. Our family dog was barking at him. Makkie was convinced the dog was going to bite him, but I explained that he would never bite as long as I was there. I said: 'Just remember, don't come alone!' We both laughed – although I don't think he ever really trusted my dog.

And here we were, six or seven years later, playing for our country together. Once again, I'd love to say it was a dream come true, but I had not even dared to dream such a thing when I was a young boy. Perhaps Makkie did. He was coping so well with all the pressure and expectation from back home. I was so chuffed for him. We won the game and it was my first experience of a victory beer in the change room after an international. Makhaya doesn't drink, but he had a few sodas and took some pictures – enjoyed the moment.

I felt so much more comfortable with my game in Australia. The conditions in Pakistan had been alien to me and I was completely unprepared for them. But, having spent time with Bob Woolmer and Dave Richardson working on my game with bat and gloves, the time in Australia was a joy. Conditions were similar to South Africa, and the bounce of the ball meant I was taking it behind the stumps at a height similar to what I was used to. I was able to involve myself in the game much more instead of just concentrating on doing my job.

I had started to build relationships within the squad and had also started to earn the trust of the players. I was still just a youngster, but they started to see that I had the potential to do the job. Hansie and several of the senior players mentioned that Dave wasn't going to play for much longer – he announced his retirement at the end of the tour. They said to me: 'You have very big shoes to fill, but don't be in a hurry. Take your time and enjoy the ride. You've been working hard, which everyone has appreciated, and we think you're ready to step up.' Apart from Hansie, who was firm but always fair and supportive, I must mention Brian McMillan, Pat Symcox, Gary Kirsten and Jonty Rhodes, who were a constant source of encouragement. They all made a special effort to help me believe in myself.

I'd scored a few runs and batted well in the warm-up matches, and kept wicket tidily, too. I had provided some evidence for their optimism and they had obviously started to relax. It was clearly a big concern for those guys who had only ever played with Dave behind the stumps. It wasn't just batting and keeping; it was his knowledge of the game and the calming influence he provided in tight situations. I probably didn't realise the full extent of the void he was leaving behind, which was a good thing. I was intimidated enough as it was.

Record partnership

Soon after we had played Australia, Pakistan came to South Africa for the return series. It might have been the same opposition and the same personnel, but it couldn't have been more different for me. I wouldn't say I was confident yet, but I was certainly a lot happier with my game. At least I knew that I wasn't going to sink in international cricket or make a fool of myself. I was looking forward to playing in South Africa.

The first Test at the Wanderers (14-18 February) was delayed for a day because some of the Pakistan players had been involved in a 'misunderstanding' at a downtown nightclub. (I wasn't sure of the details back then and I'm none the wiser now.) We were in terrible trouble on the first day, having collapsed to 166-8. I was left at the crease when Lance Klusener was dismissed, and there didn't seem much chance of reaching a respectable total. Out to the wicket strolled Pat Symcox, which made me smile. I briefly thought about that line he gave me before my Test debut in Sheikupura, but I certainly wasn't about to bring it up at that moment.

I had developed a strong relationship with Symmo, almost like father and son. I loved keeping wicket to his bowling, but also just being around him. Symmo was always a funny guy, and enjoyed a relaxing drink after the game. The younger guys used to huddle around his corner in the change room because he had all the stories. He was a good team man with a lot of knowledge about the game of cricket. So I knew that batting with him would be interesting if it lasted any meaningful length of time. He had a calming influence on me. I was quite aggressive at times during the innings, and he would stroll down the wicket to see how I was doing, just a 'check call' to see if I was still in control of myself and my emotions. If he was satisfied that I was, he said: 'Good, well done. You're in now, so keep going for a while.'

Shoaib Akhtar had just arrived on the international scene – with quite some fanfare – and was bowling as fast as any human being has ever done. It was also a hard, bouncy Wanderers pitch – a hell of a challenge. Symmo wasn't spared the short stuff even though he was batting at number 10. After a couple of frightening bouncers, which almost took his head off, Symmo wandered down the pitch to have a chat: 'Listen here, Bouch,' he said, 'I think I've got a plan for us. When this guy bowls a bouncer Moin Khan is standing so far back I think we take a cheeky single to the keeper. That way we can keep the scoreboard ticking over and it will also really piss these guys off, and we can keep growing the partnership as well.' I said: 'Great, Symmo – let's do it!'

The very next ball, Shoaib bounced him again and Symmo just took off for the non-striker's end without a call – he simply put his head down and ran. I responded and ran down to the striker's end. Excellent; it worked. So I assumed that was the game plan from then on, or at least until the Pakistanis did something to change the situation.

A couple of balls later, I was facing and Shoaib bounced me. I looked back to see Moin taking the ball above his head about 30m away, so I took off for another bye. But Symmo stood at the non-striker's end leaning on his bat with his arm out like someone directing traffic. 'No' was all he said.

I recalled the Peter Kirsten scenario a couple of years earlier. All that talk about rotating the strike and growing our partnership ... Just like Kirsey, Symmo was quite a bit closer to 40 than 30 and he wasn't entirely enjoying facing the quick stuff at 155kph. So I realised what was happening, and I thought 'fair enough'. I never said a word, though. We just tapped gloves at the end of the over and I tried to give him a smile that said: 'OK, I know what's going on here, and that's totally fine with me.' But we just moved on.

A few overs later, the brilliant off spinner Saqlain Mushtaq was brought into the attack. Symmo went berserk, smashing him to all parts of the ground. He belted 20 or 30 in a couple of overs, and also whacked Mushtaq Ahmed for four while I was trying to stay alive at the other end. It may have seemed like Symmo was looking after himself but, actually, it was the best thing to do for the team. I'd trained a bit harder for the quick stuff and I was up for the challenge. Pat always backed himself against the spinners, so he was happy and I was happy. The result was a world-record ninth-wicket partnership of 195.

It seems strange now, but I didn't make much of the record at the time. I knew Symmo could bat, so it didn't feel like he was a number 10. All I could think of was the team's position. Afterwards my main emotion was relief that we had escaped from a deep hole and that I'd managed to contribute.

Pat came over to me at the end of the day with a handful of shirts and told me to sign them. Clearly he could see my indifference: 'You don't understand, and you will never understand until the day you retire, what a great feat this is,' he said. He was right. It wasn't until many months after I retired that I thought about what an achievement it had been. I looked at the shirts we'd signed back then and for the first time they meant something to me. The Test finished in a draw but it might not have done if we'd been bowled out for 150 on the first day.

Symmo managed to score a hundred – only the third man ever to do so batting at number 10 – and it was applauded as loudly in the change room as almost any other. The only louder applause I ever heard was for Jacques's maiden double century at Centurion.

I knew I'd played my part in turning the game around for us, and I was over the moon with my 78. It was exactly the sort of performance I needed, under pressure, to convince both myself and my team-mates that I could perform at international level.

England tour, 1998

There are many 'landmark' tours and tournaments that international cricketers aspire to be a part of, and a full Test tour of England ranks among the most prestigious of these. The 1998 tour was just South Africa's second since the end of isolation. The thought of playing a Test match at Lord's kept me awake at night, but it was for the right reasons.

I'd been to Pakistan and Australia and, although I hadn't played many games, I no longer doubted my abilities.

We were playing against Gloucestershire in Bristol in the final warm-up county game before the 1st Test at Edgbaston in Birmingham. Daryll Cullinan had been out for dinner one evening and had evidently had a couple of glasses of wine. Around 10:30 that night he called me to his room and told me to sit down and shut up.

'I don't know how you got into this side,' he started, 'but Nic Pothas is a far better cricketer than you.' He went on to tell me that I wouldn't last the tour and that in two months' time I would be lucky to get a job selling second-hand cars in East London. I was shocked – too shocked to respond in an aggressive or defensive way. Besides, Daryll was a senior player and I wasn't about to pick a fight with him. I just said: 'Daryll, I appreciate your honesty. I have always looked up to you as a senior player and obviously I watched you playing for South Africa when I was a schoolboy.' Then I stood up to leave.

'Where do you think you're going? I'm not finished with you,' he said. He continued to abuse me and tell me how useless I was for another five minutes. Eventually I stood up and said: 'Daryll, listen here. I have to play a Test match in a couple of days' time with you standing at first slip, so I think I've taken enough abuse for one evening.' I walked out of the door feeling a mixture of anger, sadness and a small amount of pride that I had had the courage to stand up for myself without causing conflict. I left it at that.

Not surprisingly, it was pretty tough walking out to play Test cricket with Daryll standing next to me and knowing what he really thought of me. He had made it obvious that he thought I didn't deserve to be there and he reminded me of that every time I made a mistake.

I should take this opportunity to thank Daryll for what he did. His outburst drove me to become a better cricketer. I was on a mission to prove Daryll wrong. It irked me even more to think that he was also an ex-Border boy. As fate would have it, Daryll was working as a commentator for SuperSport when I played my 100th Test match at Centurion about a decade later, and the producer nominated him to interview me. Very few people knew about our prickly relationship, so there was nothing deliberate or 'set up' about it. Daryll had never spoken more than a single sentence to me at any stage in the intervening ten years, and yet there he was having to say 'congratulations' to me on live television. We never spoke about the incident.

He is, and always will be, a former team-mate. But it still troubles me that he never apologised. We all do and say things that are wrong and that we regret, and sometimes we have legitimate reasons for doing them, but there is still room for an apology. I probably do still feel a bit aggrieved that he hasn't phoned me or had a private chat – it's not as though we haven't bumped into each other from time to time. I would have let the issue go immediately if he had done that. Still, I guess I should just remain grateful for how much drive and determination it gave me.

Perhaps he had a point? Maybe he just went about it in the wrong way? I don't believe my wicket-keeping was up to the required standard at that stage of my career. I was a work in progress and I *was* working really hard on it. Keeping wicket in England, for a youngster with no previous experience there, is a tough job. The ball tends to wobble on its way to you after it has passed the batsman – Bob Woolmer used to call it the 'corkscrew effect'. Unless you have done the job, stood behind the stumps and caught thousands of balls, it's impossible to prepare. It often doesn't even show up on TV, but, I can assure you, the ball does some strange things depending on the atmospheric conditions. It only needs to deviate by a couple of inches as it approaches your gloves to make life tricky. During one game, a delivery from Jacques swung incredibly late and I didn't lay a glove on it. Didn't even touch it. He burst out laughing – he'd clearly seen it before. He told me to forget about it and concentrate on catching the ones that mattered.

Trent Bridge, 23–27 July

Allan Donald's spell of fast bowling to Michael Atherton in the 4th Test at Trent Bridge will stay in the memories of everyone who saw it. Many people have said it was one of the most riveting pieces of cricket theatre they have ever seen. It was inspired by a let-off for the former England captain, which left AD livid with rage. Atherton had gloved a lifter from Allan to me and I took a decent catch. The umpire gave it not out, but replays were conclusive. There was absolutely no doubt that he had gloved it. (Some time after the match, Atherton came into our change room with the offending glove and showed AD the red mark the ball had made when it hit him! Not only that, but he asked him to sign the glove, which AD gladly did over a beer. You cannot take on-field war off the field.)

Allan bowled as fast as I had ever seen for the next few overs as he looked for revenge. Actually, I don't think he was as interested in Atherton's wicket as his blood. Nasser Hussain nicked one to me not long after the incident. It was an absolute sitter, and I dropped it.

I wanted the ground to swallow me up. I was devastated, because I'd kept tidily and taken some sharp catches during the Test. A couple of balls had wobbled away from me, but none were edges.

As I picked myself up off the ground, the first thing I saw was Daryll's icy glare. It didn't help. It was hard to get through the rest of the day. AD made his feelings obvious with a couple of gestures in my direction, which upset me a little bit because I'd always been taught to keep my feelings about team-mates private. It was the heat of the moment, though.

Fast bowlers hurt. It is not a natural thing to do and their bodies remind them of that all the time. They become 'red-eyed' in the heat of battle and they cannot always control their emotions – and shouldn't be expected to. Allan recovered pretty quickly and made a special effort to encourage me. He put his arms around me and said: 'Keep going, you're doing fine. We all make mistakes.'

At the end of the over, after that catch had gone down, I saw Hansie walking towards me. I thought he might pat me on the back or put his arm on my shoulder. It was obvious that I was in a bit of a state. I thought he might try to encourage me. How young and naive I was back then. There was nothing the captain could say or do to make me feel better, and he knew it. His face was emotionless. 'This is no time to let your head drop, Mark,' he said. 'You've cocked up; now stand up and be counted. There is no place to hide in Test cricket, so stop trying to.' Then he walked away. It was a massive moment for me and I never forgot it.

It wasn't just the message that was important; it was the realisation that he was treating me like a man. There was no concession to the fact that I was a youngster with just a few caps to my name, not even a thought about trying to protect me. It was, in a way, a compliment to me that Hansie treated me that way.

That lesson shaped the way I played international cricket. I lived by those words and they became a motto for me. There really is no place to hide in Test cricket. You will be found out. It may be quick or it may take a while, but your weaknesses *will* be exposed. There are certain places to 'hide' in other formats, but not over five days.

If I thought a team-mate wasn't facing up to his responsibilities or being honest with himself, I would tell him so – and that didn't always win me friends. But I felt it was in the best interests of him and the team. If he made a mistake I told him not to look for a 'way out', but 'look for a way back in – a way you can make a difference'. It's never nice to drop a catch or score a duck or bowl a bad ball, but it happens. They are certainties in the game of cricket. The test is how you get up after being knocked down. Hansie taught me that lesson. If I'd been a bit weaker mentally, I would have carried on sulking and dropped the next one that came my way, and that could have been the end of my career.

Hansie visited me in my hotel room that night as well and said that he knew how I was feeling but that the team needed me and it was my responsibility to pick myself up and get over it. The series was tied as we headed towards the 5th and deciding Test match, at Headingley. It worked, too. The next day I was so geed up to play. I was determined to put it right, and convinced that I could.

Allan Donald

The two things I get asked about most are the 1999 World Cup semifinal run-out with Lance … and Mark's dropped catch off me at Trent Bridge a year earlier! Let me just clear this up: it was Nasser Hussain he dropped, not Mike Atherton. He caught Atherton off his glove but the umpire gave it not out. I was furious and full of adrenaline. We were defending a low total and desperate to win the Test match. When the catch went down it was like a balloon bursting, as the tension went out of the match. I reacted badly, but when I got down to fine leg at the end of the over and started taking heaps of abuse from the crowd, I calmed down and thought: 'This is bullshit, Allan. This is no time to be selfish. You need to help the guy through the next few overs.' So I ran up to him, put my arm round his shoulders and said: 'Don't worry – another edge will come and this will just be history. Forget it now, let's move on.' But he looked desperate, and I could see he wanted the ground to swallow him up. It was the only catch he dropped in the whole series.

England is the hardest place in the world for an inexperienced keeper. It was a hell of a tough learning experience for him, but he caught everything that had any wood on it – apart from that one.

When he first walked into the team room in Pakistan I thought he had an unusual air of authority and confidence for someone so young. It's traditional for a debutant to make a short speech before being awarded his cap the night before the game and he delivered a statement about what he wanted to become, and to achieve, which really impressed me. I thought: 'Shit, this kid really means business.' He was a scrapper and a tough little shit back then, and fortunately for South African cricket that is the way he stayed. But he was never, ever afraid of taking responsibility. He didn't look for leadership roles in the sense of someone who was ambitious in that way, but he would do anything for the team. He could read a game and work out tactics as well as anyone I ever played with. It may have taken a couple of years before he was a full member of the team's 'think tank', but I remember his first contribution coming a lot earlier than that.

I was in Australia on his first tour when Dave Richardson was keeping for the last time. We had Australia in a bit of trouble at 18 for 3. I had just had Greg Blewett caught at slip by Brian McMillan. Steve Waugh was the new batsman and Mark ran on to the field with some drinks as 12th man: 'Why don't you bowl him a slower ball first up; he won't be expecting that. He'll be on the back foot because he knows you want to knock his head off.' My first thought was: 'Who the hell is this kid?' But I thought about it and decided to give it a go. Waugh was on the back foot, and he only just lunged forward in time. He looked up at me with raised eyebrows and an expression that said 'You almost got me there.' After that I was happy for Bouch to chip in with ideas whenever he had them. I backed myself to sift out the good ones from the ones that were absolute garbage. As the years went by there were less and less of those.

He was very serious about performing to the best of his ability and about winning, but he didn't take himself too seriously. He could be on the receiving end just as easily as he could dish out both humour and criticism. He asked great questions at team meetings and never demanded anything of a teammate that he didn't demand of himself. He hated players who expected to be spoon-fed, and believed that people should toughen up rather than complain. But he also stood up for the rights of more South African cricketers, and for players going through a hard time, than almost anyone of his generation.

He was responsible for a lot of good times and mini-traditions in the team, and he always had the same words of advice for every debutant as they walked on to the field: 'Don't f*** it up.'

Gary's 275 at Kingsmead

The Boxing Day Test match against England at Kingsmead in 1999 was the first chance Boucher had to display his mental resolve. Having watched England pile up a painstaking 366 in 166.4 overs, South Africa were bundled out for a paltry 156 in reply. The follow-on innings would require, at the very least, two days of batting to save the game. Gary Kirsten was in danger of running out of partners at 244-4. But a young Boucher (as nightwatchman) stymied England's march to victory during a 192-run partnership with Kirsten that spanned four hours and 50 minutes. Boucher finished with 125 and Kirsten was bowled by the last ball of the Test for a national record-equalling 275, long after the game had been saved.

I wasn't ever fighting for me – that's my recollection. I was fighting only for Gary and the Test match. Gary was in a bad place. Everyone was aware of it. His last few Tests had been disappointing and the talk before the game was that it was his last chance. There was talk of him retiring after the game if he failed again, and he had discussed it with his wife, Deborah. He was only 32. Ridiculous.

Gary was my senior partner, but I spoke to him as my equal. I started acting like the senior partner, getting a bit ahead of myself because I was so desperate for him make some runs. I was reminding him all the time to show the bowler a straight bat while I played a few shots at the other end. Most of my focus was on Gary, though. I kept telling myself that it was his responsibility to make sure he didn't lose concentration and give his wicket away. I really wanted him to stick it down the throats of those who were talking about dropping him. I was far more emotional about it than he was. Gary was calm about the situation. He believed in fate, but I believed in making sure he played straight!

Cricket is a team game played by individuals; it's unlike most other sports. In contact sports you can physically help your mates; in cricket you can't bowl or hit the ball for him. Once or twice, when Andy Caddick was bowling bouncers to Gary, I could see he was itching to take him on. As a batsman you cannot allow a fast bowler to dominate you.

I said to Gary that I would take on Caddick and try to hit him out of the attack. Fortunately it worked. We met between overs a little while later, just after Caddick was taken off, and Gary said: 'Well done, Bouch – good work.' They were simple words but they were wrapped in gold for me. A huge moment. First you prove you're not out of your depth, then you prove you belong. Then you prove you can be useful!

Gary Kirsten

I loved batting with him. He was energetic, aggressive and always keen to take the lead whenever he could. The most memorable occasion was during my 275 at Kingsmead. I was busy trying to save my career, as well as the Test match, and he could see I was pretty exhausted when he came to the crease. There was still a lot of work to do and England were still strong favourites to win. He said: 'Leave this to me, Gazza. I'm going to take Caddick on and see if I can hit him out the attack. That's not your job, it's mine.' We seemed to move from a position of serious trouble to saving the Test match very quickly while he was at the crease.

He was always a man for the big occasion, and, although his team-mates have always known that, I am not sure that that quality has been as widely recognised as it should have been. I can think of dozens of occasions when he made a crucial 32 in a Test match or 28 off 24 balls in an ODI. His total might not have stood out on a scorecard but his team-mates all knew those runs were crucial to the momentum and the result of the game. He was an X-factor player. His keeping was average at the beginning but he became one of the best glovemen in the world for the last half-dozen years of his career. He may not have been 'pretty' or flash, but the only thing that matters is that he never actually dropped a catch. Sure, there was that one at Trent Bridge in 1998, but that just proves my point – people can still remember a catch he dropped 15 years after he started.

He always had a strong opinion in team meetings and found it hard to accept a different point of view if he was convinced he was right. There was never any grey area or much room for polite discussion. But it takes two people to create friction, not one, and the wisest people soon learnt that Mark was right more often that not, and that it certainly wasn't worth arguing with him on the few occasions he got it wrong.

Mark loves a party and was the life and soul of a good few that I will always remember. He believed victories should be properly celebrated and it was a philosophy I found hard to disagree with. I used to call him the 'dop and dialler' because he often had an overwhelming urge to share the joy of victory with a mate or an old buddy at one or two in the morning. I think a few ex-girlfriends may have been on the receiving end, too.

The highest compliment I can pay Mark Boucher is that he got the best out of me – and the 'best' of Gary Kirsten was a small target to hit.

Chapter 5

The fall of Hansie Cronje

I always had a good, strong relationship with Hansie. He knew how to treat me as a player, and he knew how to get the best out of me. Just about everyone who played under him will say the same, and it's true. I fully understand how those sentiments might make some people feel uncomfortable, given what happened at the end, but that's the truth. He was a good captain and a very good leader of men. Are we supposed to pretend that he wasn't?

Hansie was a tough character. He enjoyed taking people out of their comfort zones every now and again. One time was after the victory in the Lord's Test match in June 1998. Every game at Lord's is special, of course, but so was our performance and the result on that occasion.

We'd been 46-4 before lunch on the first day. Jonty led the fight-back with a brilliant century and Hansie made 81. When England got rid of them and still seemed likely to bowl us out for a below-par score, Lance and I made decent 30s to reach a total of 360. I already had experience of a major 'get out of jail' situation against Pakistan at the Wanderers, but this time we really made it count.

AD joined Jonty on the most famous honours board in cricket with 5-32 and we bowled England out for 110. I took five catches, too, but there's no place on the Lord's Honours Board for wicket-keepers!

England followed on and we were left with a target of 15 to win the match, which took seven balls. It was amazing to win so well.

After a few beers in the change room, we went back to the hotel to change and then out for dinner and a few glasses of wine. We had night-caps back at the hotel and didn't get to bed until about 4:00 am. Still, it was worth savouring the moment, and at least we had the luxury of a long lie-in. Or so we thought.

Hansie had joined in the celebrations, although not for quite as long as the rest of us. But he had booked a 6:00 am wake-up call for the whole squad and proceeded to take us on an 8km run. It was cold, and the guys were hungover and confused. There was a lot of moaning and groaning. Nobody could understand why the hell we were doing it. But that was Hansie; he liked to challenge people.

He was a big prankster, too. There are many stories of his jokes on tour. But he wasn't quite as good at taking the medicine as he was at giving it out. I'd heard about a few times when he hadn't taken 'retaliation' in the same spirit that he'd played his own joke. The day after that 6:00 am run, Jacques and I organised a 5:00 am wake-up call for Hansie. We were leaving London that day, and when he climbed onto the bus it was obvious that he was pretty pissed off. Jacques and I, as juniors, didn't think it was really our place to own up to that, so we kept quiet.

You never really knew exactly where you stood with Hansie. One day he would be joking and laughing, and the next he would have a face like thunder. You never knew whether it was serious or whether he was kidding. Some days, he would have that face and then suddenly crack and laugh. The next day, he would have it again, and you would laugh with him, but it was like poking a stick at a crocodile. You thought he might take your head off. But he was a great captain, completely different to any other I have played under.

Some of my doubts about Hansie were created by this uncertainty. There was one time when he, maybe, made a play at Lance, Jacques and me. We were having pasta in our room, in India. We'd had it made to our dietician's orders and there was a ton of it left over, so we called him to ask whether he'd eaten and whether he would like to join us. So he did.

The offer was very light-hearted. It seemed like a complete joke. He said: 'I've just been offered $200 000 to fix the game.' (I can't recall the exact figure. It was something around there.) Anyway, we didn't take him seriously. As always, if in doubt with Hansie, just laugh. In hindsight, he probably summed us up very quickly. If any of us was going to 'bite', we would have said something then and there. I think, and hope, he knew it was barren ground. He finished his pasta quickly and left to complete his captain's commitments.

There is only one situation in a game that, in hindsight, I believe he manipulated. We found out, many months later, that the game (vs India in Nagpur, in 2000) was suspected of being fixed. Hansie was bowling and he called me up to the stumps to look for the stumping. I had never done it before to him. I thought: 'He's just playing with the batsman's mind.' The first ball he bowled after that was about half a metre down the leg side, which was inconceivable for a guy of his accuracy. It went for four byes. I hardly saw it, never mind having a chance to catch it. I must say the ball had started reverse-swinging at that stage of the innings, so it is possible that he just got it badly wrong, but I never saw him bowl a ball that wide again in the rest of the time he played.

It was the same match in which Herschelle had agreed to get out for below 20. He played some great shots, like only Hersch can. I got 68 in that match and I ran Herschelle out! It was quite funny reading about it afterwards. Herschelle made 74 off 53 balls.

We used to joke about Hansie being tight with money. He didn't use his captain's allowance on drinks for the team, that's for sure. But there was a different side to it, and one which I benefited from. He sat me down very early in my career to ask what I was doing with my finances. I didn't have a clue. He asked where my money was going. What investments did I have? Did I have an offshore bank account? Many questions. He gave me some of the best advice I could ever have received as a youngster. I have little doubt that I would have blown a lot of the money on a bunch of things I didn't need. He said: 'Mark, the first opportunity you get to put money overseas, you must do it. There's nothing wrong with investing in South Africa, but it's more secure overseas. And, besides, the money you earn at this age is not yours – it's for the family you will have one day.'

It didn't all make sense to me because he was talking about my kids and school fees, varsity fees – and I was only a kid myself. But he explained that I would become used to a certain lifestyle and that, unless I planned straightaway, that lifestyle would change when I retired and had bills to pay and no regular income. It was very good advice, and I'm grateful to him that I followed through with much of what he said.

The 'bust'

When the story of Hansie's involvement with Indian bookmakers first broke, in April 2000, he called us all in to the team room in the Elangeni Hotel in Durban, where we were preparing to play Australia in a three-match ODI series. It had been organised after the 1999 World Cup semifinal (which was tied, not lost!). He was upset, but he promised us that the story was not true. As a team, we gave him our unconditional, 100 per cent backing. Nobody, so far as I was aware, had a single doubt. A couple of the senior players told him that we all supported him and that he was our captain.

The situation remained unchanged – to me – until the following evening, when I received a phone call from team manager Goolam Rajah asking me to come to his room. Goolam told me that Hansie had written a letter pretty much confessing everything and was now on his way home.

I was too numb to comprehend. I thought: 'Right, so he'll be back in a few days.' Then it began to sink in. He had admitted that it was *true*! He had just dropped a letter off and gone home? How about talking to us? I felt shocked and let down in equal measure, but that was quickly followed by thoughts of what a mess his mind must be in. As a friend – and I considered myself a good friend by then – I was genuinely concerned. Even 13 years later it's still hard to describe how I felt. Each moment I felt anger, I felt sympathy. And whenever I felt sympathy, I felt a lot of anger.

I was asked to take over as vice-captain. Polly was made captain. I didn't know if I was ready for the job, or wanted it, but it was just a case of trying to support Polly so I said yes. It was a ridiculously tough time. We were playing Australia in two days and there was a lot of talk from the players of cancelling the series.

There were many strong words spoken in team meetings. Polly said that we needed to stick together and that we had always done well when our backs were to the wall. We spoke about the expectation that people would have for us to bounce back, and how weak we would be to cave in at that point. We didn't want to use this crisis as an excuse. We spoke a lot about how South Africa needed us to get its good name back. Gary Kirsten spoke well, too. He reminded us that we had a responsibility to ourselves, the team and the country – and that we usually responded well when we were under pressure.

We still had no idea of how serious the situation was before the first game. We were just trying to concentrate on the three-match series. Gary was very, very strong in that first game. He made 97 and Jonty made 46 from 40 balls as we chased down 240 with two overs to spare. It was a bit of a blur for me.

After Hansie

Nobody had died – yet. But it honestly felt a bit like everyone was in mourning. Hansie was gone as suddenly as if he'd died and we were left trying to make sense of it. Once or twice, a group of us would end up in one of our hotel rooms – we didn't feel like going out in public – and talk about 'fixing'. We know now that the problem has been around for years, but we were naive about it back then. We were all asking ourselves the same question: was I involved in fixing a cricket match and didn't even know about it?

We each had one or two moments that we questioned, but only with the benefit of hindsight. Why did Hansie make that decision, or that bowling change? Why was A selected over B when B was in better form?

Even in the game that was supposedly fixed, in Nagpur, one of the 'unusual' events that took place had been a strategy agreed on by the team. It was pretty unusual for a spinner to open the innings in those days, especially for South Africa, but Hansie had suggested it during the team meeting the night before, and we had all agreed. He pointed out that our new-ball bowlers were going for between 6 and 7 per over and we had nothing to lose by trying something different. Derek Crookes, our off spinner, was keen to have a go at Sourav Ganguly because he would be turning the ball away from the left-hander.

It was no more or less successful than bowling the seamers, but at least it was something different. Nobody was suspicious about the move, but, as it turned out, it was one of the aspects of the match that Hansie had agreed on with the bookmaker.

That match was the last in the series, and we went straight on to Sharjah in the United Arab Emirates for a one-day triangular series with India and Pakistan. You can look at the scorecards of that series and see dozens of things that look 'odd'. We bowled India out for around 160 in both group matches and faced Pakistan in the final. Crookes bowled 5-0-20-1 and that was it. Hansie bowled three overs for 22. That can happen. We heard later that the ICC's anti-corruption unit were investigating the tournament, but I didn't think anything was suspicious at the time.

I did notice Hansie having meetings and a few dinners with people I didn't know, but there was nothing unusual or untoward about that. He had always been interested in business and was often involved in a property development, an endorsement or something like that. I was just happy to enjoy the relative privacy of the hotel. And the air con.

Third ODI against Australia, 16 April

Australia levelled the series at Newlands (14 April) after our emotional first win at Kingsmead (12 April), so we went to the Wanderers all-square. The decider was one of my favourite games ever. We were in a bit of trouble chasing ... against a very good Australian team.

When I arrived at the wicket, Shane Warne was mouthing off, as he does, and he wasn't shy about mentioning the match-fixing. He said that if the captain was doing it, then we were all a bunch of cheats. It was the beginning of something we all had to get used to. It lasted a long time. Many years.

Lance and I worked hard to get a partnership going and, surprisingly, we ended up cruising to victory. It will always stand out as one of my best innings because the team was under pressure. There was a mountain of emotion in the change room afterwards; we knew so badly that we had to put the game of cricket above our personal issues, and above Hansie.

Some of the crowd booed when Polly dedicated some of the win to Hansie. We knew a lot of people were angry. He had been a hero for a very long time. We quickly became aware of the hatred that some people had developed. Even those who had adored him a week earlier suddenly despised him.

From a team perspective, it was very difficult. On tour you get to know people closely; you form a brotherhood. I wasn't the only one. Many of the guys felt they had lost a brother.

We heard people talking about him being suicidal. Then our feelings changed completely. Jeez, he made a huge mistake, but no! Please don't let that happen to one of our friends. Suddenly we wanted to be by his side. Don't do something so stupid, it's not that bad – or serious. That was the moment I realised just how serious it was. National pride, the reputation of the game – nothing seemed nearly as important as Hansie's life.

He needed to answer a lot of questions, and we knew that he would. Clearly there was going to be nowhere to hide. I think it was the situation that inspired us to play well as much as it was Hansie the individual. Polly asked us just to think about a brother in trouble, how many times we had all tried to help each other in difficult times, on and off the field.

I sent him a couple of messages saying: 'Hope you are well. What you did was wrong but I'm happy to forgive and move on. Stay in touch.' Many people sent him similar messages but I don't think he was in a state to reply for quite a few weeks. I'm not sure he even turned his phone on. He did reply to us eventually. The first time I saw him after he left the Elangeni Hotel was at the King Commission. It was painful. He looked broken.

It was much better seeing him at Fancourt many weeks later. He had a strong, solid group of friends who refused to judge him. Norman Minnaar and Garth le Roux played golf with him, and there was a core group of people whose approach was: 'You've made a mistake but you are now in the Fancourt family and we'll look after you and protect you.'

He needed that. At the time he may have felt deserted by the cricket family, certainly by those at the 'head' of the family when Cricket South Africa (CSA) president Percy Sonn announced that he would not even be allowed to play beach cricket. As far as the players were concerned, much of the abandonment was of his own making. He simply found it hard to face us. Every time Jacques I went to Fancourt, Hansie would always come and say 'hi', but he was much more sheepish than he had been during our playing days.

Guilty? Yes I was.

I was never offered a bribe. I wasn't even approached – except by Hansie, if you count that one time in India. I heard Michael Atherton saying that he couldn't believe he never heard anything about fixing in all his time as captain. Maybe the thieves and gamblers are better at recognising personalities than we think? Maybe I should take it as a compliment.

Chapter 6

The King Commission and after

The King Commission of Inquiry into match-fixing and corruption in cricket was a challenge for all of us. It was the first time any of us had experienced a 'courtroom' atmosphere, even though it wasn't really a court. We had no idea what to expect. Lance, Jacques and I were briefed by our lawyer, Peter Whelan. We were all nervous, though I knew I had nothing to be worried about.

We answered questions in Peter's office beforehand, out loud. It was like a rehearsal. Even though I had done nothing wrong, it was explained to me that I might not convince everyone if I stumbled over my words or didn't know the answers to obvious questions. Peter was nervous, too. He knew we were all innocent, but he was concerned that we might say something stupid that would lead to a line of questioning that he was unprepared for, and had not prepared us for. Part of me wanted to skip all the preparation; I just wanted to go in there and tell them what I saw and what I knew. But it made sense to be prepared.

Herschelle Gibbs was also being represented by Peter, but he wasn't with us. He was being treated as a separate witness, and for good reason as it turned out.

I met Herschelle for drinks a little while before we were due to appear before Justice Edwin King. It was my suggestion, because I knew something was wrong with him. He doesn't hide his feelings well. It was only noon. We made small talk for a couple of minutes and then sat down. We ordered Cokes. I said: 'Bud, you've got to come clean here; what's on your mind? If I can see there is something bothering you, the lawyers are going to see it before you've even opened your mouth. And when they put you on the stand, the truth will come out and you'll end up looking like an absolute idiot.'

I also reminded him of the worst-case scenario, that he could end up sitting in jail. Peter and several other people had told us that we could be prosecuted in a number of ways if it was proven that we had lied to the commission under oath. After a minute or so, Hersch said that he thought we should probably order a Jack Daniel's to go with the Coke. I thought: 'Oh my, here we go.' Hersch ordered a triple. 'OK fine, Bouch, I can't hide anything from you.'

He talked me through what had really gone down with him and Hansie, about the communications that they'd had and how he'd agreed to get out for less than 20. I said: 'You've got to stop a minute, Hersch. I can't remember all this. We need other people to hear it.' I asked if I could get hold of our manager, Donné Commins, and Peter Whelan; I said it would be a very good idea if they came to the bar and took notes. They really needed to hear it first-hand. Neither of them knew what was going on.

He didn't hesitate for a second, so I called them both. Donné is flexible and used to dealing with professional sportsmen, but she was still a bit pissed off. She realised it had something to do with Hersch, but probably thought he'd crashed his car or been involved in some other misdemeanour.

Herschelle was smiling when they walked in. It could easily have been interpreted as cockiness or arrogance. How could he sit there drinking and then grin at two busy people after disrupting their day? But I knew that smile, and it wasn't like that at all. It was a nervous smile. He was thinking: 'Shit, what the f*** have I done?' There were plenty of times in Hersch's life when I could see that he wanted to cry rather than smile, but crying didn't fit into who Herschelle Gibbs was, so he forced himself to laugh instead.

I thanked them for coming and explained that we were just having a chat about India, and that they might want to hear what Herschelle had to say. So Hersch took another big sip of his drink, rewound a bit, and then started talking. Peter and Donné were very good with him. It was hard for them to hear it because it was confirmation that he had lied to them both. But they could see that he wasn't holding back now, that he was telling them everything from the beginning. They didn't comment, and just occasionally prompted him to carry on, or to clarify some detail or other. Peter took notes.

Peter and Donné left after about an hour and I stayed on with Hersch for a while longer. I assured him that he'd done the right thing and that he wouldn't regret it. His greatest concern – sometimes it sounded like it was his only concern – was for Hansie. He desperately didn't want to hurt him or further jeopardise his position. Of course, he didn't know how much of the truth Hansie was going to tell, so he didn't want to be the one who landed him in jail. That's how serious it felt at the time. I told him that telling the truth would allow him to move on with his life. If he didn't, and Hansie didn't, they would have to live with it for the rest of their lives and would always worry that it would come out one day.

To his great credit, he delivered it all again before the commission, pretty much as he had while sipping a Jack Daniel's. We had all been worried about him taking the stand. Not only was the atmosphere intimidating, but there were television cameras in there, too, and Herschelle sometimes couldn't help himself when he saw a camera. We were nervous every minute he was up there. We were all very fond of Hersch – a lovely, warm and funny guy. But he was not always the brightest when it came to what came out of his mouth, and he had a history of being let down by what he said!

We were also desperately concerned about his future and what CSA would do about his 'deal' with Hansie. He was in his prime as a cricketer, and, to be honest, cricket was all he knew. We shuddered to think what might become of him if his cricket career was taken away. Thankfully, it wasn't too bad. He spent six months out of cricket, but was quickly brought back into the national squad when he became eligible. It was a great relief, and it was good to see him back. His talent probably merited special treatment.

The aspect of the King Commission, and of Hansie's very public humiliation, that really upset me and many others, was the fact that there were other names involved – and I'm not talking about South Africans. It particularly upset Jonty, who was Hansie's best friend. Not only was Hansie portrayed as a lone wolf who had let down his team-mates and his country, but also no genuine effort was made at the time to find and prove the case against the others involved. Does anybody really believe that Hansie was the only international captain to fall prey to the bookies and gamblers in India? Many other names, from several other countries, popped up from time to time, but they stand there and smile to this day. They enjoyed full careers and retired wealthy men. Nothing will ever happen to them. Hansie protected them and took their names with him to his grave. I believe he was trying to protect the game he loved rather than damage their names and reputations.

I never questioned or doubted any of my other team-mates. It seemed to me, at the time, quite straightforward: Hansie had a 'double personality', which we sort of knew about but which we never, ever suspected involved him in match-fixing. But to this day we do still wonder whether he really did tell the whole truth. It's a subject we'd rather not discuss, but I know we think about it. If there is anything else involving my team-mates or other South African players, I believe it will come out. I'll be upset and disappointed all over again, but I believe it's better out in the open than concealed inside.

I personally never had any doubts about those names mentioned or implicated in the 'Hansie tapes' – which have never materialised. Apart from Herschelle and Henry Williams, who admitted their involvement, I didn't suspect anyone. I knew immediately that Herschelle was hiding something, and I think it would have been impossible for anyone else to have kept their involvement secret. As for Pieter Strydom and Nicky Boje, they were questioned under oath and I don't have any doubt they told the truth. Lance was even mentioned at one point, but he was in the room with me when Hansie made his 'move' and I saw how he reacted.

You trust your team-mates to tell the truth and be honest.

I was never approached by anyone to do anything on the cricket field, or even for information. Once or twice, towards the end of my career, I wondered about certain moments in matches I played in – in the IPL, for instance. But you can't be suspicious about everything strange that happens on a cricket field. Some days, it would feel like every ball was fixed. It's an unpredictable game and it makes you do strange things, which is why fixing it is so possible.

If I ever had been suspicious of anyone or anything, I knew exactly what to do. Everyone does. Either report it straight to the ICC corruption officer or to the team manager. Once or twice, our players felt strongly enough about something to report it. Mostly it was just strangers offering overly generous gifts or dinners rather than anything on the field.

Centurion Test against England, 14–18 January

The final Test against England in the 1999-2000 series featured strongly during the King Commission. The middle three days were entirely lost to rain, leaving it supposedly 'dead' and unable to produce a positive result. But Hansie Cronje and Nasser Hussain made history by forfeiting an innings each to set up a one-innings run chase. England won in dramatic fashion by just two wickets. It made no difference to the series but the consolation victory made the scoreline 2-1 rather than 2-0.

What a strange Test match that was. Jacques and I used to hate the rain as much as anyone when we were in a strong or winning position and needed to get on the field. But when it didn't matter, or when the opposition were desperate to get on the field, we loved the rain – especially in Joburg. Hanging around in the change rooms at the ground can be horrible but a lazy day at the hotel suited us perfectly. On the rare occasions that we received an early morning call from Goolam Rajah saying the ground was waterlogged and we could stay in the Sandton Sun, it was a happy day. The rooms at the Sandton Sun are so comfortable – great beds, soft pillows, a coffee machine, room service and a selection of the latest movies. And we had won the series – time to put our feet up and relax. We'd worked hard for the win, and nobody wanted England to gain any crumbs of comfort. We didn't want them to have any reason to smile. One day of such luxury was rare enough, but three was beyond our wildest dreams. We had dominated the series. This was our equivalent of doing a lap of the stadium at the end of a marathon, but we were the only ones in the stadium.

On the fifth day it was bright and sunny. After three days watching movies, we were happy enough to go and play some cricket, finish the series and collect our medals. After the usual warm-ups and stretching, Hansie walked in and said that we were going to try and make a game of it. He had spoken to Dr Bacher and it had been approved. None of us were quite sure what was going on. It could even have been one of Hansie's jokes, but he seemed deadly serious.

Then we saw him talking to Nasser Hussain out in the middle of the ground. When he walked back he said it was definitely on. I must be honest: I thought it was a terrible idea. Jacques also thought it was wrong, as did Lance. But because we were all still junior players we didn't say anything. I wasn't sure what the senior players felt, but I didn't detect any enthusiasm.

The feeling among the junior section of the change room – and we had learnt from the seniors – was that Test matches are never, ever to be messed with. You never give your opposition a sniff of victory in Test cricket, unless you are desperate to win yourselves and that is your only chance. There was a simmering atmosphere of anger, but I wasn't aware of anyone speaking to Hansie about it. We just went out to carry on batting.

I went in when Polly got out early in the day, but I hadn't had much practice at setting a target in a first-class match, one that involved a certain number of runs in a certain number of overs. If you score too quickly, you have to play out a couple of quiet overs. I became a bit confused at one stage and started slogging Darren Gough. Alan Mullally was bowling from the other end. At the end of the over, Nasser walked past me and had a quiet word: 'Bouch, do you actually know what the target is here?' I replied: 'Yeh, yeh, of course. It's ... (whatever it was).' He replied: 'No, mate, that's not it. You are 15 or 20 runs ahead of schedule. You'd better slow down or you'll mess this up.'

I knew I hadn't really been listening properly. Subconsciously I probably wanted to stuff it up. If I was angry before play started, it only got worse with the England captain telling me how to bat. I was furious.

But it got worse. I was forced to try and block the next over. Left-arm seamer Mullally was bowling slow pies. There was no point in the bowlers putting their hearts into it with a target having been agreed. I lunged forward to try and block a ball, which nipped back a little and was bowled. I went from hitting Darren Gough for a couple of boundaries (19 runs off 15 balls) to blocking Mullally (3 runs off 27 balls) – and getting out. It was a mess.

Lance finished on 61 not out, and the target was set. Lance hated doing the job but he was just following instructions. England needed 249 in 76 overs – just over 3 runs to the over. The whole thing just looked and felt worse and worse.

Polly, Lance and Paul Adams took early wickets, and at 102-4 they were struggling. They needed only one decent partnership, and Alec Stewart and Michael Vaughan gave it to them, with 126 for the fifth wicket. We kept fighting, though, and there was some drama at the end before they limped over the line. I didn't enjoy that day at all, but when the England players ran onto the outfield to congratulate the tail-enders who had got them home, and I saw the smiles on their faces, I could hardly explain how I felt. We had just handed them a Test match. It was a bitter pill to swallow.

The post-match beers after a Test match were always my favourite moment, especially if we had won. A series win is the greatest highlight – the last match of the tour, a five-match series in which you've played some tremendous cricket. We had a couple of drinks but that was it. Nobody was in the mood. We just wanted to go home.

Hansie did try to cheer the guys up, but when he said it had been 'a good game' it was very hard to agree. He reminded us that we had only been two wickets away from winning and then it would have been 3-0.

But it still didn't work. We were convinced we should never have given them a chance. You can mess around with the lower levels of the game, try to 'make a game of it' at first-class level if both teams are keen to play for a win, but not in Test cricket.

Not one of us suspected that the game was corrupt, however. It was explained to us over and over that we were doing it for the good of Test cricket, for the sponsors and for the Centurion crowd, which had not seen a ball bowled for three days. We knew that Dr Bacher had spoken to Hansie. We were told it was great marketing for the game.

At the King Commission, we all saw Marlon Aronstam, the gambler who had 'persuaded' Hansie to do it. I had never met him before, but I recognised his face. Had he ever been in the change room? It all gets a bit wishy-washy as you try to recall. Perhaps he had been around somewhere else. I didn't want to start second-guessing what had had happened. I chose to put the game as far out of my mind as possible, to forget the negatives and move on.

The fight against corruption

Hansie was caught and he was guilty. He served his lifetime ban. Cricket South Africa were harsh on him, and they needed to be. But in order for his punishment to be an effective deterrent to future generations, the other countries needed to take the threat of match-fixing seriously. They did nothing then, and they continue to do nothing today. There is a lot of shrugging of shoulders and shaking of heads.

I've spoken to the ICC anti-corruption guys and they know what's going on from time to time, and they know who the prime suspects are. But they can't do or say anything because of this or that. They'll be sued for defamation. They can't get the evidence. They don't get the backing from the national board to investigate.

The ICC Anti-Corruption Unit (now the ICC Anti-Corruption and Security Unit) had a flashy video made showing Hansie crying at the King Commission. Jonty and I were sitting together when they played it to us at some tournament – I can't remember where. We understood the message, but it was a joke the way they used Hansie. We both stood up afterwards and asked where were the other guys they had caught. I was a bit sarcastic: 'Is that it? You've caught one guy in ten years? And now you drag his name through the shit in the hope that it will stop others being caught up by the gangsters and gamblers?' I was bloody angry.

They couldn't really give us an answer. The video made it look like the problem of match-fixing was a South African issue. What crap. It is, and always will be, a potential problem worldwide, but, because gambling and bookmaking are illegal on the Indian subcontinent the majority of fixing is always likely to start from there.

I had my doubts about a number of people and some of the things that allegedly happened behind closed doors, and I heard a few second-hand comments that made me upset or even angry. But you can't speak out because the consequences of getting it wrong, and of misunderstanding or misinterpreting a comment or a conversation, are too great. If you are approached directly, offered something or invited to be part of a fix, then you can be fined and banned for not reporting it. But if you have nothing solid, no facts or evidence, then you cannot afford to compromise the career of a fellow professional. You could be sued and ostracised from the cricket community.

I can't apologise for my stance. I don't believe in second chances. We all watched the ACU video, it is absolutely clear. Any involvement in fixing, regardless of age, experience or 'innocence', and you are supposed to be banned for anywhere between five years and life. But it hasn't happened. It seems to be different for every country.

Hansie's death

When Hansie died in the plane crash, it was a very personal, individual experience for all of us. There's no doubt that we felt like we had lost a brother. We had all moved on from the match-fixing period and were in various stages of rebuilding our friendship with our former captain.

A few, perhaps only Jonty, had made up for lost time and were as close to him as they had been before, but, for most of us, it was a case of allowing time to carry on healing.

Jacques and I share a holiday house at Fancourt; we would escape there whenever we could to play golf and relax, and we saw Hansie on all of those occasions. He was always friendly, but was never comfortable around us for too long. He was remorseful, but you have to move on in life, and we could see that he was trying to do that. We never discussed what had happened and didn't feel the need to. We always thought we would, one day, but there was no hurry. We could see how he felt just from his facial expressions. But we did, thankfully, have time one evening to say that we knew what he'd done was wrong but that we didn't want to hold anything against him and we wanted our friendship back. I know he appreciated that.

I was in East London when I heard about the plane crash. Jonty SMSed me to say that Hansie's plane had hit the mountains outside George. It did not register. Although I could read the words, and they were straightforward, I didn't understand them. I think my emotions weren't able to cope. Did Hansie own a plane? I immediately called Jonty and asked him to explain. He explained that it was the plane Hansie was flying back from Joburg in. He said it had disappeared off the radar and crashed somewhere, but they hadn't found it. So there was some hope.

Half an hour after that, I got the call to say that the plane had been found and that there were no survivors. It was a sickening moment, and it took a long time to sink in. I was preparing to drive to Fancourt for that weekend, and I met Jacques at our house. There was a sombre atmosphere around the whole estate; everybody was very gloomy. The breaking news was on the television in the members' lounge. After about half an hour, somebody stood up and turned it off.

Norman Minnaar chartered a flight from George to Bloemfontein a couple of days later to take people to the funeral. Jacques and I were on board. The funeral service was one of the hardest things I've been through, but it was much harder for Bertha Cronje and all the immediate family. When the boys from Grey College started to sing 'Time to

Say Goodbye' there was barely a dry eye anywhere. The national team attended, all of us wearing our blazers and ties. When we walked past Bertha she sobbed: 'Oh no, you can't do this to me!' I don't know how we got through that. She knew we were all there, but she didn't see us walk onto the stage, and it caught her completely by surprise. When we walked past her, she just broke down.

We stood in a couple of rows on the stage fighting our emotions, aware that we were there to show support and to illustrate that we could forgive a team-mate who had done wrong. The sense of brotherhood at Grey College has always been incredibly strong, and there was a lot of emotion in the air. Jonty and Polly both said a few words and showed amazing strength. I wouldn't have been able to do that.

It was no secret that Jonty and Hansie were best mates. The whole world knew it. Yet Jonty was so strong; he smiled and spoke about celebrating Hansie's life and looking forward ... his voice never cracked. I don't know how he did it. A little while later, I walked out of the assembly hall to find the toilets. Jonty was sitting on a bench by himself. He was crying quietly. I walked over to him and sat down. I said: 'Jo, you can let it go now, if you like. You've been strong enough for a long time now.'

Some of his tears were for Hansie, but most of them were for Bertha. As he said in his speech, it is the present that matters, not the past. All he could talk about was Bertha and what was going to happen to her now that she was alone. She was in a terrible place and it was breaking Jo's heart to see what she was going through.

How did Bertha keep going? She didn't give up; she just put one foot in front of the other. She kept herself busy, too. Not long after Hansie's funeral, we returned to Fancourt to play in a golf day in his name. All the proceeds were to go to children with disabilities and special needs in a school in George that Hansie had started to work with. We played three or four of those golf days. Bertha did her best to see the school benefit, as Hansie had wanted.

After one golf day, we went to see Bertha at her house. Jacques and I sat down with her, and, for the first time, we chatted properly, in a way we had never managed to do with Hansie. She was in a much better state by then. She told us a story about a woman who had left a letter under her door. It was a story that I would never forget. I had no idea of how important it would become to me ten years later.

The woman had lost her entire family within the space of about two weeks. Husband and children. There were two car accidents, I think, unrelated but close together. Her letter said: 'Bertha, I know you are suffering and have been through a lot of pain. But you must just understand that, when you think you are really badly off and suffering a lot, there is always someone who is going through a lot worse than you. I'm not looking for sympathy or anything like that, I'm just saying that I went through all of that, and I'm all right now. I survived and came through it. You're going through a tough time, but you'll get through it – don't worry.'

I didn't stay close to Bertha in the years after Hansie. I don't think it was a conscious decision on anyone's part, but it must have been the best thing for her. To be seeing cricketers – and ex-cricketers – all the time wouldn't have done much for her. It was definitely time to move on. But whenever I have seen her since, I've been so happy for her. She is happily married with kids and a great husband. She has a smile on her face. She says all she did was get on with her life, but she's an inspiration. It can be the hardest thing in the world to get on with your life sometimes.

Chapter 7

Dreadlock holiday

On the 2000-2001 tour of the West Indies, South Africa completed a hard-fought 'double' of Test and ODI series victories. But it was a 'drugs bust' after the Test series victory that grabbed the headlines. Six members of the squad were fined for smoking dagga in Antigua after the series had been won. It was a storm in a teacup.

We played some excellent cricket on the tour, but a scandal will always grab more headlines than a win. That used to upset us all as players, but, the older you get, the more you begin to understand human nature. I can comfortably say I'll always be more interested in results, but I accept that many people are attracted by the 'sex, drugs and rock'n'roll' aspect of sports tours. It was 'drugs' in Antigua after the 4th Test, which we won by 82 runs to take a 2-0 lead in the series, with just the last Test in Jamaica to come.

Staying at the Jolly Beach Resort was an eye-opener for everyone, even for those who had visited the Caribbean on a South Africa 'A' tour a couple of years earlier. Many other international players have spoken about the 'natural hazards' that make it so difficult to concentrate on your job and to remember that you aren't, in fact, on holiday. Guests wear a wristband that entitles them to food and drink at any of the bars or restaurants, night and day. The beach is snow-white and the sea is turquoise. With girls wandering about in little bikinis and everyone concentrating on enjoying their holiday, it was tricky preparing for a Test match and then playing in one.

Another 'hazard' was the local habit of smoking marijuana quite openly. I wasn't sure whether it was illegal or not, and it didn't particularly interest me because I'm open-minded about how people want to enjoy themselves. Although there were security fences around the resort to keep non-residents out, there were plenty of Rasta guys on the beach selling souvenirs and joints. Right from the beginning of our stay at Jolly Beach Resort there were comments and jokes about celebrating in the 'traditional' way if we won the Test and the series.

It was a hard-fought match on a deathly slow pitch. The scoring rate in the first three innings was less than two runs per over. It was painful at times, but there was so much at stake – for both teams – so everyone was playing risk-free cricket and nobody wanted to take a chance.

We finally set West Indies a target of 323 and took wickets steadily. It looked as though we would win easily at 89-4 and 155-7. The snag was that Brian Lara was still there. He smashed it when he was joined by the tail-enders, and the last session became tense when the target dropped below 100. But Jacques persuaded him to slash a bouncer to Neil Mac on 91 and that was it.

Lara was the best batsman I ever saw. When he was at the crease there was always a danger of the game getting away from us – even if he was with the number 11. He played spin brilliantly in that game, when everyone else struggled. Nicky Boje was bowling well into the rough and the ball was turning square, but Lara just adapted and took him out of the game, dominated him. Lara scored 63 of his 91 in that innings off Boje. Hitting balls at will, mixing patience with aggression – it was something special to watch.

Brian was the first batsman I ever saw use the crease according to conditions. Once, at Kingsmead, the ball was going all over the place and bouncing steeply. He batted far outside off stump, exposing all three stumps behind his legs – and that was just to play himself in. On another occasion, when the ball was soft and the wicket flat, he batted just as far outside leg stump. Balls that he had been leaving were now being lashed past backward point to the boundary. For that reason he was the hardest guy of his generation to bowl to. Guys would bowl a genuinely good ball, he would leave it and it would shave off stump. A little while later, they would bowl the same ball and he would clear his right leg and slap it past point. The poor bowler had delivered the perfect six balls and gone for eight runs because he'd hit two perfectly good deliveries for four. He knew his game so well, he knew batting conditions so well. He messed around with bowlers' heads. He was a genius. Always will be.

The celebrations could begin.

They started in the traditional South African way, with a fines meeting in the change room. We had more than a few beers and there was some local rum, too. Fortunately, many of the wives and girlfriends had joined the squad in Antigua, so things didn't get out of hand, as many of the guys were keen to get back to the resort.

Many of us went straight to the beach and swam in the ocean as soon as we returned, but one of the guys must have bought a joint from one of the beach 'traders'. He was joined by a handful of other guys in one of the hotel rooms closest to the beach. They knew that dagga was a banned substance, but there was no drug testing in those days. We'd just won a series and we were probably all feeling a little bulletproof in our haven of paradise. It wasn't a big deal at all. In fact, had it not been for the wives and girlfriends, I believe a few more guys might have popped into the room just to see what the fuss was about.

I was vaguely aware that some of the guys might have followed up on the jokes from earlier in the week about 'when in Rome, do as the Romans do' but I didn't know where they were and it didn't bother me. I had a beer, or a rum punch or something, on the beach and I was in and out of the sea – I was happy, very happy. The thrill of winning Test matches, and series, was the greatest feeling I knew. Nothing could beat it.

We moved on to Montego Bay, Jamaica, for a practice match before the final Test at Sabina Park in Kingston (19-23 April 2001). Polly rested himself, so I captained the side. On the first day there was a massive bust-up between Daryll Cullinan and Roger Telemachus. It started, would you believe, with an argument about someone farting and not taking responsibility for it. Roger stood up to Daryll and told him he wasn't scared of him. Daryll retaliated and traded a few shoves and pushes before our physio, Craig Smith, stepped in to separate them. I only walked in towards the tail end of it.

We walked out after the lunch break to carry on with the game, believing that the situation had been sorted out. It was a little awkward with Daryll standing between Jacques and me at second slip, but we had become used to fielding in silence over the years. Suddenly Daryll turned on the two of us and said: 'You two as well, you never stick up for me.' I asked him what he meant and he said he deserved more support and then started swearing at us. I explained that I had just walked into the room when he and Roger were fighting and didn't really know what was going on.

But Daryll insisted that we had it in for him. He told us that we should have stood up for him and then said he'd had enough. He walked off the field, packed his bags and went out to the bus, where he told the driver to take him back to the hotel. I really didn't know what to do or say, so I didn't do anything except call the 12th man onto the field so we could carry on playing. We all knew Daryll was a fiery character, but he was clearly a lot more upset about the Telemachus incident than we realised.

When we arrived back at the hotel after the day's play we had an emergency meeting with the management and senior players – Polly, me, Corrie van Zyl, Graham Ford, Goolam Rajah and Daryll. Daryll was still seething, and it didn't take long before he started abusing us all individually and saying that we were weak and gutless. Then he mentioned about the guys smoking weed and said we should have done something about it.

The management felt under pressure to take action on the

dope-smoking story because Daryll had said he was going to 'take it further'. Nobody was sure who had been involved, so, at the next team meeting, the players were asked to own up. A couple of the guys stayed behind and they were pretty upset because it was clear that somebody had grassed on them (if you'll excuse the pun).

The UCB dealt with the matter and issued a press release on 11 May, which named those involved – Paul Adams, Roger Telemachus, Andre Nel, Justin Kemp, Herschelle Gibbs and Craig Smith – and announced that they had been fined R10 000 each. It also confirmed that Daryll had been fined for leaving the field during the final Test.

One of the players found it particularly stressful because his father first heard about the incident on the radio. It made it sound like they were taking crack cocaine, not messing around with a joint.

Chatting to them afterwards, it was clear they were just having a bit of fun. Most of them only had a couple of puffs and weren't affected at all. Craig, as part of the management, said he was there to keep an eye on the boys. If they were going to do something silly, rather he was with them than not. It sounded like a decent theory to me!

It wasn't the right thing to do, and I'm not condoning it, but I'm sure a lot of people have done similar or worse things in their youth, and I think it could have been dealt with in-house. The whole incident was unfortunate because it undoubtedly put a bit of a dampener on what had been a very good tour for us.

Drugs and cricket

While the business in Antigua was blown out of proportion and was swiftly dealt with by the authorities, the use of drugs has become more and more of a problem in world cricket. Some countries take a hard stance on it, and South Africa, rightly, is one of them. If you get caught, you're out. And I've got no problem with that. But why is it like that for South Africa and not for other countries?

There was an element of surprise among some cricketers when the

ICC signed up to the anti-doping Code of Conduct issued by World Anti-Doping Agency (WADA) in July 2006. There was a feeling that cricketers couldn't benefit like athletes and cyclists from doping. I disagree. Put it this way: you're in the third session on the fourth or fifth day of a Test match, and you need three or four wickets to win. Your premier fast bowler, who's bowled 20-odd overs in the innings, is flagging. He goes into the dressing room to get 'spiked' up with mandol – what isn't performance-enhancing about that? He'll come out and find something extra, bowl at 150kph rather than 135. It can definitely help a cricketer. I swear I have no evidence, real, circumstantial or anecdotal, to suggest that has happened. I'm just saying it's stupid and naive to believe cricket might not be affected. We used to think the same about match-fixing.

There is already evidence and proof of drug use. There have been guys who've been caught already. Shoaib Akhtar is one example that we know of, and there have been others who have been caught with drugs in their system. Shane Warne missing the 2003 World Cup – that was a decade ago. Cricketers can use drugs to help them recover from injury more quickly. It's not performance-enhancing as such, but it's illegal in every other sport, so why should cricket be any different? It's simple: just like match-fixing, you don't do banned drugs, performance-enhancing or otherwise. Simple.

There are exceptions, of course, and systems are in place to cope with them. I was massaged for a stiff neck at Centurion before a match, and my skin reacted badly to something in the arnica oil the physio had used. I ended up with a bad rash around my ear. It wasn't getting any better by the time I returned to East London. I was due to play a match that Wednesday night. On the Tuesday I went to see a sports doctor and he gave me some pills for the rash. Fortunately it started to clear up.

I drove to Port Elizabeth the next morning for the game and was getting my fingers strapped up when the team doctor came into the physio's room to inquire about the rash. I told him it was from some oil that I was using, and that the other doctor had given me some pills for it. He asked if it was working, and I said that it was working great and even showed him the bottle. He looked at it for longer than was comfortable and then, finally, said: 'Bouch, do you know that this is illegal? They're doing drug testing tonight, and if they find this in your system, you could be in big trouble.'

I was completely taken aback. Shocked. I was told to write a letter immediately, which was faxed to WADA. I had to get a letter from the doctor in East London to say that he'd made a mistake, that it was intended to clear up a rash, and that, incidentally, it was working! I had to send it all off in case I was tested. It was a pain in the arse, but I wouldn't change it. I have no complaints. As it turned out, I wasn't tested because the testing was random. I was lucky, in a sense, because the team doctor happened to be in the room with the physio. But I wouldn't advocate a loosening of the rules. Players need to accept responsibility for their own welfare and wellbeing, and there should be enough experts around to help them. If there aren't, they must find them.

I'm not saying it's easy, or simple. I have thought many times about the potential injustice and the severity of the punishment an innocent player could suffer. You are accountable for what goes into your body. Yet there may be times when you are genuinely vulnerable. If a person really wanted to mess up your career, they could slip a pill into your drink at a bar, or in your tea at breakfast. The pill dissolves, you'll never know. As a sportsman, it doesn't even cross your mind. You wake up with a bit of a headache, and you think it's because you might have had a bit too much to drink. Two days later you get tested, and it comes up in your system that you're taking performance-enhancing drugs.

The answer is that you have to be mindful of the chance, however slight it might be. Don't put your glass down in public places. Don't give people the chance. Drink out of a bottle. So what if people tell you that you're being paranoid? It happens to women all the time, and if a person has a vendetta against you and knows that you're a sportsman, he can slip something into your drink and potentially ruin your career.

WADA's 'whereabouts' clause can be tough, because it requires you to tell them where you will be at any stage of each day, for months in advance. I don't know anybody who plans their life so closely, so far in advance. You can inform them of a change in plans, but it does remove the element of spontaneity from your life. Last-minute holidays to Mauritius involve a series of emails or faxes to WADA. For the really famous guys, the fear of leaks to the media about their holidays isn't great. Sometimes you spontaneously decide to drive to George and, two hours into the drive, you suddenly think: 'I could be prosecuted for avoiding a drugs test for doing this.'

But you know what? These are the rules and regulations, and you have to abide by them. Simple.

The Board of Control for Cricket in India (BCCI) objected to the ICC's signing up with WADA and, specifically, to the 'whereabouts' clause. Unfortunately, it's another example of the belief that there are different rules for different countries. In a perfect world, you'd want to be on the same system, be punished the same for the same crimes, and be looked after in a similar way. But we all know that doesn't happen, and it's not right. I'm just a cricketer, not a politician. It's easy to say we have no choice, but we can make a difference, which is why I am involved in the South African Cricketers' Association (SACA), the body that represents the interests of the players.

Chapter 8

Transformation, selection and discipline

W e had many excellent results in the early and mid-2000s and we played some very fine cricket. But it's also fair to say that we didn't reach our full potential. Man for man, we had the talent and skill to have pushed one of the greatest Australian teams of all time harder than we did – and to have beaten the other teams more regularly. I'm not certain why that didn't happen. Results at the highest level of international sport can be decided by small factors. If there is doubt, uncertainty or mistrust, it can affect performances on the field.

I challenge anyone, however, to look at the calibre of players we had in the early and middle part of the decade and say our results did us justice. It's a long list: Gary Kirsten, Herschelle Gibbs, Graeme Smith, Jonty Rhodes, Jacques Kallis, Shaun Pollock, Lance Klusener, Allan Donald, Makhaya Ntini.

There are two things I'm certain about: firstly, politically driven racial transformation was on all of our minds for a lot of the time; and, secondly, transformation was necessary. And still is. I can't pretend that I understood that concept early on in my career, but it was explained to us at the beginning of the decade and we grew to understand how and why it was important. As cricketers of all races and backgrounds, our instincts were simply to pick the best XI on merit. I never once met or spoke to a black or coloured cricketer who believed he should be selected because he wasn't white!

What I cannot be sure of, however, is whether the issue detracted from our performances. Yes, it was on our minds and it was a distraction. But did we score fewer runs and take fewer wickets and catches because of it? Perhaps we would always have been outplayed by that great Australian team, and maybe we weren't as good as I think we were.

Part of the problem with transformation, from about 2000 onwards, was that it was rarely spoken about, and certainly not in the change room among the players. There was not that much doubt and suspicion within the national squad, but the mistrust and confusion that existed in the franchise system at that time was impossible to ignore. It meant that new players who arrived in the national squad carried quite a bit of 'baggage' with them.

There were too many instances of young players of colour who were basically specialist fielders – they didn't bat or bowl. Some coaches said they were 'gaining experience' of first-class cricket before they were entrusted with meaningful roles, but that was no way to treat an ambitious young cricketer. It was totally unfair. The coaches argued that it was equally unfair to watch a young bowler get smashed or a batsman who was out of his depth. But the CSA constitution said there had to be a minimum of four players of colour in every franchise team. It was a painful time.

At times, there were as many as five or six players in a squad who weren't sure if they were included – or excluded – for reasons other than their cricket skill. I'm fairly sure there were a few young cricketers, of all races, who were lost to the game because of the atmosphere created by transformation. If they had been left to develop at their own pace and to find their own way, they would probably still be playing first-class cricket and might well have progressed to the national team.

You have to say, though, that the depth of players in all the franchises has increased in the last ten years and the game is producing more quality players from regions that never used to feature, so progress is being made. There are concerns, and rightly, that so few black African players have made it to the highest level. Perhaps the answer lies in the period between school and a player's early 20s. Perhaps more support and structure needs to be found there.

There hasn't been so much as a suggestion of doubt about the merit of every player in the national side since around 2008, the point when the Test team started producing its best and most consistent results. When every squad member feels worthy of his place and enjoys the confidence of his team-mates, it is easy to focus all your energy on training, developing your skills and playing to the best of your ability.

I'm not completely against fast-tracking. If a young black cricketer shows fantastic promise, and has a track record at first-class level, even if it's a short one, then I would back him being fast-tracked. The crucial difference between now and 10 or 12 years ago, however, is that he would be spoken to honestly. There is a massive difference between cold silence and the captain, coach, manager or selector telling you: 'Look, you have leapfrogged a few guys, but we believe you have the ability and we back you. Just relax and everybody will back you up.'

We've turned the corner now. As long as we continue to concentrate on giving opportunities to young kids who didn't have the chance to play in the past, then we should be fine. Guys like JP Duminy, Hashim Amla, Vernon Philander – they're not just great South African role models, they have all reached the top in international cricket.

Ashwell Prince

In many ways Ashwell Prince was a pioneer, a trailblazer. He put up with a lot of crap early in his career and he didn't deserve it. Like Makhaya, he had to prove himself all along, time after time, long after he had justified his place in the team.

I started playing with Ash at under-19 level; we used to open the batting together. From the first time we played in the same team, I never,

ever looked at Ashwell as a guy who was there because of colour. I knew immediately that Ashwell could play the game of cricket, and I knew he was a bloody tough nut to crack, too. But as tough as he was, the 'political' pressure occasionally got to him. It hurt him deeply when people said, mostly behind his back, that he was only there because of his skin. It was not what the players felt – quite the opposite. Those close to him, and those who mattered, and anyone who had ever played with him, said: 'This is the man for the job.'

Even when JP played one of the great Test innings of all time, the 166 at the MCG in the 2nd Test in 2008, it was because Ashwell was injured. There was so much talk and speculation about what would happen when Ash was fit again for the return series in South Africa. I was one of the first guys to say: 'Ashwell comes back into the side because he has actually been playing bloody well and JP, unfortunately, will have to wait his turn – again.'

Ashwell played some unbelievable knocks for South Africa under pressure. I always enjoyed a player who could put it together as he did. I hope he mellowed at the end of his career, as I did. He was always at the forefront for Lancashire when the wicket was difficult.

He probably looks back on his career and admits that he was a little too angry at certain times, and at certain things, but he probably also feels justified. I know Ashwell and I know where he comes from, and I do understand why he was angry. But I also know that, as he got older, he started to calm down and recognise the bigger things in life, the real issues.

He is one of my favourite team-mates. People said he had too much to say, too many chips on his shoulder. But unless you were Ashwell Prince, you didn't know the whole situation.

I decided very early on that I would be the same Mark Boucher that Ashwell had played with as a teenager. I could see he was sceptical about people, and how they changed, so I decided to be a stable point of reference for him. I don't know if that worked, but that was my goal. He never received the credit he deserved, and that pissed me off. I always fought his corner.

There were times in team meetings when the feedback dried up. Then Ash would talk – and people would listen. He had an aura about him. He always had something to say when there was something unfair happening, but he chose his time when it came to team tactics, attitudes and approaches. He could be a bit of a wild man on certain things (much of which I agreed with), but when it came to winning games he was wise. When he was asked for his opinion, he gave it – and everyone respected that. He spoke with great truth and openness about the difficulties that players of colour experience, and everyone, of all backgrounds, benefited from what he said. He spoke the words many others didn't have the confidence to speak. I admired him so much for that.

One of my favourite partnerships ever was with Ash. We had a two-Test series against Bangladesh just before we went to Australia in 2008. Bangladesh batted first and made 250. We were 134-5 in reply. It was embarrassing. We barely said a word when I got to the crease. It didn't need much more than eye contact: that said it all. We were two proud cricketers and we weren't going to be humiliated. We added 271 together.

Sydney, January 2002

South Africa were 2-0 down in the Test series heading into the final Test at the SCG. The selection panel, headed by Rushdi Magiet, chose Jacques Rudolph to make his debut. Late on the night before the match, UCB president Percy Sonn invoked his power of veto to replace Rudolph with Justin Ontong.

Selection panel member Graeme Pollock said, in an interview on ABC radio on the morning of the match, that the South African XI was 'not the team chosen by me or the selectors', and the Australian media created great hype around the 'disharmony in the tourists' team'. Little did they know that Jacques Rudolph and Justin Ontong were not only roommates at the time, but also close friends.

We were probably an 85 per cent team playing against one of the best sides of all time. It was messy, unpleasant and unnecessary, not to mention unfair. Everybody could see that one member of the squad had been playing well and was in good form, and was also a youngster who deserved his chance. And everyone could also see that Justin, for all his talent and potential, wasn't ready at that stage of his career and had just come off a pair at the same venue. He wasn't ready. You could see he wasn't ready. You just needed to look at his face. We never thought for a second that he would *never* be good enough, just that it was so obviously the wrong time to blood him.

I don't think the XI was finalised until an hour before the start of play. It was brutal for Justin. The Australians didn't give a shit about him – that's normal for Test cricket. They sledged him brutally from the moment he got to the wicket. They called him 'Percy's love child'.

I don't care about the politicians. I care about the individuals, the cricketers. I felt deeply for Onters at that stage. He'd been thrown into the deep end by people who had no idea of what Test cricket entailed, or required. In the name of advancing the game, they set a promising cricketer's career back by six or seven years. Justin played a decent and courageous innings of 32 in the second innings of that Test when we followed on 400 behind and had a partnership of 64 with Gary Kirsten. He was selected for the 1st Test of the return series against Australia but had to withdraw due to injury.

Onters has fought back brilliantly, captaining the Cape Cobras and playing again for the national side, but he could, and should, have enjoyed a longer and better career for South Africa. It knocked his confidence badly. He does everything – bats anywhere successfully, bowls a variety of things and is a brilliant fielder. We should have seen more of Justin Ontong.

I understand that Percy Sonn was frustrated by the slow pace of transformation, and that he felt he was doing the right thing, but I'm sure he would have reconsidered if he had any idea of how damaging the consequences would be – and how long they would last.

The worst thing about the transformation years was not being able to talk about the situation. It was like denying the existence of an illness and just watching the patient get sicker and sicker. It couldn't have been more different to the way the decade finished, with Mickey Arthur and Gary Kirsten encouraging an atmosphere of total trust and transparency. Back then, if we mentioned anything, as white players, we would be labelled as 'anti-transformation' and be seen as troublemakers. So we all kept quiet. And pulled apart into our little enclaves.

I never recovered from the double standards that applied to the players and our bosses. When sports and recreation minister Ngconde Balfour said something along the lines of, 'I don't go to Newlands to watch Jacques Kallis', to me it sounded a bit inflammatory. Maybe he didn't mean it like that. But I still wondered how he could say that. If we, the players, had said something similar we wouldn't have played another day of cricket in South Africa.

Thami Tsolekile is another player, like Justin, who showed fantastic character and the courage to keep playing and to fight back from being thrown into the deep end. Thami went to India in November 2004 to play Test cricket as his first assignment with the national team. How unfair is that? For every Ontong and Tsolekile who made the headlines, how many cricketers experienced a similar fate at provincial or franchise level and were lost to the game forever? Plenty.

Makhaya, on the other hand, was the exception that proved the rule. But he was different for a number of reasons. He was exceptionally fit and was driven to the point of obsession to be as strong as he could be. He worked on his cricket skills whenever he could and he never complained. That part of him was exceptional.

Another factor was his debut, which was outstanding. Your first taste and experience of international cricket can last a long, long time. If it's bad, it can take years to get over it. But Hansie and Bob looked after Makhaya; they waited for the right moment to give him his debut and then for the right time to bring him into the attack in that ODI against New Zealand in Perth. He was as relaxed as you can be on debut, ran in smoothly and bowled beautifully to take 2-31 in ten overs. The confidence he gained from that day lasted him years.

Another factor in Makhaya's favour was that he didn't overanalyse things; he didn't think too far ahead. He tried his best every day and in every game, and that's all he could do. He'd spent his early youth herding goats – he wasn't about to start fretting and worrying about his place in the side or the consequences of having two bad games in a row. Enjoyment was a huge part of Makhaya's game. Sometimes he'd be a little bit too cheerful for a particular situation – if we were losing a Test match or had just lost a one-dayer – but he was the ultimate 'it's just a game, nobody has died' kind of person. It could really piss people off at times, but it could also be a great icebreaker.

Sometimes I thought about the pressure and the weight of expectation that Makhaya must have carried on his shoulders, for over a decade, and I wonder how on earth he coped. At other times, I wasn't sure he even noticed it. He took everything in his stride – or seemed to. When he was under pressure, he would make a joke. I knew Makkie better than most, but even I wasn't always sure what he was thinking or feeling.

Overall, the transformation years weren't much fun for anybody. There were some great moments, fabulous matches and memorable tours, but it was never long before the next spate of doubts and whispers. One of the problems was that the quotas – or 'targets' as they were wisely called – were never fully explained to the coaches or management, or to us. The CSA board, the selectors and whoever else was involved in the process preferred to see a 'willingness' from the coach and the team to transform. But if they didn't see enough willingness, they would intervene.

If the selectors were told they had to play a certain number of players of colour, I thought they should have told everyone, but they wimped out and would just tell the coaches who they should play. That was unfair on the coaches, because they weren't making the decisions. If everyone had been open and honest, and the players had known where they stood, things could have been better. I would like to think this has all stopped, but it's still there. I have never met anybody who doesn't believe the game should be transformed and spread to as much of the population as possible. I have met plenty of people, of all races and colours, who have had a problem with the way it has been implemented.

Social media and forums like Twitter have opened up the selection debate to everybody now. There's no end of people, from professional pundits to ex-players and keen fans, saying: 'X should play and Y should play – get them in the team.' But they very rarely say in place of whom, especially when they are proposing the selection of black players. So if Thami Tsolekile and Lopsy Tsotsobe must play, who must be dropped? AB de Villiers and Morne Morkel? Or Dale Steyn? Vernon Philander? It was that kind of pressure that probably cracked Mickey. Even though I am a purist, and I would like to see the best team possible play Test cricket for South Africa, I understand how satisfying it would be to see more black players wearing the Test shirt. But it's not that simple. If it was, we might see more people proposing the complete strategy rather than just the players they want in the XI.

People may say there are precedents, but I'm not sure about that. It certainly wasn't the case with Makhaya; he never played ahead of someone more deserving. He was chosen in a squad of 16 and made his debut once the team had reached the final of the ODI tournament in Australia, like me. We both played when the senior players were given a rest. And if he was fast-tracked in the Test XI, he responded immediately. That's why he played 101 Test matches.

Cliques

For much of the mid-2000s, the Proteas squad was accused of being run by a clique. Graeme Smith was close friends with Jacques Kallis, AB de Villiers, Justin Kemp and me. The rest were occasionally described by other team-mates as merely 'crew'. Several players, notably Roger Telemachus and Garnett Kruger, spoke out on the issue.

Garnett blamed us, the senior players, for not being given a chance at international cricket. We weren't selecting the team – it had nothing to do with us. But he was given a chance: he played two ODIs against Australia and one against Sri Lanka, and he was belted. Did he expect to be given an opportunity against Bangladesh to warm up for international cricket? You sink or swim at the highest level. Sometimes you get lucky and circumstances contrive to give you a second or third chance, but maybe Garnett was unlucky in that sense. He didn't take his chance and then somebody else came along and the ship had sailed.

I don't know why he slated the senior players. What could I have done differently? I couldn't bowl the ball for him. He was selected to do a job and he didn't do it particularly well. So the selectors chose someone else. Garnett didn't like that, but it was up to him to fight his way back, not blame other people.

I equate the situation in the national team to a large business or corporation. Does everyone in the workforce have their say on major decisions? No, the directors run the company and make the important, strategic decisions. A cricket team is the same, with its senior players and high performers who have served the team for many years and have learnt from their experiences. They are the directors; they are best qualified to run the team, along with the coach. You can't expect to succeed if you have young, inexperienced cricketers coming into the side and making demands about how things should be done.

Some people might like to call it a clique but that's not the way I saw it. It's no different in 2013 to what it was in 2007 when the team was run by the so-called clique. There are some excellent, well-respected senior players in the team under Graeme's captaincy and they form what is effectively a board of directors. It allows new players to come into the team and to know exactly what is expected of them and how the hierarchy works. They are talented cricketers representing their country, but they do so in a structured environment and on the understanding that they will not always get their way. And they know when to stop arguing and shut up.

In some ways, we are all a product of our upbringing and the lessons we learn early in life. Either we choose to make changes and do things differently, or we repeat the things that we think worked well. When I first came into the team, I never questioned Hansie, Symmo, Brian McMillan, Dave Richardson or Gary. I never dreamt of it. I answered if I was asked for some input, but otherwise it was a case of getting on with your job, working hard to improve, and listening to as much advice as possible. They used to have senior player meetings by themselves, while the juniors like Polly, Jacques, Lance and me would sit outside. Sometimes we'd be outside for half an hour. That was how the team was run. It worked. We'd be called back into the room to hear the conclusions and decisions they had reached. Sometimes we would be asked our thoughts, but generally it was understood that we agreed with them!

We didn't argue, and, to be frank, we didn't particularly want to make any big decisions because then we'd be held accountable for them. We trusted the senior players to make decisions in the best interests of the team – and to take ownership of those decisions and accept responsibility for the results. We knew our time would come, but we weren't in a hurry to push for a place on the board.

It came soon enough for all of us – sooner than we expected. Lance was the World Cup man-of-the-tournament just a couple of years after his debut and a year after that Polly was captain and I was vice-captain. After that we were taking responsibility for everything! When you come home from another World Cup 'failure', it's the senior players who get castigated in the media. And that's fine – it's part of your job.

Wild card

No matter what you have done at first-class level or below, I cannot believe there has ever been a cricketer who automatically felt comfortable and at home in an international change room until he had produced some results at that level.

I enjoyed reading the comments made by Kyle Abbott after his Test debut against Pakistan in the first home season after my retirement. He was called up only as cover for Dale Steyn but ended up playing in place of Jacques when he injured himself at the end of the final practice session. Kyle spoke glowingly about the way the senior players had received him and how much he had been welcomed into the family.

I have it on very good authority that his account was entirely accurate – except that it came *after* he had picked up 7-29 in the first innings!

Despite bowling well in domestic cricket, Kyle was a wild card selection of note. He had never been mentioned as a candidate before, and some excellent figures for the Dolphins saw him jump ahead of three or four fast bowlers who'd been in the queue for quite a while. When he was called up I'm sure there would have been a few reservations among the coaching staff and senior players. Not about Kyle personally, but about the difference between domestic cricket and Test cricket.

It was a stunning debut. He was able to bowl in much the same way as he had been doing at first-class level and the wickets started tumbling.

Not many cricketers are good enough to earn that much respect so quickly – no wonder he said he was made welcome. There would have been a lot of guys thinking: 'OK, you've proved that you've got what it takes at this level. Well done.' But they wouldn't have been saying that before he bowled.

Polly explained it to me early on. He'd played for a couple of years before me and he knew how I was feeling: 'Bouch, you will always question whether you're good enough until you actually perform. If and when you do, then you'll feel confident and like you belong. Then your team-mates will feed off that confidence and then you will start to relax and believe in yourself. Then your performances will get even better. That's the way it works. And it's the same if you don't perform. You will lack confidence and the team will pick up on that. So, perform!'

It's the same throughout life. You have to find your way, discover whether you're going to be able to cope. There is fear. It's to be expected. Some people help, but it's your own journey.

Disciplinary issues

I was never afraid of disciplinary action. All my life, from Selborne College onwards, I was taught – and believed – that you reap the consequences of your actions. The only thing I ever asked for was a fair hearing.

I had a couple of disciplinary hearings in my time, but I sat on more committees than I was subjected to. And I accepted the results, even if I believed them to be wrong and unfair. Except on one occasion.

It was in 2007, just before the start of the inaugural ICC World Twenty20, and there was speculation about the composition of the national squad. Ngconde Balfour had made his uncomplimentary comment about Jacques, and I was pretty upset about that. Jacques was left out of the team and there was a pile of wrangling going on about who, in fact, had selected the squad and who had overruled whom. Coach Mickey Arthur said he had asked for Jacques to be included. But when Norman Arendse, by then president of CSA, approved the squad, Jacques was not there. Nobody really knew what was happening, but we did know that Jacques was desperately keen to play. There had been some confusing talk about 'resting' him.

At that stage Jacques and I were neighbours in Cape Town (we subsequently bought different houses). I was walking across the road to borrow some braai wood from him when *Business Day* journalist Mark Smit called me. He asked: 'What's your take on the squad which has been announced?' I said that Jacques was an unbelievable player, one of the best all-rounders in the history of the game, that he would have been a very useful addition to our squad, and that he had the skills to adapt his game to suit T20 cricket. I said it was just a matter of time before he dominated this format, as he had the others.

I returned home and lit my braai with Jacques's wood and thought nothing more about it. It was a good braai, too. Two days later, I received a phone call from Gerald Majola, the chief executive of CSA. 'What the hell have you done?' he demanded. 'You have abused our selectors and been disrespectful to the administration ... there will be a disciplinary hearing.'

I couldn't believe it. I hadn't seen the article but realised I had better get my hands on a copy as soon as possible. I immediately called Tony Irish, the CEO of SACA. He said he had seen the article and was hoping it would slip through the net and go unnoticed. He said my quotes 'weren't great'. Now I was even more confused. I was sure I hadn't said anything controversial – I certainly hadn't meant to. Sometimes I deliberately took a chance with a quote or two, but not this time.

Tony sent me the article. Mark Smit wanted to make a couple of strong points about the selection and the attitude of Ngconde Balfour, who had had said he wouldn't go to Newlands to watch Jacques Kallis play. A couple of my quotes were taken out of context and thrown in to back up the writer's opinions.

I phoned Mark and told him that I was in a bit of trouble and that I would appreciate him explaining to my employers that there had been a lot of cutting and pasting of my quotes. He apologised profusely and admitted, in retrospect, that he might have been a bit too opinionated and used some of my quotes to support his point of view. I asked him if he would mind putting that in writing, and he agreed. He said he would email Gerald Majola and copy Tony in so that we had a copy when we went to Joburg for the hearing.

Mark did write the email and, although he said he had not done it deliberately, admitted that he had misrepresented me and that my quotes had only ever been in support of Jacques as a cricketer rather than critical of CSA or the selectors. He admitted that he should have written the story as an 'opinion' column rather than tried to get quotes to 'fit'. He also said that I had not spoken disrespectfully or disparagingly about anyone at CSA during the interview.

I was grateful to Mark for setting the record straight and felt pretty confident that the situation had been explained. It was regrettable, but we all make errors of judgement. If I wasn't completely cleared, I certainly believed the need for a disciplinary hearing had been removed.

I called Gerald to ask whether he had read the email and whether I still needed to come up to Johannesburg. He said he wanted nothing to do with it. I was shocked. I'd always had a good relationship with the CEO and, for whatever other faults and problems he had, he was always good with the players. He was usually a good listener and always believed that the team would win more if the players felt supported. He said: 'I'm not interested; you have said what you have said – now you must go to the disciplinary hearing and sort it out.' That hurt.

So Tony travelled with me to Joburg and we introduced ourselves to Judge Kuper and CSA's Brian Basson. The first thing we did was to present Mark Smit's letter in mitigation. Tony and I suggested that it might make the proceedings a bit shorter if they wouldn't mind reading it. It was obvious to me that Basson's mind was made up. He was hostile to the point of aggression and spoke in a patronising way, as a teacher might to a naughty eight-year-old. If he was trying to upset me, it worked. I wasn't even guilty. He took the letter and as far as I could see placed it on the desk without even looking at it. And then they carried on with the hearing. CSA was seeking a ban.

As we walked out, I turned to Tony and asked: 'What the hell was that? I didn't even get the chance to explain myself!' Tony, who is a lawyer, looked at me with half a smile and said: 'Bouch, I'm afraid it looks like someone in a high position has got it in for you. I'm sorry to say this, but you can expect to get the book thrown at you. I know that you are not guilty – I have seen the email – but the way that Brian Basson was with you in there suggests that someone wants to teach you a lesson.'

In fact, the judge threw only half the book at me when he passed sentence a few days later. A ban would have ruled me out of the T20 tournament, but he opted for a fine – a huge fine, and not just one, either. I was fined 60 per cent of my match fee for every game I played.

At the centre of the argument were my comments about Jacques. I said: 'He is our best all-rounder ever and a far better one-day player than people give him credit for. People either have an issue with him, or have a chip on their shoulders, or they have ulterior motives.' These were comments made in reply to a general query about Jacques that was not asked in the context of his non-selection for the tournament. The judge said: 'Senior players have a responsibility to CSA and to cricket in general. Their responsibilities are set forth in the code [of conduct] and in their contracts and one is entitled to expect punctilious performance of their obligations.'

I still don't know what 'punctilious' means.

Chapter 9

Dropped from the squad

L ike most tours to Sri Lanka, our visit in August 2004 was a disaster as far as results were concerned. Having kicked off with a morale-boosting, high-scoring draw in the 1st Test in Galle, we travelled back to Colombo for the 2nd Test at the Sinhalese Sports Club, the 'Lord's' of Sri Lankan cricket. Mahela Jayawardene's double century in Galle had gone to waste but his friend Kumar Sangakkara's one in Colombo set them up for a huge win by over 300 runs. Muttiah Muralitharan didn't even play in that game; Sanath Jayasuriya and Chaminda Vaas both took five wickets and we were bowled out for under 200 in both innings.

There was some brave talk about bouncing back in the one-day series that followed. We had been drilled. Lost five out of five. We desperately needed to change things around. We weren't a particularly happy squad, either, but that was mostly because of the results. You don't find many losing teams that are happy.

Just a couple of years earlier, during a bizarre but enjoyable one-day triangular tournament with Pakistan and Sri Lanka in Tangier, Morocco, Eric Simons had impressed upon me the need to take a greater leadership role and to start driving our fitness sessions. If you're pushing hard from the front, he said, then the rest of the guys will follow you.

That was very much in my mind during our struggles in Sri Lanka. I could see the problems and I wanted to *do* something. I thought back to my squash touring days and remembered something that had been useful. There were just five or six guys in the team and a manager. We knew we were going to be in each other's faces for weeks at a time and that little niggles and irritations could become big issues unless they were tackled. So, every four or five days, sometimes more and sometimes less, we would get together for a meeting to catch up on things. Each guy could make two points about everyone else: one good, one not so good. We promised each other that we would do our best to take the 'bad' point as constructive criticism and to use it to better ourselves.

Generally it worked very well – not just because we could get things off our chests, but also because it gave us a chance to say thank you or well done. That part is easy to forget, so we had to think of something we appreciated in our colleagues as well as something that was a problem or annoyed us.

During the one-day series in Sri Lanka, I suggested the senior players get together and try something similar. They all agreed. I kicked off with a general comment – that that there were relationship 'triangles' developing in the squad and losing was making them grow more divisive. I suggested that the squad wasn't very 'healthy' as far as trust and understanding between players was concerned, and that it wasn't going to get any better until we, the senior players, started backing each other and sharing the same agenda. I don't think anyone really knew what to do, because back then there wasn't the culture of honesty that existed after 2008. There were guys who had just never learnt to be honest.

I felt quite proud, not that it was my idea but because it seemed to be working. Although some guys may have been a little uncomfortable, they seemed to be trying. At least, I thought they were. They could have walked out. Nobody locked the door.

I distinctly remember taking a deep breath and telling Hersch that he was an unbelievable player with so much talent, more talent than anyone else in the team, but ... I told him that I believed he had a tendency to get carried away and to play for the crowd rather than the team. He took it really well.

He approached me afterwards to talk about it. He wanted to hear more – and to just make sure he understood me. He was an entertainer, after all, so 'playing for the crowd' was natural for him. I told him I also loved to watch him bat. But I was also a team-mate, and he had nine other team-mates whom he had to think about. When he started getting into the crowd vibe and the adrenaline started pumping, he had to think about the team. Too many times he threw away his wicket when the team needed him. I was pleased with the chat. Even if we were being pumped by Sri Lanka, at least we had achieved something.

People said things to me that I had to take on the chin: I was too quick to criticise, I was too hard on the younger players. And I did take it all on board. I explained that I really was trying to act in everyone's best interests and for the good of the team, but I promised to try and be less confrontational. I was genuinely interested in being a better person – and a better cricketer.

But there's no doubt that some of the guys were just a bit too uncomfortable. They didn't enjoy the environment, and they didn't appreciate the truth coming out about certain attitudes and deficiencies. Perhaps it wasn't the right thing to do at that time, but, if everyone had got on like best friends and agreed with each other, did that mean the exercise was pointless or unnecessary? Perhaps that discomfort was needed. The truth can hurt, as we all know, and it's hard to choose pain and be positive about it. All I said was what I believed – that if you are in a team environment you need to trust one another, and you can't trust others if you can't be honest with them.

After the tour, eventually, I heard that Omar Henry, the convenor of selectors, had told someone that I was a 'troublemaker'. He said the squad was unhappy, and that I was the main cause of it! The squad was unhappy, for sure, but I was one of the people trying to fix that. Omar was probably only trying to show the country that he was 'doing something'.

Being dropped

In October 2004 Eric Simons was replaced as coach and I was left out of the tour of India. I got the news when Omar called me on my mobile. I was standing on the outfield at Buffalo Park either preparing for a practice or packing up after one. He told me I wouldn't be going on the tour. I had been left out of the squad.

I asked why. He said it was for disciplinary reasons. I asked him if he could, please, tell me what I had done wrong. He said I would have to speak to the coaching and management staff. I asked again. As the national selection convenor, he was ultimately responsible for the team. Couldn't he tell me? He just wouldn't answer me.

So I called Eric Simons and asked him if he knew the reason. He said it had nothing to do with him – that he had said nothing to the selectors. Eric never, ever lied. So I called a few of the players to ask if they knew anything about it. They didn't. Then I received a phone call from interim coach Ray Jennings that changed our relationship forever.

Jet had always been a Nic Pothas fan, and everyone knew that. That was absolutely fine with me; he wasn't the only one who thought Pothas had been unfairly overlooked. But Ray had said a few things in the newspapers that I thought were a bit harsh, so I assumed we were unlikely to make it onto each other's Christmas card lists. But when he phoned me that day, he said he had spoken to a couple of senior players and none of them had any problem with me being in the side. He said he asked them if I was a bad influence and they had all said 'no'. They said the opposite was true. That's what Ray told me. They said I was vital. So if they want me in the side, then he wants me in the side. He said the 'disciplinary' stuff was mostly lies and bullshit. He said he wanted me to put that crap out of my head and focus all my energy on producing the performances that everybody, including me, knew I was capable of. He made it absolutely clear that I was the best wicket-keeper/batsman in the country and that, if I performed to my potential, the selectors would have no option but to choose me again.

Then he said: 'Listen, Bouch. We may have had our differences in the past but there is absolutely nothing standing in your way back into the team. I have never held a grudge, so get out onto the park, do your best, and let your performances do your talking. Get your head down – and get on with it.'

And that's what I did. My father had always taught me about personal responsibility. If you're not succeeding, don't point fingers at other people; look in the mirror and point the finger at yourself. I went back to the drawing board and looked again at everything from technique to ambition and motivation.

This may sound strange, but I was probably taking too much responsibility for things I had no control over. I wasn't enjoying my cricket as much as I used to. I was a senior player, but that didn't mean I had to stop working on my own game and devote most of my time to others. When I wanted to go and hit balls in the nets, or catch balls, I didn't do that. Instead I would grab a couple of younger guys and run shuttles and sprints with them. So, when I was dropped, I realised it was time to work on my own game and perhaps be a little bit more selfish.

It was a quick transformation. I returned to the Warriors, scored runs, kept wicket well – and kept a smile on my face. Ray was right. I was reselected.

Christmas 2004

This was the first Christmas and festive season I'd had off for seven or eight years, and it was great. Part of me longed for the action and the thrill of being involved, especially as I was missing a tour to India followed by an England tour at home. But I'd made peace with the situation and I knew I had the backing of the coach – as long as I performed.

Some cricketers who have long careers go for a couple of decades without spending a normal family Christmas at home. There are always matches over the festive season, both international and domestic. I made the best of the situation, spending time on the beach and reflecting on my career and deciding what I wanted to be and to achieve.

Jacques and Graeme and a few of the other guys called me quite often from India saying they wished they were at home, too. And I said: 'I wish I was there with you!' I was really missing it.

I would wake up on match days and fight the urge to switch on the TV. If I did, I would be there for much of the day and feel pretty ordinary by the end of it. I forced myself to go to the beach with my fishing rod and to really enjoy the time, and I never, ever regretted it. I knew I would be better off clearing my head of cricket thoughts and taking a complete break. I spent a lot of time in Morgan Bay on the Wild Coast. I recommend it to anyone.

I was angry at first because I had been lied to. Or, at least, I had not been told the truth. Where had the 'disciplinary reasons' come from? I guessed there must have been some truth in it, but why wouldn't – or couldn't – anyone be honest with me? Throughout my career I always said to people: 'If you have something to say to me, say it to my face. Don't beat around the bush.' That's a big part of my character. It works both ways, too. I don't enjoy talking behind other people's backs. I'd rather get it off my chest so we both know where we stand. If it means an argument and hurt feelings, I'd rather have that than lingering resentment or suspicion. My preferred method of resolving disputes is to sit down and have a chat over a drink. That wasn't always possible with some guys, and perhaps I could have been more sensitive to that.

In the early days I just couldn't understand why people couldn't be the same with me, because it was just about being honest, about being a man, and man enough to speak your mind. I hope I became a little better at appreciating that people work in different ways.

I couldn't help feeling that there was something that many of the people I had spoken to weren't telling me. Especially Omar Henry. Being convenor of selectors can be a tough job, which involves breaking bad news to players. It's not pleasant. But that comes with the territory; it is a responsibility you accept when you take on the job. If he felt I needed to be dropped, he should have fronted up and told me why.

After Ray's phone call, I had calmed down a lot. I had focus and a direction, which is exactly what I needed. From feeling bleak and a bit desolate, I was confident that my destiny was back in my own hands.

If the idea had been to scare me, I have to say it probably worked. You get dropped for the first time at the age of 27 or 28 and you think: Is this it? Is it over? What the hell am I going to do now? I can understand how some people might think that could be beneficial to a player, but I cannot understand the lack of communication and honesty.

Ray had been forthright to the point of aggression. He knew how to speak to me. We are similar personalities, a bit 'hard' and very upfront. When I started to speak on the phone he interrupted: 'Shut up and listen to me! I'm trying to tell you what you need to do, so stop trying to talk and just listen.' I needed that. I thought about it a lot while I was fishing.

But I did have doubts. It wasn't pleasant to think that there were, or may have been, some of the team who didn't think I was the right man for the change room. As hard as I might have been as a cricketer, there was a side of me as a person that was vulnerable and insecure. Ray knew that – even though he wouldn't allow me to say it.

I learnt subsequently that some people weren't able or willing to take me at face value. I was too harsh and 'in your face' for certain players who didn't share my philosophy on what it took to win. I was too young to think about the damage or disharmony I might have been causing. If I had any doubts at all, I would have done whatever was in the best interests of the team. Or I hope I would have.

I realised later on in my career that you do need to take a backward step and approach certain situations in a calmer, quieter way. We are not all the same. Some team-mates who I thought were a bit weak or soft, weren't. They weren't. They were different. Difference can, and should, be a strength, not a weakness.

AB de Villiers

The first time I saw Mark play on TV was probably when I was 12 or 13 years old. Even as a schoolboy I knew that Nic Pothas was probably the obvious choice, but I remember thinking how the selectors had made a really good call because there was a lot of talent and fight in the guy. Early on in his career he played with so much freedom and had so much natural ability. Even as a kid I could see he was a serious player.

When I turned 20 Mark was dropped, for whatever reason, and Thami took his place. That's when I met him for the first time, when the Titans played the Warriors. We chatted and he 'logged' me as one of the next keepers coming up. He said Thami was a terrific talent but I must push him hard, because he thought I had just as much ability.

I have seen him be a really grumpy person and really hard on other people, but for some reason he just liked me and we got along really well. I had so much respect for him as a player and as a person. It's hard when you get dropped, but he was so kind to me from the word go. When it was announced that I would make my debut, we went out and had a chat about what was required and had a few beers. After that I thought: 'I want to be friends with this guy for a long, long time ahead.' I'm happy to say that has been the case.

I didn't last long as an international wicket-keeper for the Proteas because there is a big gap from first-class level to Test level. After a couple of Tests he was brought back and I was reinstated to opening the batting. As a 20-year-old, I had a lot to learn and Mark did everything he could to help me.

It was amazing to see the effect he had on the team. He was a captain, without being the captain. People listened and followed. He provided belief and confidence when, perhaps, it had been missing.

Dale Steyn

It was just my third Test match, against England at the Wanderers. I had played OK in my first two at St George's Park and Kingsmead, but I'd just had a bad spell at the Bullring. Coach Ray Jennings gave me an absolute bollocking during an interval. I felt terrible, almost on the point of tears. Then I saw Mark approaching me and thought he was coming to put an encouraging arm around my shoulders. He sat down and said: 'The same thing happened to me. You'll be OK. But you do know that you were shit, right? You deserved to hear that. Don't bowl like that again.'

It didn't feel very nice at the time, but it was exactly right. There's no point in sugar-coating the truth or talking bullshit. Mark was always the first person to tell the truth, never mind how difficult or awkward it was. Some people couldn't handle it, but they were poorer cricketers for that.

By the time I was a regular in the side, he had been there for years and had become the finished article as a wicket-keeper. Young keepers have to concentrate on watching the ball and catching it, whereas Mark was able to watch the bowlers all the time and see how the ball was coming out of their hands. He could pick up the slightest change of action and notice things that the bowlers themselves had no idea about. If anyone knows my action better than him, then I would like to meet that person, soon. He was insanely good at getting the best out of me. He would call me 'Pringle' if I was bowling pretty away-swingers at 130kph. I love watching the ball swing, and sometimes I forget to bowl the ball at 145kph. Bouch would say: 'You are not Meyrick Pringle, and you don't swing the ball as much as him anyway. You're Dale Steyn and you kill.' He could really piss me off, which is when I bowled my best.

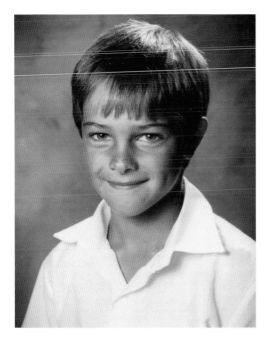

So much for the 'hard man' to come; butter wouldn't melt in my mouth. HEATHER BOUCHER

Squash champion: South Africa number 1 at under-13, under-15 and under-17. HEATHER BOUCHER

Selborne College, Standard 8: Sportsman's Dance with Hayley Stephen (now Hayley Wyer), still a good friend today. Not sure who chose my wardrobe that night ... Mom? GEOFF LOVE

Earliest days wearing the Proteas badge.
Am I good enough? HEATHER BOUCHER

A day I'll never forget. My first cap and blazer, awarded to me by Hansie
Cronje in Pakistan. DUIF DU TOIT/GALLO IMAGES

Pat Symcox and I enjoying a commemorative moment following our world-record 9th-wicket stand of 195 against Pakistan at the Wanderers in 1998. The picture was taken at the next Test match, at Kingsmead. TERTIUS PICKARD/ GALLO IMAGES

Another moment never to forget. First Test century – against the West Indies at Centurion, January 1999. We won the series 5-0. Allan Donald looks considerably happier than me, or was it relief? DUIF DU TOIT/GALLO IMAGES

Awards ceremony at St George's Park, 26 December 1999. Looking at pictures like this will always remind me of the highs and rewards of playing international cricket. You've won, and it's about to be made official. GALLO IMAGES

You can score 100s and you can score 50s, and you can score 27 not out. When the last one means you win your first series in India, there's no better feeling – 26 February 2000, Mumbai. GALLO IMAGES

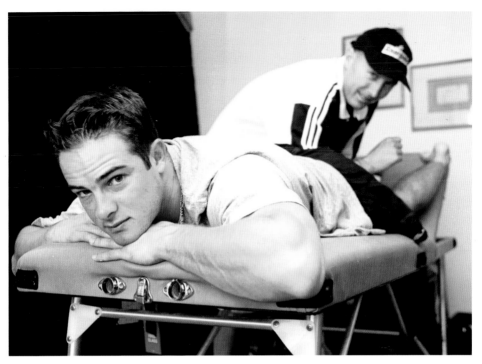

Part of the job. Many hundreds of hours were spent on the physio's bench, and Craig Smith was one of the best. DUIF DU TOIT/GALLO IMAGES

Not what I expected from international cricket, but I had nothing to hide at the King Commission of Inquiry into match-fixing. Lance Klusener is on the left and Dr Ali Bacher on the right. Cape Town, 12 June 2000. GALLO IMAGES

Wavell Hinds is run out, Port of Spain, 12 March 2001. This was my 153rd Test dismissal, taking me past the great Dave Richardson's South African record. DUIF DU TOIT/GALLO IMAGES

Manager Tim Southey, Jonty Rhodes, Allan Donald and me indulging in some drumming during a pre-World Cup team-building session, January 2003. DUIF DU TOIT/GALLO IMAGES

The Boucher family. From left to right (back): Mandy Carr (Boucher), Mark, Verdon (Dad), Che van Heerden (Boucher). In front is Heather (Mom). HEATHER BOUCHER

It didn't get any better than this – hitting the winning runs in the 438 game.
It was a long night after that ... DUIF DU TOIT/GALLO IMAGES

Chapter 10

The cricket bubble

There are two sorts of 'bubble' in which, to a greater or lesser degree, all professional cricketers exist. There's the one that cuts out all distractions while you're on the field of play and allows you to focus on the ball or the batsman. Sledging is used to break that bubble, to distract the opposition and make them play poorly.

The second bubble is the one in which you live a lot of your day-to-day life. It separates you from many aspects of the real world, so that you focus all your energy on playing the best cricket you can. The second bubble is mostly seen as a good thing by coaches and team management, but can be burst by many things – not just your opposition. Newspapers, commentators, over-enthusiastic fans, friends, sponsors, marketing people – they can all 'throw' a cricketer's concentration and play on his mind.

At the back end of my career, when my confidence was sinking, I became more and more susceptible to this kind of distraction. I listened to criticism and took it personally, whereas I used to pay no attention. So, the more vulnerable I became, the more vulnerable I was.

I appreciated the team management's attempts to shield me from the outside 'negativity' and to strengthen the bubble around me. However, now that I have retired, I realise that the policy can create an environment in which everything is about me, me and me. It inflates your sense of self-importance – and it comes at a high price. You forget about close friends; you forget family birthdays; you don't phone people back. And all because you are too tightly wrapped up in the cricket family. Only once I left the bubble and the cricket family circle did I realise and recognise the consequences.

For cricketers, the game is not just a massive part of their life – it *is* their life. The financial rewards are greater than ever and will probably climb even higher, but it's not just that. For me, and for so many others, it is the thrill of representing your country, of competing on the greatest stage, and of winning. There is nothing comparable to the thrill of winning. No amount of money could ever buy the feeling of being a member of the first South African team to win a Test series in Australia after a century of trying, or of hitting the winning runs in the 438 game.

But cricket will not be there forever. That is guaranteed.

Afterwards I could see the damage I did to friendships, relations with the public, and even family ties because of the bubble. I look at my former colleagues now and can see them doing similar things. You can fix some of them, but some are broken beyond repair. Sometimes I think about bursting the bubble around my team-mates so they do not experience some of the regrets I have, but what if that is detrimental to their careers? Perhaps they really do need the bubble to perform at their best. Maybe I did.

It's been said that some of the greatest players in history had the ability to climb in and out of the bubble whenever appropriate, and never needed to burst it. It's a great thought. But when do you climb in and out? How do you explain to your mates that you wanted to be in the bubble when they needed to talk to you but you're outside it now?

At the end of your career, you realise how many people you pushed away, and for how long, and you wonder how you might be able to get them back as friends, to reaffirm their confidence in you, that you can be relied on. Inside the bubble you believe you are untouchable, invincible. That arrogance is useful in the game of cricket, where you are destined to fail as an individual far, far more often than you are likely to succeed. Statistics confirm this. The problem is that such arrogance is a major hindrance in life once your cricketing days are over.

I don't know how to get the balance right, but I'm confident that knowing there is a balance to be found, and understanding why, is better than living in the bubble. Although I'm no expert, I'm confident that I could make a positive contribution to players in the future.

Gary Kirsten and Paddy Upton did a particularly good job of this in my final couple of years. Gary encouraged players to take responsibility for their own lives and their decision-making both in cricket and outside. As performance director, Paddy made sure the younger guys didn't just sit in their rooms each day, and he discussed with them the road they were on and the options that lay ahead. His role was coaching life skills rather than cricket skills, and he managed to do it in a way that didn't feel like a lecture! Ultimately, if you like yourself a little more, and respect yourself a little more, that will inevitably filter into your game and you will become a better cricketer.

An artificial world

International cricketers live in an artificial world, and there isn't much they can do to change that. Some are more grounded than others, but it's not a normal lifestyle. Even for young, single men, it is not right to be away from home for up to 250 days a year, for year after year.

The way we are treated isn't always healthy, either. I can understand the logic behind making life as easy and simple as possible for the players, but perhaps they need to think about something other than cricket. Perhaps it would provide them with some valuable perspective.

Every effort was made to shelter the players from the real world, especially the night before a Test match. This was appreciated by everyone at the time, but it didn't suit everyone. Certain players would be shielded from the media in case there was adverse criticism. They would be kept away from newspapers the following day so that they wouldn't be distracted or upset. Any issues that cropped up before or during a Test match would be dealt with by the management. Nobody outside our immediate friends and family could get hold of us.

The idea was to maximise on-field performances, but I wonder whether the effort would have been better spent in teaching players how to deal with the real world rather than protecting them from it. Ideally it would be better for a player to know about an issue, and to be able to deal with it, rather than to be shielded from it. You can't protect him forever. I'd rather a player learns the skill of leaving baggage in the change room when he walks out to bat or field.

Mental strength

I will never question the use of a psychologist in sport. I may have done as a naive youngster, but not now. But I do believe it is a matter of personal choice. There is nothing wrong with having a team psychologist, as long as everyone is aware that people function differently when it comes to on-field performances.

Paddy Upton did a great job with the national team, and I spent plenty of one-on-one time with him. I don't believe he could have improved my temperament or performance in pressure situations, but he helped me in other ways. He was a good sounding board, a good guy to chat with about relationships and perceptions. Once I'd realised that we all work in different ways I enjoyed discussing differences with him!

But in terms of rising to the occasion and performing under pressure, I relied upon self-talk and self-belief. It came from my earliest days on the squash court, doing my training routines at 4:30 am. I knew nobody else was doing that. Many times I didn't want to be there. It hurt and I was cold and tired. But there was nobody else there to encourage me, or push me. Only me. It was just me. I used to talk to myself, asking whether I wanted to give up, asking how strong I was.

Jacques always said that the strongest cricketers, mentally, are the ones who have been through some strong challenges early in their lives. Jacques pushed himself very hard as a youngster and also had the tragedy of his mother's death to deal with as a nine-year-old. His father believed in many old-fashioned virtues, but top of the list were hard work, discipline, good manners and respect. When he passed away, in 2003, Jacques may have been alone but he had his father's guiding influence to help him.

There is a common and successful technique used by psychologists that involves writing down your off-field worries or concerns in a diary and leaving them in your kitbag or locker when you walk onto the field. I can see how and why that works, but I preferred to keep everything 'real', to take those concerns onto the field with me but then separate them from the game once I was there. It was a test of mental strength for me. Some cricketers return from a game and successfully deal with problems they have isolated for the day – or the match. For me it was a test of mental strength to isolate those issues while I was on the field rather than pretend they weren't there. I couldn't pretend they didn't exist. I might not have wanted to speak to anyone about them.

I learnt a lot from Jacques. It is impossible to forget about something completely. If something happens on the morning of a game, it is always there when you walk out onto the field. At times it can become an advantage, because you can take whatever has angered or hurt you and use it to increase your determination to succeed. There were times when I was upset about things that were said about me, but I put them in a box on the side of the field. When I was feeling a bit loose in my game, I thought of that little box and reminded myself that I was playing to try and show that person in the box how wrong they were. Towards the end of my career, I found that a little bit tougher, but I would say to myself: 'I have been through tough times before; let's not pretend you don't have any. Just deal with them later. Now concentrate on your job.'

I used to think that if I trained hard enough, for long enough, I wouldn't get tired at the end of a long, hot day in the field. It took a while before I realised that was impossible. Instead of trying to 'ban' tiredness, it's more important to recognise it and work with it, not against it.

Anybody can make life easier for themselves by learning how their bodies operate best – what to eat, when to eat, how much to drink. Some people make the mistake of going on instinct, eating and drinking when they think they need to. By then it can be too late to make a difference to your performance on that day.

Cramp is a cricketer's nightmare. Some people are more vulnerable to it than others, no matter how they prepare. I only cramped once in my career, and it was all my fault. I was boiling inside after a hot morning session in India – one of the 'oven cities' like Chennai. I climbed into an ice bath at lunchtime and stayed there for most of the interval. I didn't feel hungry afterwards so didn't eat anything. Big mistake.

Some time before tea, I started feeling weak and a bit faint. I had blurred vision but, with a big effort, was able to focus my eyes for each delivery. I was calm and rational. I had to decide whether the team would be better served by me in this condition or by a stand-in taking the gloves without preparation in difficult wicket-keeping conditions. I had to get through it.

It was important that I conserved what energy I had and used it only when necessary, so I stopped running up to the stumps after every delivery. It was more important that I was strong and focused as the bowler delivered every ball. The wicket-keeper is a little different to the other fielders; I couldn't call the 12th man on. Everyone knew I was cramping: they could see me hobbling between overs, although I was trying to hide it. Self-talk got me through it, together with a bit of pride and a lot of self-belief. Nobody else could have said anything to help me.

Nobody ever really asked me about dealing with pressure situations during my playing career. Perhaps professional sportsmen are reluctant to ask their peers or team-mates. After I retired, many people asked me what made me cope, even thrive. Although my team-mates backed me and were happy for me to be at the crease when things were tight and the game was on the line, they never asked what made me tick. Perhaps they didn't care. As long as I was happy to be there, that's all that mattered.

Chapter 11

Security issues

Having endured a miserable tour of Sri Lanka in 2004, the Proteas had a quick opportunity for redemption with a return tour just two years later. If the players thought the 2004 tour was bad, this one opened their eyes to greater depths.

Jacques Kallis and Graeme Smith were both injured and missed the tour. Ashwell was named as captain of the Test side, which was a huge issue for CSA and the media but was nothing more than logical for the players. He was the right choice – and he happened to be South Africa's first non-white Test captain. But because he wasn't in the one-day team, I was named as captain of the ODI squad.

Strangely enough, I didn't think we played too badly in the Tests, although the first one (27-31 July) will always be remembered for the highest partnership of all time for any wicket, between Mahela Jayawardene and Kumar Sangakkara. We gave them the perfect start by being bowled out for 169 in 50 overs. Dale Steyn then removed both openers in his first two overs and we thought we were back in the game. The two big men were at the crease before tea on the first day, and we had Ntini and Steyn with a brand-new ball. They batted for the next two days.

They put on 624 for the third wicket. At one stage it seemed certain that Jayawardene would break Brian Lara's world record of 400. Nicky Boje bowled the unluckiest 65 overs in history and took 0-221, which was also a record for South Africa and second worst overall. Jayawardene did have the decency to single Nicky out afterwards to say he'd actually bowled well and had been unlucky. I distinctly remember Jayawardene playing forward to one ball, which turned and bounced over the shoulder of his bat. He was on about 300 at that stage.

Nicky bowled particularly well with the third new ball! It was gripping and bouncing, but still there was no luck for him. When the first two balls had become older and soft, the batsmen were in complete control. I wondered whether they were toying with us at times, hitting deliveries into gaps that, really, shouldn't have been possible. They were masters in those conditions.

Sangakkara finally nicked one off Andrew Hall on 287. Although nobody had ever seen or experienced anything like that partnership before (there were only a couple of us who had fielded for two straight days), the attitude was incredible. Nobody gave up. The bowlers, led by a young and hostile Steyn, ran in all day. Both days.

It was painfully hot and humid, the pitch was flat, we dropped a couple of catches – and the batsmen were in the best form of their lives. They're also best mates and have that understanding that allows them to keep each other going. But, still, it was the greatest display of concentration I had seen since Gary's 275 at Kingsmead seven years earlier.

On the second day of the partnership, the Sinhalese Sports Club set off fireworks to celebrate each landmark and milestone as they passed them. Double hundreds, 400 partnership, Sri Lankan record, world record ... there seemed to be fireworks going off all afternoon. The only one left by the end of the day was for Mahela's world record. At the start of play the next day, the players were presented with cars as reward for their efforts. They were driven onto the field of play, where the keys were handed over to the batsmen. It was unusual, to say the least, but I enjoy the appreciation that players are shown in India and Sri Lanka. Records are celebrated properly.

As much as I did not enjoy standing behind the stumps and getting dehydrated for two days, I did enjoy watching them bat. In cricket you get a sense when something is about to happen. A couple of rash shots, a batsman looking tired ... you get a feeling when a wicket is going to fall. It just never happened on those two days. Once or twice I thought 'maybe now', but the feeling soon went away. And then, finally, it was over. Completely out of the blue. Mahela missed one from Andre Nel. Even though we were dead on our feet, we wouldn't have minded seeing him reach 400. But he missed one from Nella and that was that: 756-5 declared.

Most teams would have capitulated in their second innings under that sort of pressure. A first-innings deficit of 587 runs – it's too big to comprehend. It might as well have been 1000. But we put up a hell of a fight, with Jacques Rudolph and Hally putting on 165 for the first wicket. We really started to believe we could bat for a couple of days to save the game. We finished the fourth day on 311-4 with Ashwell and me at the crease. We had batted 105 overs – just another 90 to go. On a fifth-day wicket against Muttiah Muralitharan.

Murali bowled 64 overs in that innings, just one less than Boje. Except he finished with 6-131. We took until close to tea on that final day, but the result was still a thrashing. We lost by an innings and 153 runs. All things considered, we had fought back well. Only in Test cricket can you be hammered and still keep your dignity and self-respect.

The second Test (4-8 August) was a thriller – the closest I ever came to playing in a tied Test. Ashwell led from the front with 86 and AB de Villiers made 95 in our first innings of 361. Dale and Makhaya then took nine wickets between them and we had a lead of 40. At 207-6 in our second innings we were a bit short of what we needed, but I scrambled 65 and we got to 311, setting them a target of 352. It was a huge target and we were pretty confident of levelling the series – but not over-confident.

We couldn't believe that Jayawardene was doing it again. He picked up exactly where he had left off a week earlier and made 123 until, finally, Boje got his man. But at 341-7 the game looked over, with just 11 runs needed. But Hally picked up two more wickets and the last man, Lasith

Malinga, came to the wicket with two needed to win and scrambled a couple of singles to win the game.

I loved Sri Lanka; it was one of my favourite places to tour. Galle is one of the most beautiful venues in the world. The people are humble, generous and hospitable. Strangely enough, although we struggled on the field against a team that was always highly skilled and tough to beat, this never detracted from our enjoyment of the country. Except for what happened after this Test series.

Difficult decision

During the build-up to the tour, there had been quite a few security problems relating to Sri Lanka's civil war with the Tamil Tigers, and these had continued during the Tests. When the war was contained in the north of the country it was safe for teams to tour and play in Galle and Colombo, but when terrorist-type activity started spreading south towards the capital, that's when the situation changed.

We had spoken about it at team meetings, and I had tried to assure everybody that we were well looked after by our security company. They would not allow us to be placed in a dangerous situation.

A couple of days before the first game I met our manager, Goolam Rajah, in the team room downstairs in the hotel. We had a conference call booked with SACA CEO Tony Irish, and with Graeme and Jacques, who were looking after our interests back in Cape Town. Tony confirmed that a number of bombs had been detonated in and around Colombo in the preceding week and that our security consultants, Nicholls Steyn & Associates (NSA), had stated that there had been a significant change to the security status of the city.

Bob Nicholls and Rory Steyn are among the best in the business and had been used on a regular basis by the ICC. They knew their stuff, and we trusted them completely. So when they said they believed the city to be unsafe for us to play in, we were a bit rattled.

There was concern that we had to follow the correct protocol, which involved informing the ICC of our security report and going through diplomatic channels. The Sri Lankan government also promised to boost their security for the teams to 'presidential level'. The recommendation from NSA was that we commit to staying for another 48 hours; if the situation did not change, we would postpone or cancel the rest of the tour and return home.

For the next two days we were effectively under house arrest. Or rather hotel arrest. It wasn't nearly as bad as it sounds because we weren't confined to our rooms and there was a very pleasant shopping arcade next door to the hotel that was accessible through the lobby. There was plenty of security there, too. We were allowed to go to the arcade but not outside the actual building.

There was some local hostility towards us at that stage, but people made the mistake of believing it was the players who didn't want to play. We were simply following instructions from those in charge of our safety and security. At lunchtime on the first day I went to the arcade to buy a couple of baguettes from a French patisserie. (They were really good and had become a favourite for many of the guys.)

A newspaper photographer took a picture of me and it appeared the following day with the caption: 'Do these cricketers look terrified?' The picture made it back to South Africa, too, and there was a backlash from people saying that we should just get on with it and play the tournament. Several people declared, from the comfort of their lounges, that we were making a fuss about nothing, and that there was violence at home, too, so what is the problem? What were we scared of?

Editorials and comment pieces in Sri Lanka suggested that we *were* scared – but only of playing against Sri Lanka after the beating we'd taken in the Test matches. 'Running scared – of losing' was one headline I recall.

That night, a letter had been pushed under my door. It was addressed to: 'Mr M. Boucher, SA Cricket Captain'. It was from one of the Tamil Tiger leaders. The letter stated that they had no desire to hurt us and that we had nothing to do with their war. But he said that a bombing campaign was under way in Colombo and that it would be very unfortunate if we were affected. He said they could make no promises or guarantees for our safety and recommended we leave the country as soon as possible.

I immediately called our security man, Faisal Dhajee (from NSA), and went downstairs to meet him. He informed me that, earlier that day, a bomb had been detonated in a shopping centre just a few kilometres from the hotel – and that two of the journalists covering the tour had been there about 20 minutes earlier. We had all been shopping there on our days off.

Faisal needed to verify the letter, and the Sri Lankan authorities soon confirmed that it was authentic. It felt like a net was drawing tighter. At what point do you say 'enough'? Faisal made the appropriate calls, including to Tony Irish and Cricket South Africa, and the decision was made to return home as soon as flights could be arranged.

A television news team was at Cape Town airport when I walked through passport control. The camera was in my face within a few seconds and the line of questioning was hostile, to say the least: 'Are you scared of playing Sri Lanka? Why did you come home? What do you think this will do for South Africa's reputation?' They had no idea of the facts. It was sensationalism. I thought about trying to explain, but I knew they'd probably run only 30 seconds on the news that night, so I didn't say anything. That probably looked bad, too. Sometimes you really can't win. When some minds are made up, you can't change them.

It was a difficult time for everybody but, as captain, I felt I was carrying a ridiculous load. It's one thing making team selections and bowling changes, but you don't expect your decisions to have the potential of life and death! I was never scared of playing against any individual or team. Even when we were being hammered by one of the strongest Australian teams of all time, I always wanted another go. So it really touched a raw nerve when it was suggested we were running away from a contest.

Three years later, when the Sri Lanka team was attacked in Lahore, I thought immediately about how some of their players had intimated that we were showing weakness in leaving their country. We chose to leave when it had become dangerous; they chose to go to a region when it had become dangerous. It probably wasn't even their players who chose to go. The decision would have been made by men in suits in comfortable offices.

At our team meetings before we returned home, there were one or two players who asked whether we were overreacting. They were young and ambitious and were keen to play for their country. I totally understood where they were coming from. I tried to explain that we were cricketers, not security experts, and that was why we employed experts to make these decisions for us. All I asked for was that we stick together and abide by whatever decision was made. We all agreed that we would not make any rash decisions, and we didn't. But the letter from the Tamil Tigers convinced the last few doubters.

We tried to rationalise everything. We asked lots of questions, like: what does 'presidential security' mean? The answer is bigger numbers – more troops, more vehicles and more weapons. Which also means a bigger target for the Tigers. And more chance of us being caught in the crossfire. I wasn't ever worried that a Tamil Tiger would walk up to me and put a bullet through my head. The letter was very polite in explaining that we were not a target. It even said that Tamils love cricket!

Pakistan, 2007

South Africa were the last non-Asian nation to tour Pakistan before the fatal attack on the Sri Lankan team in Lahore in March 2009. There was a great deal of debate about whether the tour should go ahead, given the security concerns in the country and the region as a whole. In the end a tour comprising two Test matches and five one-day internationals did go ahead – and without significant incident.

There were major security concerns, as everybody expected, in the months leading up to the tour. The speculation about whether it would go ahead raged on and was a constant distraction for all of us. The team was taking shape under Mickey Arthur and Graeme Smith, and we were keen to play, but not if safety was an issue. There was just too

129

long to think about everything. One day we'd be absolutely certain that we would just concentrate on playing cricket and leave the security to the experts, and the next we were saying there was no way on Earth we would go.

As always, the final decision was left with Bob Nicholls and Rory Steyn. We knew they would pull us out if the situation became unsafe. Our faith and confidence in them was always high, and it had increased even further after their decision to pull us out of Colombo 15 months earlier. A lot of political and diplomatic pressure had been applied to keep us there, but they knew what the right thing to do was and they had the courage of their convictions.

Bob and Rory completed their survey of the Pakistani stadiums, facilities and security plans, but they wanted some final questions answered before giving the green light. In the past they had been promised many things verbally, only to arrive and find nothing had been implemented. So they asked for everything to be signed off in writing and double-checked. The offer from the Pakistan Cricket Board and the government was 'full presidential-level' security. Bob and Rory, thorough as always, wanted to know exactly what that entailed. We arrived to find a small army had been assigned to look after us. Often we assumed that a certain patrol had nothing to do with us, but, more often than not, they were a part of our assignment.

Our main fear was being targeted in a case of mistaken identity. But we felt we could limit the chances of that happening if we hung out in large groups, making it fairly obvious that we were South African. We tried to make sure we wore something with a South African flag on it at all times – team kit has never been worn so much in leisure time before. Subtly though, we weren't thinking of singing 'Shosholoza' in the hotel lobby. But there was a lot of crossfire, and there was bugger all we could do about that.

'No Fear'

The whole tour proceeded without any security incident to speak of, but it was still an eye-opener for most of us. Even by the end of six weeks in the country we had not grown accustomed to being surrounded by so many soldiers. We had confirmation of what we had suspected in Sri Lanka – that 'presidential security' just meant 'more'. Not more sophisticated, or more planning, just 'more'. At one stage, our consultant had an issue with a particular aspect of the security – a potential weakness in the system. It was a technical or logistical issue, nothing to do with manpower. The solution provided to us the following day was … 150 more troops.

The Special Services troops assigned to protect us proudly wore black T-shirts emblazoned with the words 'No Fear'. They all carried machine guns. Many of us couldn't help thinking what a tempting target they would be for terrorists wishing to make a statement. Three hundred security troops all in close proximity – with us in the middle somewhere. It made you want to keep your distance from them. None of us had seen anything like it before, and none of us were comfortable. Having said that, they were good people, always ready to pose for a photo with us and rarely without a smile.

After one of the ODIs there was a bit of trouble outside the stadium, where some protestors burnt an American flag. We could see it through a window in the back of the change room. All the doubts and worries about the region quickly returned. It was the only occasion on the whole tour where it occurred to me that things could get out of control.

During the Karachi Test (1-5 October) I had a room next to the lifts where our trio of all-night security troops were stationed. They talked and talked and talked, eating watermelon seeds and keeping each other entertained. I guess it was an easy assignment. I asked them three or four times, as politely as possible, to keep the noise down and showed them that I was trying to get some sleep. They would go quiet for about five minutes and then the volume would pick up again. Eventually I lost my patience and asked them to move, which they did – leaving the lift unguarded and open for whoever wanted to visit the floor, which was exclusively reserved for the players and management. They moved around the corner and I could still hear them chatting away, but I managed to get to sleep.

I was up early for breakfast the following day, after about four hours of sleep, and I wondered where they had got to. It was very quiet. I walked round the corner to find them fast asleep on the corridor carpet.

Return to Pakistan?

I haven't had the opportunity to speak to the Pakistan players about the chances of international cricket tours resuming, but the captain, Misbah-ul-Haq, did speak with some passion, when they came to South Africa soon after my retirement, about how much the country needs them. He said the game is dying without international exposure, and I can understand that. It's hard enough, as a player, spending half the year away from home, but when you have to play your 'home' fixtures in the UAE it must be close to impossible to have a normal life. It is unfortunate, but I know Misbah wouldn't want to put players' lives at risk.

With enough security personnel, it should be possible to guarantee safety. But who wants to play cricket like that? It used to upset me when I heard of visiting teams being too scared to leave the Sandton Sun at night because of Joburg's reputation for crime. Fortunately, South Africa remains a favourite tour for most teams, and they take away happy memories of beaches, game parks, good food, golf courses and, of course, Table Mountain.

The security experts talk about 'acceptable risk'. As a cricketer, I'm inclined to think than no risk is acceptable. I remember people telling us that we would never be targeted because 'Pakistanis love cricket'. And I believed them, because I saw the passion for the game there. But there are others who wouldn't think twice about using cricket as a target.

I am not overly cautious or security-conscious. I'm not a scared or timid person. But I do believe it's reasonable to have a fair say in how safe you are, to have some control over your own destiny. I don't think that is the case in Pakistan for a touring international cricketer.

The stream of information from Nicholls Steyn & Associates was a great comfort on the tour. Players could take as much interest in the situation as they chose. Some were happy to leave it to the experts and others wanted as much information as possible. I was more interested in the process of gathering intelligence and how they kept up to date with developments around the country.

The 2007 Rugby World Cup final was played while we were in Pakistan. The television production crew managed to tap into a satellite feed of the game and to stream it into our team room, and we watched the whole build-up and the game until well after midnight. A couple of the South African journalists watched the game with us – the perfect opportunity to build bridges! We had originally planned to move on to the next destination at 7:00 am the following day but management soon changed that. It was a 'dry' weekend so we didn't have any beer to celebrate but it wasn't the first time. Jacques had earlier celebrated the incredible feat of scoring hundreds in both innings of a Test with a couple of bottles of sparkling water!

There was a lot of hotel room time on that tour, though. Too much. You have to keep your mind occupied to avoid cabin fever setting in. We played a lot of board games and cards. I started as a backgammon novice but was hard to beat by the end.

Such a confined tour can be a superb way of getting to know your team-mates and strengthening the bonds between you, but there is always the danger that you can encroach too far into one another's personal space – often through no fault of your own. It just happens. You have to be able to be honest with each other and to discuss your feelings in an unintimidating or threatening atmosphere. We were just beginning to get there. It wasn't a major problem but it was also an opportunity missed. The process of reaching that point as a squad began a year or so later and gathered more momentum when Gary Kirsten took over as coach in June 2011.

Chapter 12

Facing Australia

South Africa lost the 2005-2006 Test series 2-0, yet there was so much more to the script than simply being outplayed. A high-scoring draw in Perth proved that the Proteas were able to compete. Defeat by 184 runs in the Boxing Day Test at the MCG in Melbourne ended the team's hopes of becoming the first South African side to win a series in Australia, but they were determined to salvage some honour in the final Test in Sydney. However, Graeme Smith became just the second captain in history to declare in both innings and lose the game. The great leg spinner Shane Warne pronounced the Proteas 'the worst team to have left South African shores.' For the tourists, the words hurt – mostly because they were patently untrue.

I t was a tough tour. We believed we had a decent team, albeit a bit inexperienced. It was still the great Australian team that had dominated the world game for a decade. There was some talk of the era coming to an end but, frankly, while some of the players may have been in their mid-30s they had lost none of their magic. Having lost on the two previous tours, I was apprehensive about losing again. The other senior guys were realistic. We didn't believe we necessarily had the firepower to take them on from the first ball, but we truly believed we had the fight to take them deep into every game. And when you do that, you always give yourselves a chance.

We did compete, too. We could easily have drawn that final Test in Sydney, but Graeme was adamant that he'd rather lose 2-0 in pursuit of a 1-1 draw than settle for a 1-0 defeat without trying to do something about it. It was his decision to declare, but there were no dissenters. I still think it was the right thing to do, and always will.

Mickey and Graeme sat together on the plane back from Australia. While some guys slept, some of us were already planning for the next tour. We may have lost 2-0 and been labelled as useless by Warne, but we knew better. We all knew better.

A major part of Mickey's planning involved a rethink on the mental side of the game. He was so passionate about doing well against Australia, because he said it was the way history would judge you as a coach or captain. There's no doubt that we had allowed ourselves to be affected by some aspects of playing in Australia – other aspects were unavoidable, like the scars from losing the previous six series against them, home and away.

The 438 game

Australia toured South Africa in the summer of 2006. Coach Mickey Arthur and captain Graeme Smith have both written about the extraordinary developments before 'the greatest' ODI in history – the so-called 438 game at the Wanderers on 12 March. Opening batsman Herschelle Gibbs had suffered a relapse in discipline the night before the series-deciding match, and had not located his hotel room until the early hours of the morning. There was a lengthy meeting of team management over breakfast to decide whether Gibbs should be dropped from the match. He made it by the skin of his teeth. And then played one of the greatest innings in South Africa's ODI history.

I wasn't aware of the situation with Herschelle before the game. That was probably a deliberate ploy by Mickey and Graeme. I would have been pretty annoyed if I'd known that he'd been half-drunk at breakfast after getting to bed in the early hours of the morning. The only two things I was certain of were that he was prone to doing stupid things and that he was really, really pumped up for that game.

It's understandable that most people forget the background to the game. We went 2-0 up in the series quite easily and could easily have won it 4-0 by the time we got to the Wanderers. Australia fought back bravely and won the third game by 24 runs before winning the fourth by one wicket.

We were particularly dejected after the fourth game in Durban (10 March). The last wicket pair needed 6 to win and we blew it. Australia should never have won that game. But I couldn't help admiring them for doing it. In your bleakest moments, ask yourself how the opposition might be feeling. If you say 'lucky', then you really have blown it. If they are saying 'We fought hard and deserve it,' then good for them.

We were all nervous before the Wanderers match. We were 'up' for the game, because everyone loves to play in the Bullring, but we were tense, too. There is negative tension and positive tension in sport. You don't like to admit it at the time, but you can tell the difference. This was definitely positive tension.

The stadium was packed. It looked like a belter of a pitch, but it almost always does at the Wanderers. It looked especially good, though.

Adam Gilchrist made his usual blazing start, but then Andrew Hall took a blinder of a catch at mid on to send him back for 55 with almost 100 on the board after 15 overs. I thought that might calm things down a bit.

But Ricky Ponting played the innings of a lifetime. His hooking and cutting was just spectacular. Simon Katich even hit a six, so everything was hitting the middle of the bat. Mike Hussey smashed ... and Ponting was just unstoppable.

At one point, Hersch was gazing at the scoreboard between overs and looking a bit confused. He walked over to me and said: 'Bouch, they could get 400 here!' I just shook my head: 'Try again, Hersch. Do the maths. We're going to do bloody well to keep them to 400.'

The boundary was unusually short on one side of the ground, but, the truth is, that made almost no difference whatsoever. The sixes weren't just dropping over the rope; they were landing on row 18. The ball was running on the outfield like snooker balls on a table. The pitch was as perfect for batting as any surface in the world. You can't measure how 'good' a pitch is (or how 'bad' for bowlers), but the scores at the Wanderers would suggest it's probably in the top three in the world. As we got deeper into the innings we started thinking and feeling things we had never felt before. This was such a massive game for us and ... we looked at the scoreboard and didn't know whether to laugh or cry. When it said 380, or something like that, I had to look hard at the 3 because it didn't look right. Surely it had to be a 2? There were moments when we did have a quiet laugh, though. You had to. No point in crying.

Roger Telemachus had an interesting time with the ball, poor guy. He'd bowled superbly for eight overs and had gone for just 47. His figures stood out like a beacon on the scoreboard because they were so respectable, while everyone else's looked like they'd been in a car crash. Jacques had figures of 6-0-70-0! Unfortunately for Roger, he was our nominated death bowler in that game. If you get it just slightly wrong in those conditions, you end up in the stands. Poor Roger – after a couple of fours and sixes, the wheels completely fell off. There were no balls and wides added to the mix, and at one stage I was worried that he wouldn't be able to finish the over. He was shaking. His 10 overs cost 87. It was not a day to be a bowler. Much later, Roger's figures were made to look half decent by Mick Lewis, who conceded a world record 113 from his 10 overs.

The Australians were high-fiving each other and celebrating all over their change room balcony. There was a lot of laughter and a sense of disbelief. The only thing they were absolutely certain about was that they had won the game. But I knew it was only half-time and ... no, just kidding. I thought they'd won the game, too.

There were plenty of empty seats when the innings ended, and I saw a lot of people filing out of the stadium. Maybe they were just going to get lunch or a beer, but it seemed like more than that. Leaving at half-time. It was a terrible thought. We had really stuffed it up.

As we sat in the change room there was little noise – just the moans and groans of sore bodies and battered spirits. It is well known that Jacques says very little in team meetings or in the change room, but when he does everybody else shuts up. When he speaks, it is worth listening. We were all quite surprised when he stood up after a few minutes. Everyone looked at him.

'OK, guys, I think the bowlers have done their job. Now it's up to the batsmen,' he said. He kept a straight face, so we weren't immediately sure. Then he said: 'They're 15 runs short; this is a 450 wicket.' A great weight was lifted off our shoulders. The big man had spoken and had made a joke out of a desperate situation; it allowed everyone else to laugh. Suddenly there was a lot of laughter and plenty of swearing, but at least it wasn't bottled up inside. We had nothing to lose. What the hell – let's give it a go. Before that moment, I don't believe anybody would even have talked about trying to win. It seemed too ridiculous.

I think I was one of the first to try and take the run chase seriously. I said to Mickey: 'Coach, we can't just say balls-to-the-wall and to hell with it; we need to make a plan. Let's try and draw up something and try and stick to the plan.' Mickey was funny: 'Sure, Bouch. A plan to chase 434 – I've done loads of those.' But we did it. We were writing down numbers that made us laugh. Usually, if you're chasing 300 – which was pretty much considered the limit back then – you would start with a target of 60 from the first 10 overs with no more than one wicket down. This time we wrote 100 off the first 10. It was a liberating exercise. Mickey always enjoyed thinking out of the box. We both did. Then it was 180 off 20, or something similarly silly.

We lost Boeta Dippenaar very early and the bad thoughts started. What if we lose another wicket? But Graeme and Hersch just went berserk, and it went on and on ... You reach that point where you know it can't carry on, because you've seen and played in enough of these games. Someone will get out. The partnership reached 100 at 10 runs per over. Then 120, 150 ... Eventually, on 187, Graeme was caught in the deep for 90 from just 55 balls. Amazing.

Herschelle was still going strong, and was even accelerating. At the 20-over mark we were about 40 runs ahead of our projected target. It was completely surreal. I looked at the coach and said: 'Maybe it's time to start getting more strategic here. Take our foot off the pedal a bit, actually start believing we can win this.' Everything was moving at such a fast pace; we would start to analyse where the game was and it would move again. It was like a highlights package. My fear was that Herschelle would struggle to change his game. He was flying in sixth gear with his foot hard down. We all knew how he struggled to change back down the gears when he was in that mode.

Hersch played an unbelievable innings, and we could never have got within a hundred runs without it. At that stage he was the only person in the country who could have played it. But he wasn't the one to take us home. He could take us so far, further than anyone else at that stage, but as soon as he realised we had a chance, he would get out. When it became serious and no longer just him having fun and dazzling everyone with his skill, it would be too much. So I spoke to everyone else left in the change room and said: 'Look, Hersch will get out now but he's given us a chance. Let's not panic. The tail is going to have to wag big-time, but we've done it before and we can do it again. This time it'll be the biggest day of our lives.'

An over later, he chipped one down to Brett Lee at long off and it was down to the rest of us. I said: 'We have our targets, let's just stick to them. Forget about the total. We know what we have to do.'

As I left the change room to replace Hersch it was 299-4 with just less than 20 overs to go. I looked at the guys and said: 'We've scored this many before with six wickets left – and we're going to do it again. This game is ours for the taking. That was the moment when the whole mood in the change room shifted. I could sense that everyone was thinking: 'Shit, he's right. We can actually win this.'

Targets were sent out as regularly as possible, but I was aware of what they were and my biggest concern was that we were ahead of them. I was concerned that we might get caught in the no-man's land of trying to stick to them or carrying on as we were. If we kept wickets in hand, I was confident we'd get home. In hindsight, we should probably have made an effort to relax Hersch and encourage him to keep having fun. We should have told him to keep enjoying himself and we'd bat around him. We might have won with three overs to spare if we'd done that! We could have avoided all that last-over agony.

Jacques and I knew we had to calm things down a bit because we'd just lost AB and Hersch in successive overs and we were way ahead of schedule. The plan was for Jacques to bat through until the end, with me and the rest of a strong lower middle order taking more chances and looking for boundaries. But when Jacques hit a return catch to Andrew Symonds, Mickey's last words before I went out to bat came back to me: 'You bat until the end, Bouch, and we win the game.' It was definitely up to me to be there at the end.

The guys coming in behind me were unbelievable: Johan van der Wath smashed 35 from 18 balls, Roger made 12 off six, and Andrew Hall hit the four that seemed to have won the game at 433-8 with four balls to go. Then he hit one to mid on. Oh no. But all three of them had been calm when they got to the crease and they all said the same thing: you must stay here; we will take the chances. They took the pressure off me completely. I managed to find a couple of boundaries, but they were the real heroes at the end because they all managed to smash it from ball one.

When Hally hit that boundary off the first ball of the last over I walked down the wicket to reassure him. The last thing I wanted to say was: 'Just look for one.' The field was up saving singles and the 1999 World Cup semifinal flashed back from a dark corner of my memory. So I just said: 'Hally, if you could keep it on the ground that would be good, but if it's in your area then don't second-guess yourself – have a go. Just please keep it on the ground.' My advice had the opposite effect. Instead of being clear about what he was doing, I think he was caught in two minds. He tried to keep it down but couldn't get on top of it. The irony is that, if we'd needed six, he could probably have hit it for six. Instead it was another chip to mid on.

So it was down to Makhaya. I was hoping it wouldn't come to this, but the situation is what you make of it.

He walked in, spinning his bat. But it wasn't out of confidence; it was a reaction to the terror he was feeling. I swear he was turning white with fear. Seriously, I was watching a black man turn white. I walked over to meet him and his eyes were all over the place. He was looking at the stands, the crowd, and spinning his bloody bat. I said: 'Makkie, listen to me ...' but he was gone.

I said: 'Makkie, *look* at me!' That seemed to do the trick. 'He is probably going to bowl you a yorker, to get you out. So keep your bat straight and get it down nice and quick. When you make contact with it, do not worry about where it goes and do not look at the fielders. Just look at me. If I run, you run. If I don't run, then you dive back into your crease and stay there. We still have three balls, so don't panic.' I was terrified for him. I couldn't bear the thought that this historic game had come down to him. He didn't deserve this.

The crowd was going berserk. The noise was deafening. All of a sudden I was aware of how packed the stadium was. Had everyone who left early come back? There had been about 10 000 empty seats two hours earlier.

So Brett Lee ran in, and Makhaya seemed momentarily frozen in time. It's an in-swinging leg stump yorker. To this day, I cannot understand how he managed to work it down to third man. It defied all the angles and logic of cricket. And it came off the full face of the bat. It was truly a great shot. The best single run I ever saw. Seconds later, Makhaya was running past me screaming at the top of his lungs. And he is loud. I could even hear him above the roar of the crowd. We couldn't lose. The reality really hit me as I reached the striker's end. Makhaya could never be blamed or remembered as 'the guy who lost the 434 game'. It was down to me. I was the only one who could cock it up now. The two World Cup ties went through my head. I wasn't going to have another tie. I had two balls to make sure of that.

I looked at the field. Everybody was up saving one. I was surrounded. As Brett stood at the top of his run-up, the noise disappeared. I was aware of the crowd jumping up and down, but I couldn't hear a thing. Now it was me who seemed stuck in a time warp. Then he started to run. It took forever. I hadn't formed a clear plan. I was worried that, like Hally, I would be caught in two minds. Actually, I could have been caught in about five minds. Where are the weaker fielders? Do I push it to one of them and sprint? Do I block and sprint? Do I go over the top? Do I ...?

Three steps away from the delivery, I made up my mind. I don't know how you can have so many thoughts in such a small space of time, but I thought: 'We've played this whole game in such an aggressive and fearless way, why am I now getting all this other crap in to my head about "block and run"? I've been hitting the ball sweetly.' My very last thought was something a little crude which Peter Emslie used to say to me on the golf course when faced with a high-risk, high-reward shot: 'Commit to it 100 per cent because the faint-hearted never f***ed a fair maiden.' That was my final thought. If it was pitched up, I was going after it. At that stage I couldn't care what the consequences were. At least I could look at myself in the mirror afterwards and say: 'I didn't bottle it, I played without fear and I committed to the shot.'

That's exactly what happened. It was in the right area, I made sweet contact and it sailed back over Lee's head.

I looked at Makhaya and the colour was coming back into his cheeks. I could hear the crowd again, louder and louder. After hugging Makkie, I looked at the change room and the guys were tumbling over the balcony balustrade trying to get onto the field. Much of what happened after that was a blur for the next hour or so. It was completely unreal. I wish I'd had the chance to run around the ground to thank the crowd; they were unbelievable that day. I did a TV interview and was shaking like a leaf. I'll never forget Polly coming up to me with a tear in his eye and congratulating me – he was injured and didn't play in the game, but he was still desperate to win and it meant everything to him. Emotions were running very high.

After-party

I'd learnt to savour great moments and great victories, so I took it easy in the change room and watched the crowd and the enthusiasm of my team-mates while I sipped a beer or two. The afterglow of a match like that takes a long time to disappear, and this was one I wasn't going to spoil with too many beers, too soon. The feeling is hard to describe, and the usual words – satisfaction, enjoyment, achievement – don't do it justice. It's a more a blanket of contentment that wraps itself around you, protects you from any harm, but allows you to see out and appreciate the world at the same time.

The Aussies didn't take long to come to our change room. It takes two teams to produce a game like that and, once the disappointment had worn off and we had had enough time to ourselves, they decided they were entitled to join the party – and rightly so. We'd had our traditional end-of-tour fines meeting with a few beers and some champagne, and then we had a few more beers with the Aussie boys. Goodness knows what time we left the ground – sometime after 10:00 pm probably, which wasn't late considering the game hadn't finished until around 7:30 pm.

Nobody was in a mood to go to bed so we all reconvened in the sixth-floor bar at the Sandton Sun. 'Binger' Lee had his guitar and we sang songs and chatted about the day and the game. By then we had all got the adrenaline out of our systems and were happily not caring about much. The drinks had released all the tension from the day, and I realised I needed to go to bed.

It's not far from the bar to the glass-backed lifts at the Sandton Sun. You watch them go up and down all the time – people getting in and out, heading out or to their rooms. It's part of the entertainment in the bar. So I made my farewells and headed for the lifts. I'd been keeping myself awake for the last half hour so I didn't miss out on anything. 'Tired' doesn't begin to describe how I was feeling.

There was a bit of a wait – probably 30 seconds, but it felt like 10 minutes. When the lift arrived, it felt like a long way from the sixth floor to the 20th. My legs were tired, so I thought it made sense to sit down.

143

Soon after my legs started enjoying the rest, so did my eyes. I was asleep within five seconds.

Lifts are normally private environments, but this one was very public. After a few minutes, someone in the bar noticed me asleep in the lift, going up and down. They saw people getting in and, seeing me asleep, backing away in case I was a hobo. This, apparently, was a source of great amusement. A few of the players said they wanted to wake me up and take me to my room, but they were shouted down. The amusement was too good.

It was Brett, in the end, who said enough was enough. He told everyone else that I didn't deserve it after what had happened that day, put his guitar down and walked to the lift where he waited for me to reach the sixth floor for the umpteenth time. Then he woke me up and took me to my room. I was fine. I'd had plenty to drink, of course, but it was more the impact of the day that knocked me out. That's Brett Lee for you. A special guy.

Chapter 13

England 2008

It was always going to be a tough tour. England always is. Enjoyable, but never easy on the field. There was a strong sense of unfinished business for those of us who'd been on the previous tours. We'd lost in controversial circumstances in 1998, when umpire Javed Akhtar gave all those lbw decisions against us during the final Test at Headingley, and then we threw it away in 2003 when we were 2-1 up going into the last game at The Oval. Graeme's back-to-back double centuries at Edgbaston and Lord's had given us a flying start, but we ended up losing that final Test to square the series 2-2.

It had been a long wait, one that Jacques, Graeme, Makhaya and I had thought about often. Jacques and I wondered if it would be our last tour to England; we were both in our 30s, and you can never predict the future a year ahead in cricket. The recurring question from the English media was about our failure to win on previous tours. We said that, if we got into a position like that again, we could guarantee we wouldn't make the same mistakes.

By 2008 we knew we had the batsmen and the bowlers to compete with England. We also had an unprecedented level of team unity and honesty, thanks to a pre-tour camp at Pezula Golf Estate in Knysna.

Psychology at Pezula

In preparation for the tour, Mickey Arthur did some fantastic work on helping the players to understand the strength of diversity within a squad. He brought some wise, experienced people to Pezula. Mickey was determined to do everything possible to make sure we stayed strong through the tour – mentally far more than physically. We spoke about how long tours drain your emotional reserves and how many teams suffer in the final weeks. We admitted that that had been the case in 2003. Mickey brought Jeremy Snape on board, and from the start he was a great success. Not only was he a sports psychologist with a solid record in the field, but also he'd had a long first-class career and had played for England. Graeme had met him in the first season of the IPL earlier in the year.

It was a clever move to hold the camp at a prime golf resort. The camouflage was brilliant. Most of us were keen golfers and that was pretty much all we thought about. However, we did some psychological exercises that transformed many players' attitudes, including mine.

Mickey took some chances during that camp, but I guess he had nothing to lose. It was still a while before we were due to leave for England, so any damage caused would have plenty of time to heal. Also, because we hadn't won there in three post-isolation tours, he wasn't defending a great record.

Mickey made guys like Robin Peterson and JP Duminy feel like senior, valuable members of the squad. They had both been around and involved for a long time, but there was baggage that was hard to shift. They had been made to feel that there were other reasons for their inclusion in previous squads, and that was crap for them. Transformation was hardly an issue by then, but the scars from it needed to be dealt with. Mickey made that happen.

When we left Pezula everyone felt a deep sense of team spirit. They still say the same today. It was the best it had ever been. No wonder we went on to beat England.

Mickey Arthur

My first memory of Bouch was when he had just come on the scene for Border and we [Griquas] played against him in a day-night game. We had them in trouble and in came this cocky young man who played with the authority of a veteran. You just knew he was destined for great things.

I coached the Warriors in the first year of franchise cricket, and this coincided with Bouch being left out of the squad for Thami Tsolekile. This was where our relationship really began and I worked really hard with him to get him back into the national setup.

I have many special memories of Bouch. When he was waiting to bat against England in the Edgbaston Test and we were in a bit of trouble chasing, we needed somebody to stay with Graeme. Bouch just said to me, in his way: 'Don't worry, coach, I have waited too long to win a series here. I will walk off with them at the end of the game.' And he did. Another fond memory was winning the series in Australia, and Bouch and Kallis in tears on the bus leaving the MCG – that was how much that series win meant to him.

Yes, I did always have to fight for Bouch, and I never minded that because he was worth fighting for. The reason, I think, was that he could be unintentionally divisive. I always said to him that a positive Bouch was a great lift to the team and really galvanised the side, but a negative Bouch had the ability to break the team, and I think he understood that. If he wanted to question authority, I always asked him to come and see me privately. Bouch did not suffer fools gladly, and I guess this got him into trouble a bit. If ever I wanted to implement something, I would bounce it off Bouch first, because I knew that if I had his buy-in it would make everything that much easier.

First Test at Lord's

For all the preparation and planning, however, it still went badly wrong at the start of the first Test at Lord's (10-14 July). The aura of the venue was something we were concerned about, especially for the first-timers. Mickey even organised for the squad to visit the ground as tourists three days ahead in order to take photographs and spend time in the change room and the famous Long Room in the pavilion. But there is nothing like a capacity crowd to provide real atmosphere. It wasn't the same on a grey Monday with nobody there.

There had been a lot of media hype about our bowling attack, with one newspaper comparing Steyn, Ntini, Morkel and Kallis to the great West Indian pace attacks of the 1980s. It was silly. We bowled poorly and England made 600. Fortunately, they took a long time doing it and used up many overs, finally declaring shortly before the close of play on day two.

Our first-innings reply was poor. Ashwell made a gutsy hundred but there were three or four poor or careless shots played. Probably the worst came from AB who chipped a soft catch to mid on. Mickey deliberately threw protocol out of the window after the innings and had a go at most of the batsmen individually, in front of everyone else. He saved his strongest words for AB, and Graeme backed him up with a few of his own. Why target one man more than others when it was a collective balls-up? Because he was the most talented.

He didn't take it well. He is a very proud cricketer. He wanted to say the shot was on, but not in the match situation. Sure, he could have hit it over the fielder's head, but he hadn't. It led to a collapse that saw us bowled out for less than 250 and a deficit of thousands. Or so it felt.

AB plays with such flair and freedom; it is a pleasure to watch him. The last thing you want to do is take that away from him, but there is always a time and a place. He was in the transition stage from regular player to senior player, and everybody was looking to him to take more responsibility. We were battling for our lives in that game. Nobody had any doubt about how hard it would be to win the series if we lost the first Test of four. He rose to the challenge in spectacular fashion and scored

170 in the next Test, at Headingley (18-21 July). It was just another step on the road to complete honesty that had started at Pezula.

We didn't panic at the prospect of trying to save the game. We had to bat for two days. It always helps when there is a chance to win a game, but Steve Waugh's words came back to us on that occasion: 'Good sides can win Test matches, but great sides can save them, too.' It was a phenomenal effort from Graeme, Neil Mac and Hash – all three scored hundreds and added their names to Ashwell's on the Honours Board. We had discussed what an impact it would have on the England bowlers if we could keep them in the field for two days with the second Test just three days away, and they were buggered by the end of it. Monty Panesar bowled 60 overs without taking a wicket and the seamers bowled over 30 each.

Headingley Test

I'm sure AB will always say that his sensational 174 at Headingley had nothing to do with the 'chat' at Lord's, but I will always be convinced that it did. The fact that he faced 381 balls is enough evidence of that. If he'd been playing his 'normal' game he would have scored 300. But he was patient and bided his time. It was one of the most composed and authoritative innings I had seen, given the importance of the situation.

England were in some disarray on the morning of the match, with obvious disagreement over the selection of 'no-name' seamer Darren Pattinson. Half the England players had to introduce themselves to him beforehand. I took that as a sign they were worried, even panicking. Dale Steyn and Morne Morkel took four apiece, and England were gone for just 203. Control of the entire series was at stake when AB walked to the wicket at 143-4. We would surely get a lead, but if it was 20 or 30 then it was meaningless. It ended up being 319 and there was no way back for England.

After we'd won the match, and celebrations were just beginning, Mickey and Graeme made a point of handing AB a beer and saying: 'Now *that* is how you bat and what you are capable of when your team really needs you.'

An incident on the first day had added to the pressure on him and made his innings even more impressive. AB had grabbed a reflex catch at third slip and tumbled over, losing sight of the ball. When he rolled over he felt the ball in his hands and stood up. The rest of us celebrated as usual because we assumed he'd caught it, but he said: 'I'm not sure.' That was missed by most people, and the crowd made the assumption that he'd tried to claim it.

Later, England captain Michael Vaughan had a go at AB in the players' dining room and said there was no reason to cheat. It was ironic because AB is one of the fairest-minded cricketers I've ever played with. He was booed by some sections of the crowd during his innings, but he used that as motivation rather than allowing it to become a distraction.

We all know that cricket, like life, has a habit of throwing things back at you. When we batted, Hashim drove a ball to Vaughan at mid off, where the England captain claimed a low catch. Hashim was ready to walk until he saw some of us indicating for him to stay. The third umpire ruled 'no catch'. We all have moments like that in our careers. He was under pressure as captain, for sure. But it's important to remind yourself that your time for revenge, when the tables are turned, will come later, not at that moment. If AB had cheated, Vaughan could have comforted himself with the knowledge that he would pay for it later. Yelling at him in the dining room wasn't going to achieve anything.

I didn't see the incident, but became aware of it when Kevin Pietersen asked me if it was true. I've never had a problem with KP; I respect him for everything he has done. He emigrated and changed loyalties for professional reasons, and he's done brilliantly. He made some comments about South African cricket when he was a young man, which he regrets, but he's grown up. He is South African and always will be.

Edgbaston Test

The third Test (30 July-2 August), in Birmingham, is probably my second favourite ever behind the MCG Test a little under six months later. This time, however, I was able to play a role on the field rather than behind the scenes.

The misfiring sightscreen at the pavilion end was the major talking point throughout the match. There was a blind spot just above it with a dark background – at exactly the height at which Andrew Flintoff delivered the ball. We hoped Morne would be similarly difficult for the batsmen to see when he bowled, but he was a bit too tall.

Neil Mac was the first to go, ducking a ball that hit him on the ankle. He never saw it, and when that happens your instinct takes over and you dive for cover in case it's a beamer. He walked into the change room and said he'd never been so embarrassed on a cricket field. At that stage we thought it was a one-off incident, and we all had a good laugh at Neil's expense.

Then I got one – exactly the same! Didn't see it any stage. Thank goodness it went down the leg side. It was a major issue, not just in terms of the match but also of safety. It's hard enough avoiding a Flintoff bouncer when you can see it, never mind when you can't. We were desperately trying to resolve the situation because it was patently unfair. Goolam Rajah went up to the President's Suite above the sightscreen and tried to hold a white towel there, but the match referee sent the fourth umpire to ask him to move it.

The match referee, Ranjan Madugalle, consulted both captains to see if there was a consensus that playing conditions could be changed. Even though England had been bowled out for just 231, none of their batsmen had suffered any problems with the sightscreen. Naturally, Michael Vaughan refused to allow any changes.

Fortunately we built up a lead of 80-odd before England batted again, and this time they had a similar experience. Morne bowled from the pavilion end and tried to bowl from the same position on the crease as Flintoff – suddenly it worked. Ian Bell was the batsman who 'lost' the delivery and he was quick to admit it: 'I see what you guys were worried about now – we should have fixed it,' he told us between overs.

At 104-4 England were in terrible trouble, leading by just 21. But KP and Paul Collingwood got a partnership going, slowly at first but gaining dangerous momentum as the bowlers tired towards the end of day three. Kevin had changed the entire complexion of the match in a little over an hour.

England's lead had grown to 140 and we were worried. Another hour of him and we would have been gone, and we knew it. Then he gave us the keys to let ourselves out of jail.

It was a classic setup, but I would say it was born more out of desperation than anything else. We had discussed playing on KP's ego for weeks before the tour even started, so it wasn't a new plan. We knew he wanted to dominate – or maybe *needed* to dominate – all the time. So we played on that in the hope that he would get carried away, which he did. But it wasn't just a random hope. It was specifically planned to get him to make a specific mistake. Graeme sent AB two thirds of the way to the mid-on boundary and Paul Harris bowled tight in at KP's pads to make the drive difficult.

Harro had been riling him on and off throughout his innings. Nothing rude or personal, just simple things like: 'Come on, KP, take your skirt off, you can hit it further than that.' When he reached 94, Harro saw an obvious opportunity: 'Chance to shine, KP! Chance of glory, you can get there in style, they'll talk about this for years, reaching it with a six! You're KP – you know you can do it!'

AB took the catch at deep mid on.

Harro was one of my favourite and most underrated cricketers. We didn't need a spinner ripping it square and taking 3-50 in 10 overs. We needed a guy who could bowl 10 overs for 20 runs and maybe pick up one wicket. And that's exactly what he gave us. Control.

We gathered around in a huddle and Graeme reminded us about what we had said before the tour, about not letting a winning position slip again. We all knew it was the key moment of the series. Part of the skill in winning the key moments is recognising them when they arrive. The work wasn't over by any means, but there's no doubt the whole game changed after that.

Paul Collingwood made 135 and made some useful runs with the tail. The target was 281 – a lot more than we were hoping to chase when England were effectively 21-4.

The chase

It was one of the most nervous cricket teams I have ever seen in the change room before the chase started. The old change rooms at Edgbaston, before it was rebuilt, weren't great. The players were hidden away at ground level surrounded by the crowd. There was a small and uncomfortable viewing area, but most players preferred to stay in the change room, where it felt safe and you could be in your own space.

The noise of the crowd was deafening that day, especially when we lost a wicket. The sense of gloom deepened with every roar. It was obvious they weren't cheering for boundaries.

Neil Mac was listening to the commentary on a mini-radio, which many of the crowd use in England, so he would relay the most important information. I never enjoyed watching. I spend so much time during a match watching the ball that the last thing I needed was to watch every ball when I wasn't playing. I found it exhausting. I'd rather be relaxing, conserving energy. Each time a wicket fell I would watch the replays to see what I could learn.

Flintoff was in overdrive. The capacity crowd was roaring him on and he was bowling a couple of the best spells of the series. All we could do was hope he didn't bowl a yorker out of the blind spot again. He did – to Kallis, who wasn't amused as he stomped off.

At 93-4 the Birmingham crowd were in full voice and the beer was flowing. They were chanting: 'Freddie, Freddie ...' Flintoff was loving it.

AB and Graeme steadied the ship well under intense pressure, and their fifth-wicket stand of 78 brought us back into the match. I would have been happy for AB to stay and finish the job, but, at the same time, I was desperate to get out there. I wanted to be where I could make a difference. I felt the situation was tailor-made for me. I was tense, but not in a nervous way. More like a sprinter in his blocks.

Then AB was caught at slip and I was on my feet and down the few steps to the field in no time. Again the noise was deafening but I thought: 'Let's see if you're still cheering in an hour's time.'

When Graeme met me I was struck by how calm he was. He spoke with such complete certainty, there was no way anybody could doubt him. I was never so certain, before or after that moment, that somebody would not get out: 'Just stay with me – I need you to stay with me,' he said.

We needed 110 runs. If Graeme didn't get out then we should be fine – because I wasn't getting out, either! I had been in these situations before, although not with quite as much at stake. I wasn't worried – not until I got the first one from Flintoff out of the blind spot. Didn't see it all. I had to do something. I had to at least try and give myself some control over that. So, for the first and last time in my career, I changed my technique in the middle of a match.

I always used to crouch low, but, during that innings, I adopted Jacques's style, trying to stand tall to get my eyes above the blind spot. The weakness of that would be a fast yorker, but I had to back myself to get the bat down quickly enough. It worked well. I felt more and more comfortable with it as the innings progressed.

Gradually we started to wear the bowlers down. We had to absorb some pressure, although I was always looking for scoring opportunities. For me the atmosphere started to change with somewhere between 50 and 60 runs needed. The tension changed to excitement. We were going to win! I thought it was important not to show outwardly what I was thinking, but inside I didn't mind at all. Far from being a distraction, the thought of winning made me concentrate even harder. We were going to put right all the frustration and mistakes from the last three tours of England. I recalled one of the first conversations I'd had with Graeme when he joined the national team; he said he'd dreamt of winning in England since he was a kid.

James Anderson then pushed a bit too hard for a wicket and went for 17 off two overs. I said to Graeme at the end of the over: 'We've got this now, you know that, don't you?' He said: 'Don't give it away; just play normal cricket, but up the tempo if you can and let's put them under pressure.' At that point the umpires went to Graeme to ask whether he would like to claim the extra half-hour or come back on the fifth morning to complete the match. Graeme walked over to me and I said: 'Don't even ask – don't even think about it. We're having beers tonight.' He agreed, and told the umpires we'd finish the game that evening.

When KP came on to bowl, we both knew that was it. Freddie had one more over towards the end, with about 20 runs needed. He tried two yorkers, one of which I hit down the ground for four, the other I chipped to mid-wicket for two. Freddie was taken off. Graeme hit KP for a four to win it.

Graeme's instincts as captain were at their best that day. He knew it was down to him and yet he also knew that he had to be calm, to show his team that it was going to be OK. Maybe his heart was pounding, but you would never have thought so. It was one of the greatest innings in South African Test history.

I never thought about losing. I couldn't. Just the thought would have been too painful. I forced myself to play my natural game, to be positive. If I'd even thought about going to The Oval with the series all square I know I would have become tentative, and that usually spells the end.

Some days I walked to the crease quite slowly – that was usually an indication that I wasn't 100 per cent confident. That day I almost jogged to the crease. My body language was confident and aggressive – more for me than for the England players. It was my way of banishing the fear of failure and forcing myself to play positively.

That evening we had a fantastic fines meeting and celebration in the change room. Graeme gave Mickey his man-of-the-match medal. Years later, it took pride of place behind Mickey's bar in Perth. It was the greatest feeling. For two or three hours life was as perfect as it could be. I knew who I was and where I was going, and nothing could deflect from the deep satisfaction of having won that series. In those couple of hours it felt like this had been my destiny. It certainly felt like it had been Graeme's too, after that innings.

The following morning, the fire alarm went off in the team hotel at about 6:00 am. Some of the guys looked pretty groggy as we all stumbled out into the car park. They felt even worse. Ordinarily I would have been one of them, but this time was different. I had wanted to savour the feeling of achievement and joy, so I had gone to bed at a reasonable time. It might have been different if my girlfriend hadn't been with me.

We were driving to London the next day when we heard that Michael Vaughan had scheduled a press conference for midday. It could only mean that he was resigning. It was an understandably tearful occasion. He said later that he had been absolutely convinced England would win once we were set 281 to win.

It is never pleasant to watch a great cricketer end like that, especially a captain who had done so much for English cricket. After winning The Ashes back just three years earlier, he was a national hero.

We had gone at him hard during the series, but that was only natural. He was an inspirational captain who enjoyed the complete respect of his team. Bring him down and you've pretty much got the team. He knew that and understood it. Teams have been doing that with Graeme for a decade.

I had no hesitation in sending him a text message to express my respect for him as a player, a person and a captain, and that he should be proud of a great career. It was a pity it had ended like that, but you can't always manufacture the perfect ending. I became a bit of an expert on that subject a few years later.

Fourth Test

There was a lot of discussion, debate and media speculation about the composition of the team for the 4th Test at The Oval (7-11 August). The job of a lifetime was done, for many of us, and it would be hard to lift ourselves back up to the level we'd reached during most of the previous three Tests. If Vaughan hadn't retired it might not have mattered. It would have been the victors against the vanquished. We had their measure. But KP was appointed captain and there was a new vibe around the England team. It was a new beginning for them, with places at stake and reputations to be built – or rebuilt.

Steve Harmison was brought back into the side with a point to prove. He hit us hard immediately. He was a great bowler from time to time in his career. After each of the first two days, we tried to regroup, talking about needing to get back into the game. But it was almost like we had no power. The desire was there and the will was there. We said the right things, and believed them. But the tank was empty. It wasn't for lack of effort.

Should we have rested a few players and given the reserves a Test match? The overwhelming feeling was that Test caps are the most treasured and prized awards in a cricketer's life. You don't just hand them out. I spoke out about the precedent it might set. If we played guys just because the series was won, it would happen again in the future. You fight for your life in Test cricket; that's the way it should be. You are one of the best XI in your country. If we gave the impression that players could be given Test caps as 'replacements', what message were we sending to future generations?

The responsibility for the performance, and for the defeat, lay with us, the players. Not with the coach or selectors for picking the same team. We were weak. We should have been stronger. It was our responsibility to show the world, and future generations, that every Test match is as important as the last and the next. We failed there.

We learnt quickly. As beautiful as it was to win the series, we didn't need the sour taste of defeat to end it. Six months later, we also won the series with a Test to spare, and, although we lost the third one in Sydney, we fought to our last breath. We gave it everything.

Chapter 14

Tour of Australia 2008–2009

had never been in such a relaxed squad. It helped that we had just become the first post-isolation team to win in England, at the fourth try, but this time we were attempting something no South African team had ever achieved in eight tours spanning a century.

One part of the mental side of the game that we had never tackled properly was the media. Yes, we'd always talked about it and made new players aware of the intensity and effect of the Aussie media, but we'd never had a strategy. It was like saying: 'Beware of the mambas.' It didn't help. This time there was a plan in place. We would stick to an approach that suited us all and that we were comfortable with.

We knew the 'chokers' issue would be raised as soon as we landed – and wouldn't go away for the rest of the tour unless we started winning. We had tried denying it, downplaying it and admitting it. This time we said nothing, but we were as polite, friendly and accommodating as could be. We stayed strong in our sense of self-belief. That's why, when we did win the series, the media respected us and there were so many good words written. We hadn't gone in there kicking and screaming and talking about winning. Every comment or answer to a question had been thought through and discussed in our meetings. There is a difference between rehearsing answers and just thinking about your general position on something. So the answers that came from Graeme and the senior players were still spontaneous and natural, but we all knew what message we were trying to convey. It helped a lot. Every topic was covered and discussed by Mickey and Snapey and our position on the answers was talked through.

Duncan Fletcher was also a huge influence for ten days at the start of that tour. Mickey had shown his own self-belief and confidence in persuading CSA to hire Duncan on a consultancy basis and had never given a thought to being outshone or undermined. Duncan had been on Ashes tours to Australia and had learnt what it took to beat the Aussies three years earlier, when England had won The Ashes for the first time in 18 years. Apart from his technical brilliance, his greatest contribution to the tour was to make us aware of the Australian 'bully mentality'. It exists on several different levels, from the most obvious, which everybody can see, to the very subtle, where you don't even realise you're being bullied until it's too late. He had seen visiting teams quietly muscled away from their practice area before a game, or given inferior nets. And he had learnt from experience how agitated Aussie cricketers can become when they don't get their way.

The first-time tourists to Australia asked me, before we left South Africa, what it was like facing them and how aggressive their sledging could be. I always replied that words alone were pretty harmless. Sure, they could call you names and make reference to family members, but that wasn't the point. The messages you give and receive from body language can be more important and longer-lasting.

There were a couple of examples on the previous tour, which I spoke about. Nantie Hayward was a clean hitter of the ball, thanks to his baseball background, but he was also scared of it. He backed away against Brett Lee so much that Lee forgot about the stumps entirely and just tried to hit him on the head. It reflected on all of us and gave the entire Aussie team a lift. Sure, Nantie had plenty to say when he was bowling and gave everyone a few choice words, but they sounded a bit hollow.

Fletch also identified our major potential weakness and spoke openly about it. 'All the Aussie bowlers can bat,' he said. 'You have a long tail.

Series like these are always close, and if their tail is worth a hundred runs and yours is worth 20, that will cost the series.' It made a hell of a lot of sense to me, and I vowed to carry on working with guys like Paul Harris, Dale Steyn and Morne Morkel after Duncan left the tour following the first Test.

I told the bowlers that their wickets were even more valuable than they realised. Runs were important, but the way they handled themselves, and how hard they made the opposition work to dismiss them, could have long-lasting and far-reaching consequences. So I asked Mickey and Graeme whether I could work with the bowlers and try to make them a bit more than tail-enders.

Harro was funny to work with because he was prepared to take the blows to the body and he didn't lack courage, but he genuinely didn't have a scoring shot. He couldn't just stand there being turned black and blue, and he couldn't just rely on edges to get down to the non-striker's end and keep the scoreboard moving. I tried to get him playing the pull shot, but that wasn't a success. We tried working on a couple of other 'fall-back' shots, but he wasn't a natural. So we decided that he was, in fact, better off defending as solidly as possible while we worked on scoring options with the guy at the other end.

I started with tennis balls to get their reflexes working a bit faster than they were used to when batting. I threw the ball first, then dipped into my tennis memory and delivered a couple of high-kicking serves. It was fun, but then we moved into the nets with cricket balls and a bowling machine turned up to 145kph. They were all hit a couple of times. They all had some bruises and they had a few choice words for me, but I was certain – like Fletch – that it might make the difference between winning or losing the series. And they all began to play a lot better.

In the 1st Test in Perth (17-21 December) we were blown away in the space of a couple of overs by Mitchell Johnson, and our bowlers were all hit by short balls and bouncers. After that, they never questioned the extra work. Johnson had bullied us and it was time to stand up and fight back. We won the Test after a brilliant, record-breaking run chase of 414, with hundreds from Graeme Smith and AB de Villiers and 50s from

Hashim Amla, Jacques Kallis and JP Duminy. But I was still convinced the bowlers would be needed. I wouldn't have minded if they hadn't been, but we knew Australia would hit back.

The second Test was in Melbourne, the traditional Boxing Day Test at the MCG, and one of the great spectacles in the game. There was no festive season for us, though. For three days before the Test, the bowlers would finish their work in the outdoor nets and then head for the hard, indoor nets and the bowling machine for their daily dose of medicine. I loaded the machine and swore at them whenever I managed to sneak one past the bat and gloves into the ribcage. I laughed at them and told them the next one would be more painful. I told them to wake up and watch the ball if they didn't want to get hurt any more. But they stayed; they weren't going to walk away. I was only giving them what I knew they could expect from Brett Lee, Peter Siddle and Mitchell Johnson.

Once or twice, when they were really struggling and hating me a bit too much, I padded up and went into the nets. They took charge of the bowling machine and turned it up to top speed. Understandably they wanted to inflict some pain in return for everything they had received.

Australia batted first, and Ricky Ponting made a brilliant hundred in front of what is always, by far, the biggest Test match crowd of the year. Dale bowled his heart out to take 5-87 but we didn't bowl them out until shortly before lunch on the second day – and 394 was a big score.

In reply we crashed to 184-7, still 11 runs away from avoiding the follow-on. It was an absolute disaster. All the work with the tail was supposed to help us squeeze 100 runs out of the last four wickets. Now we only had three left and we were over 200 behind. Hopeless.

The following morning JP added 67 with Harro for the eighth wicket, which wasn't quite enough to put a smile on our faces but certainly lessened the gloom. Harro made 39, including four boundaries – one was even a pull shot, which definitely did put a smile on my face. But we were still 140 behind when he was out, and the drop-in pitch at the MCG meant batting would become more awkward as the match progressed. That sort of deficit would be hard to recover from. What happened next will stay with me for the rest of my life.

Dale demolished his previous career-best with an innings of 76 and JP, in just his second Test match, made 166 – one of the finest innings in South African Test history. Together they added 180 to turn the match on its head. Even Makhaya, who had put in as much batting work as everyone else, faced 29 balls in adding another 28 for the last wicket after Dale was out. We had made the greatest comeback I had ever seen in a Test match. Although I scored only three, I felt as pleased and proud as if I'd scored a hundred.

Every time they ducked a bouncer, or played one, even if they took one on the body, I felt a swell of pride. Jacques and I sat in the same position all day, not daring to move. That's a cricket superstition. If a partnership gets going, don't change the karma.

Not only did we win, but we won by nine wickets at lunchtime on the final day. In all the thrill and excitement of winning the game, and the series, many people forgot what an incredible performance Dale had delivered – with the ball! Like all bowlers, he was far more excited about being 'just four hits away from a century' but his ten-wicket haul was even more important in winning that game. It was a sign of just how good a bowler he had become. Performances like that were almost expected of him.

At the end of that incredible match the bowlers all grabbed a beer and came over to my corner of the change room to say cheers and thank you for all the hard work. I reminded them that it was their hard work that had paid off, not mine. But they insisted that I was the reason we had scored enough runs to win the Test match, and the series. It produced the first of many tears that day. I remain as proud of that memory as of anything I did with bat or gloves on the field of play. It represents what I have always believed, and have been taught by people like Jonty Rhodes: that cricket really is a team game.

I was also especially pleased for Mickey, who had dreamt of winning that series every day for three years since the last tour. He had been my coach at the Warriors when I was dropped from the national squad for the first time in 2004, and he was instrumental, along with Ray Jennings, in getting me back up and running. I admired him immensely for a number of reasons. His technical knowledge may not have been the greatest, but he more than made up for that with his man-management skills, which were outstanding. And he was never afraid to tackle his shortcomings; his recruitment of Fletch was a masterstroke and confirmed he would do anything for the team, no matter if there was a chance it could reflect awkwardly on him. The team felt like a very tight unit in the moment of our greatest Test victory, but he deserved much of the credit for the feeling of brotherhood we had.

Some things about Mickey were unusual for a coach in a high-profile job. Calmness under pressure and an ability to ooze quiet confidence at tense times are great assets. Mickey had neither. He was a glorious panicker, and the reason was because of his passion for the team and how much the job meant to him. He was a bundle of nerves on match days, and that used to pull the players even closer together. If it meant that much to the coach, we'd better make sure we played out of our skins and won the match or he might have a heart attack.

He couldn't shout at players. His weapon of choice was disappointment rather than anger, and it was often more effective. You'd hate to see Mickey disappointed. I think he knew he couldn't 'do' anger very well, so he didn't bother trying. He'd long given that up. He was different to a 'conventional' coach in many ways, but that simply contributed to his success.

I looked around that change room at the MCG and I saw four or five different races and cultures, and vastly different backgrounds, and I realised I hadn't really noticed or thought about that for many, many months. We were just team-mates who respected each other, gave each other time and space – and fought for each other. And it was largely thanks to Mickey.

We had spoken a lot about the importance of humility – in both victory and defeat. Many teams forget about their opposition when they win a highly charged, emotional victory, and we had certainly been guilty of that in the past. But this was a new era, and we had pledged that we would honour the game and respect our opponents, no matter what happened.

That's why we weren't over the top when the Melbourne Test ended. The whole series had been played in such a good spirit, and that takes two sets of players. We had both played as hard as we could, given everything and stopped at nothing, but we didn't take it off the field.

JP's innings

Another memory I'll always hold dear about that match was what happened at the start of the third day's play when JP was due to resume, with Harro as his partner. It had been my career-long practice to start getting ready for fielding when we lost our seventh wicket. Jacques, too, used to start getting changed when the seventh wicket fell.

Being seven down overnight, I started taping my fingers preparing for a day in the field. Jacques was in his whites with his bowling boots on. (JP says he didn't notice at the time, and thank goodness for that.) We weren't sending a very positive message. By lunchtime the whole team had noticed that I had sat the whole morning with my fingers taped and were laughing at me. Never had I been happier to be laughed at. Cricketers are superstitious people, and we weren't about to change anything. After lunch everybody returned to the same position they had been sitting in during the morning session, hoping we'd get another few minutes of batting. Nobody thought for a moment we'd be there for another two hours, until tea!

No praise can be too high for JP on that day. He'd been given out for a duck, caught behind off his helmet, in his debut innings in Perth before hitting the winning runs to reach 50 in the record run chase. The composure he showed that day was hard to comprehend. We all knew how good a player he was, and nobody had the slightest worry when he stepped in at the last minute when Ashwell was injured, but I'm not sure anybody thought he was capable of something like that – not in his second Test match, anyway.

JP Duminy

I honestly wasn't aware of Mark and Jacques being ready for fielding when we went out to bat. But it's understandable; I only had Harro with Dale and Makhaya to come. It's fair enough that they were prepared for an early end. I certainly didn't know that Bouch had already taped his fingers. They must have felt strange five hours later without gloves on!

He was always a positive influence on the change room. The team called him our 'bulldog'. He was the man we'd choose for a tight situation. I don't know how many tough, vital 30s he made for the team. There aren't statistics to show that.

Our relationship has grown over the years to the point where we are close friends. He took a close interest in my career right from the start, which was special for me. It gave me confidence. But it wasn't just me; he played an influential role in many of the guys' careers. He was so knowledgeable about the game, especially about the intricacies of Test cricket. Once he'd finished his own work he would spend time in the nets with the bowlers before a Test, making sure they were comfortable with their games. He would do anything to take the focus off himself and make sure everyone else was feeling confident and strong.

He was a strict, old-school disciplinarian, but that didn't mean he was inflexible. Early on in my career I was part of the ODI squad for a home series. We played a day-nighter at the Wanderers and had a pretty late night afterwards – we were flying to East London the next day and then had three or four days before the next game, so it was fine to have a few beers that night.

I didn't hear my alarm. I wouldn't have heard a fire alarm. Mark woke me up and then waited in the kombi outside the Sandton Sun. Mickey Arthur said: 'That's it, he's 15 minutes late – we're going. He can find his own way to the airport.' But Mark believed that I deserved a bit of leeway as it was my first offence and I was still new in the side. I think he actually had quite an argument with Mickey. Mark was right. I was never late for a bus again.

My favourite wicket in the Test undoubtedly belonged to Michael Hussey, but purely for the humour he provided afterwards. Like JP, Huss was hit on the head by a bouncer. But unlike JP, it wasn't a thin, glancing blow to the keeper. Hussey went on the hook against Morne Morkel but missed it. The ball hit him with such force on the side of the head that he was caught by Hashim at mid-wicket! Thank goodness for helmets, although I'm still amazed that he didn't suffer any concussion.

Having walked for about 20m after being given out, Huss suddenly stopped and looked back at us. He had a half-smile on his face: 'It might have been a shit decision,' he said, 'but that was one quick delivery.'

Sydney Test, 3–7 January

I hate losing. There is no such thing as an acceptable loss. But the Sydney Test may have been the closest I ever came. We fought our backsides off until the very end, which was personified by Graeme's one-handed heroics in the final hour. I was as determined as ever, and wanted to save that Test – to the point of obsession. It was born out of my desire to make amends for the loss to England at The Oval Test six months earlier.

Having made 89 in the first innings, I knew I was in form, and I was certain I could bat out the final day and keep one end locked up. I had planned my approach and done my mental preparation. Soon after arriving at the crease, I received one of the worst lbw decisions of my life, from Sri Lankan umpire Asoka de Silva. It was dreadful, one of those that wouldn't even divide a roomful of people 99:1. Not a single person could doubt the ball was missing leg stump. It actually *hit* me outside leg and was going further down.

When I returned to the change room, I smashed a couple of things and swore a lot. It's a hard enough game without that sort of crap. But it wasn't just me that had become obsessed with not losing – we all were. Maybe I was on the more extreme end.

The thing is, if I hadn't been given out like that, then maybe Graeme would never have been needed at the end. Maybe we would all have been denied one of the most amazing moments of competition between South Africa and Australia. Some things are fate, destiny. I would take a rubbish lbw decision every day just to witness that moment again. The character of the team, and of the captain – to walk out to bat with a broken hand in the heart of Australian cricket, and to have the SCG crowd to rise to their feet and give him a standing ovation all the way to the middle – it still brings a lump to my throat.

Being part of the process of getting him ready is also something I'll never forget. Once I had calmed down, the talk began. Would he? Could he? First we decided to get him ready. We'd make the decision nearer the time. Because he was injured, he didn't have any of his kit with him. It was all back at the hotel. He was never, ever going to bat at the start of the day. Harro had a shirt a similar size, but he'd spilt a load of tomato sauce down it at lunchtime. So Graeme was busy trying to wipe the tomato sauce off the shirt saying: 'I can't go out there wearing this.' And I was thinking: 'OK, never mind facing Mitchell Johnson with a broken hand, let's worry about the tomato sauce instead.'

Graeme didn't know what to do, so we tried to take the decision out of his hands, so to speak. We told him we would decide if there were too many overs left by the time the ninth wicket fell. We didn't want him to mess his hand up for good, and there was a real danger that could happen.

When it got closer to the end, he started to pad up. Or, at least, the guys started putting his pads on for him. It was incredibly tense. He sat at the back of the change room, out of sight of the Aussie team. We didn't want them to know if he was going to come out. When the ninth wicket fell, it was him, of course, who made the decision. He just stood up and started walking.

I noticed a couple of the Aussie players running towards the stumps to grab a souvenir, but someone must have said: 'Hang on a minute ...'

When Graeme emerged from the change room, the members sitting in front of us stood up immediately and started applauding. There was a ripple effect around the SCG, everybody standing and applauding. What a sight. What a feeling. Three years earlier, they had booed and jeered him. Now they were applauding him every step of the way. None of us will ever forget that.

Mickey moves on

A little over a year later, Mickey resigned as coach of the Proteas, and was replaced on a temporary basis by Corrie van Zyl. When I look back, I realise you can't just end a friendship or a close relationship on a technicality. Just because Mickey moved to Perth and then became coach of Australia, that didn't mean we didn't speak to him any more. He was national coach for five years and stayed in touch with quite a few of us. When he came back to South Africa he was the first man to invite me round for a braai – or invite himself around for a braai.

The way his time as coach came to an end was disappointing for everyone; he deserved better than that. But he also knew that his time was coming to a natural end. There is only so long you can do a job like coaching the Proteas, and four or five years is probably the natural life span. There were administrative and CSA board issues that were becoming increasingly frustrating for him, and it was affecting his coaching. He wasn't himself around the players, with so many frustrations on his mind. He'd just had enough.

I had reached a stage of my career where I was concentrating on trying to be the best cricketer I could be, and was trying hard not to be distracted. I didn't want to get involved for two reasons: I was too scared of incurring disciplinary action for telling the truth, and I didn't want to draw attention away from what the team had achieved with the victories in England and Australia. I wanted to support Mickey in whatever way I could, but I wasn't naive enough to think I could have made a difference. Besides, Mickey wouldn't have wanted the players to become involved. He wanted us to concentrate on doing what we did best, which was to play.

Occasionally a reporter would ask me what they thought was a potentially awkward question, like whether there was any truth in the reports that Graeme and Mickey weren't seeing eye to eye on certain important issues, and that they had fallen out. My instincts were to jump to their defence, but it wasn't worth complicating the issue by adding an irrelevant voice. Who was I to comment on their relationship? It was exclusively their right to respond to those queries. Given everything that they had achieved as a partnership, and that we had achieved as a team under their leadership, I wasn't interested in commenting. Their record spoke for itself. As far as I was concerned, playing under those two was the peak of my career.

Mick and I were close, and he was absolutely consistent in his respect for my need for honesty. He would tell me whenever there were board members or other people with influence gunning for me. It happened from time to time. No matter who you are, if a result or two goes against the team, there are always people saying: 'Let's make a change.' It even happened with Jacques, believe it or not. Mickey used to tell me because, as he said: 'You always perform best under pressure!' That wasn't the sort of pressure I enjoyed, but it probably worked all the same.

There were times when he put everything on the line to keep me in the team. He never lied or spared me the truth. I knew, for certain, that he wanted me in the team because he believed I was the person for the job, not because he had a personal allegiance to me. He was loyal to many players, but he also knew when the time was right to make a change, and he didn't lack the courage to do it. The most obvious example of that was when Polly was dropped from the squad in 2007, before the Karachi Test. But Mickey fought hard for me and then told me that I needed to put in some big performances to keep 'the wolves at bay.'

One of my best knocks in those circumstances was the 50 I made against India at Newlands in January 2011. We were in a lot of trouble and I added 100 with Jacques. It was only 55 for me, but it felt like a century. I was full of negative, pessimistic thoughts before the game and I was surrounded by speculation that the end was nigh. Newspapers were carrying articles comparing the various franchise wicket-keepers as though I had already retired. It was a battle to turn those negative emotions into fuel for the fight, to turn them from energy-sapping thoughts into energy-giving ones.

If anyone had looked at my scores for a little while before that, it would have been reasonable to conclude that I was out of form. But that's the trouble with looking at numbers in isolation. Was I out of form? Or was it more of a case that the top order were in such great form that I wasn't getting to the crease until declaration runs were required? I was playing big shots, holing out for 10 or 12 and inadvertently putting myself under pressure while the team was still succeeding. But that was my choice. I had made my bed; now I had to lie in it.

If I had been dismissed cheaply in that match, we would almost certainly have lost and that would have been a home series lost, something India have never achieved in South Africa. No doubt heads would have rolled, mine among them. It was tight, and I owed both Mickey and myself a big performance. Corrie was coach by then, but I still felt indebted to Mickey for all the support he had given me. That was one of my favourite innings.

Every member of the team had been through a lean patch during that period but the team wasn't affected because everybody was making a contribution off the field and we backed and supported each other. The confidence we had in each other was unquestioned and we all knew it would come right. I look at the team now that I have retired and I see a team with a record lead at the top of the world rankings and yet I still see and hear people wanting to make changes. It makes no sense. Yet it still happens. Form is temporary; class is permanent.

Chapter 15

Ups and downs at the World Cup

The weight of expectation on the team was huge during the three ICC Cricket World Cups I played in. But there can only be one winner. I count myself among those who talk about 'losing' the World Cup, but we didn't lose any of them. You can only lose a World Cup in the final. Some of the expectation from administrators and supporters bordered on entitlement: we were entitled to a place in the final and the players knew that. We may been guilty of many things, but overconfidence wasn't one of them.

It certainly helps if you have one of the best teams at a World Cup, but you do need a bit of luck to go your way as well. The toss of a coin can go a long way to determining whether you win or lose a pool game, or a quarter- or semifinal. It helps if the opposition batsmen and bowlers don't produce their 'once in a lifetime' performance against you, too.

On all three occasions, in 1999, 2003 and 2007, I wanted to retreat into my shell and hide for a good few weeks. I didn't want to be seen in public. If I had to be, then I avoided people's eyes. I wasn't embarrassed or ashamed, because I'd given it everything and tried my hardest, but I knew the level of disappointment that people felt, and, in many ways,

I couldn't help feeling I'd let them down. I didn't want to look into a stranger's eyes and see an expression that said: 'You choked again.' Being knocked out of a World Cup brings you back down to earth in a painful way. I lost a lot of self-confidence, not only as a cricketer but also as a person.

When South Africa was knocked out in the group stage of the 2003 World Cup, I knew it wasn't my fault, but that didn't stop me feeling somehow guilty. Many people *thought* it was my fault, and they blamed me for blocking the last ball in the match against Sri Lanka at Kingsmead, but they didn't understand what the Duckworth/Lewis method was all about – it was still pretty new to the scene at that stage and we were all getting used to it. It was just too much to accept on the back of the 1999 semifinal, when we tied with Australia. Two consecutive World Cups and two eliminations – without losing either game. It was hard for everyone to swallow. I played well in the game against Sri Lanka and brought us back into the game when it seemed to be slipping away from us.

England 1999 – semifinal tie

We had a massively talented squad in 1999, perhaps the best one-day squad South Africa has ever sent to a World Cup. I made a couple of naive mistakes with the bat, but it didn't make much difference as I was batting at number 9. We never played to our potential in the group matches, but Lance Klusener was incredible, absolutely fearless. Time and time again he pulled us out of trouble, even during the semifinal itself.

I haven't spent much time looking back at the game. The pain stayed for long enough afterwards. There is a saying among players that personal achievements mean so much less if the team doesn't win, but it was never more obvious with Polly, AD and Jacques, who took 5-36, 4-32 and scored 53, respectively. They would have given anything to have changed the course of the match.

Australia had been on the rack from the start. Even half-centuries from Michael Bevan and Steve Waugh hadn't rescued them. When Shane Warne walked to the wicket it was 158-6. We would have taken a total of 213 right then. Experience teaches you, however, that you don't chase targets in big games, you just chase the next run. Never was that more obvious than in that game. Hansie got a shocker in the run chase, the ball bouncing off his boot to be caught at short leg off Warne. How different our lives might have been if that decision had been correct.

The atmosphere in the change room afterwards was the gloomiest I ever experienced. Guys had their heads wrapped in towels and had no inclination to engage with anybody. They just wanted to be left alone. There were tears and a lot of anger and frustration. Bob Woolmer managed to say a few words, and Steve Waugh came into the change room to shake Hansie's hand. I think he just said: 'Hard luck.'

Dr Bacher walked in ready to talk to us; he looked around, tried to make eye contact and catch our attention, but nothing happened. He said: 'Gentlemen, I'm very proud of you ...' but that was all. He wanted to say more but realised he was talking to himself.

As I looked round the room it occurred to me that you could tell each player was thinking how many more chances he might get in his career to put this day right. The worst affected were the guys who knew they would never get another chance. I knew it was bad, and it hurt me deeply, but, as a youngster, I was burning with determination to get it right next time. I used that as my coping mechanism.

I realised that this was a match that would never be forgotten by the players when we returned to our hotel in London to regroup and, of course, disperse. We had a logistics meeting, which Bob chaired. He was so well balanced, and always had the ability to see the positive side and calm people down when they were over-emotional. He could always provide a different perspective on things. But when I walked into that room there was nothing like that. Everybody was hurting just as badly deep into the next day as they had been immediately after the game. Nobody had anything good to say. We just tended to our own wounds, did what we had to do, and then went to our rooms. The next day we all moved on. Gary and Debs went to Paris. A few guys took a break in Europe. The rest of us went home. But not soon enough, as it turned out!

We were still in the hotel on the day of the final, which meant we were there when the Aussies returned from Lord's, having demolished Pakistan to win the cup. I didn't resent their celebrations at all. They deserved it; they were world champions. But that didn't stop me thinking about how easily it could have been us. In the decade afterwards I often thought about how the 'choker' label would never have materialised but for one or two tiny, critical moments.

The semifinal was ridiculously close; both teams were bowled out for 213 – Australia in 49.2 overs and South Africa in 49.4. Australia choked far more than we did in the closing overs, but the one moment of indecision cost us the game. They dropped a catch, bowled a no ball that wasn't called, missed an easy run out two balls before the end ... But that's the way it was.

How could anyone blame AD for not running? And Lance was the man-of-the-tournament, with barely another contender. Lance gave us the chance of playing that semifinal. The noise made the call hard to hear ... both guys have different recollections of their chat when they came together. I can only sympathise. Something vaguely similar was to happen to me four years later. I don't like saying things were down to fate, but maybe they were that day.

Almost a decade and a half later, Lance said he 'would always have to say sorry' for what happened. I hope he doesn't feel that is a burden he will always have to carry. That would be unfair and wrong. Cricket is a team game, and we should never have been in that situation in the first place.

Cricket has an unerring way of bringing you back to earth the moment you think you've got the hang of it. Of course it scars you. I have plenty of scars, as do plenty of players from my generation. But everybody carries scars of some sort; the only difference is that ours are inflicted in public, and people – including our opponents – like to remind us of them.

I was told many, many years ago that it's not the sad, bad and ugly things that happen to you in life that define who you become, but how you bounce back from them. Scars heal, but you have to acknowledge them and give them time. Anyway, who's to say we would have won the World Cup if Lance had scored one more run? We still had to play Pakistan. They might have put up a half-decent display against us, unlike the one they put on against Australia.

South Africa, 2003

South Africa were eliminated at the group stage in bizarre circumstances when they tied their final match against Sri Lanka at Kingsmead, with Boucher blocking the last ball of what transpired to be the final over from spin wizard Muttiah Muralitharan in the belief that the Duckworth/ Lewis target had been reached. The target that had been relayed to Boucher and his batting partner, Lance Klusener, was in fact the par score rather than the winning score. Having reached that total with rain pouring down at Kingsmead and the umpires poised to take the players off the field, Boucher pushed forward to Murali's last delivery in the happy contentment that he had probably won the game – unless the rain relented and the players could return to the field.

For months before the tournament even began, and then throughout the first couple of weeks, everyone, from politicians to actors – even CSA president Percy Sonn – spoke about the World Cup as though all we had to do to win it was keep turning up on time. There were so many distractions – functions, signing sessions, sponsor commitments, media interviews. The only time that belonged to us was training sessions and when we were asleep.

Some distractions could have been avoided, however. After we'd lost a high-scoring game against New Zealand at the Wanderers, Herschelle was quoted the following morning as saying that he thought the team 'was missing Hansie, both as a player and a captain'. Local media jumped on it, but that was nothing compared to the international media, who leapt at the chance to dig up as much Hansie stuff as they could.

If it had come from anyone else I think the players would have been appalled, especially with the disrespect it showed to Polly as captain, but, because it was Hersch, it was assumed that he'd just opened his mouth for the umpteenth wrong time, in the umpteenth wrong place. It wasn't meant to be derogatory or disrespectful. It was Hersch being unable to think before he spoke, and definitely unable to think about what he was going to say. The media reaction was an unpleasant distraction, but there was no problem at all between the players.

We had no doubt that the World Cup on home soil had the potential to change the country fundamentally. We had all seen it eight years before, in 1995, when the Springboks won the Rugby World Cup. But, just in case anyone forgot, we were reminded on a daily basis of the significance of our performance. Personally, I enjoyed it. A bit of extra responsibility never hurt anyone.

South Africa vs Sri Lanka, Kingsmead, 3 March

When it started to drizzle at Kingsmead we already were in a bit of trouble – five wickets down and quite a way behind the required run rate. I said to Lance: 'What's this rain likely to do – will it blow over? You're the fisherman; you should know.' He looked around, shrugged his shoulders and said: 'If I had to guess I'd say it won't turn into real rain ... but who knows Durban weather?'

We weren't exactly sure how we should play it; if you try to catch up with the Duckworth/Lewis target too aggressively and lose wickets, the total can quickly become unreachable. But we caught up, slowly but surely, and all the time the drizzle grew thicker until it was proper rain.

The Duckworth/Lewis target score wasn't always displayed on the scoreboard. We were relying on signals from the change room, but also looking out for the D/L number when it appeared between overs. Dr Bacher, who was tournament director, still blames the ICC for the confusion that led to our elimination. The target score should have been displayed at all times – which it was at every subsequent ODI, thanks to the chaos and controversy caused by this game.

Muttiah Muralitharan was bowling what turned out to be the final over. The rain was coming down and we were expecting to be taken off at any stage. I pretty much knew it would be the last over of the match unless the rain stopped immediately, which wasn't going to happen. The number we had in our heads before the over started was 13. That was how many we believed we were behind the D/L target. We had been quite a bit further behind but we'd made great progress in catching up, thanks to Polly, who made a calm, well-paced 25 in a sixth-wicket stand of 63. It wasn't looking good at all at 149-5 chasing 268, but the game was back on an even keel at 212-6 when Polly was run out by the tiniest margin.

I decided we needed those 13 runs in that over – all of them. Lance was playing himself in and knew the importance of not losing another wicket. As always, he backed himself to hit the ball out of the ground later on provided he was 'in'. I was worried there might not be a 'later on'.

I took a single off the first ball, but Lance couldn't score off the next two. Twelve off the last three balls was going to be difficult. Our luck seemed to have changed when Murali, who was struggling with the wet ball, saw a quicker ball slip down the leg side and run away for five wides. Now we just needed seven from three balls. Lance nudged the next ball for a single. Six off two. I backed myself. I was well set, seeing the ball well and I knew Murali was battling.

The moment I hit it, I knew. It came straight out of the middle of the bat and disappeared over mid-wicket. There was no sense of triumph or anything like that, but, for the first time in the match, we had finally played ourselves into the driver's seat. It was the first time any of us had felt we could control our own destiny. At that point Lance walked down the wicket and said: 'OK, that's the D/L target reached. The last thing you want to do now is get out.' The rain was absolutely chucking down at that stage. It was obvious the umpires were going to take us off. The Sri Lankans were suddenly and clearly dejected. The plan from there was to block the final delivery and then start lobbying the umpires to get us off.

But I couldn't help noticing that Marvan Atapattu was fielding right on the edge of the circle at mid-wicket. You can't help looking at run-scoring areas and opportunities when you're at the crease. I thought: 'That's a pretty straightforward single, there. But we don't need it. Imagine if you slipped going for a quick single and were run out ... or fell lbw playing a sweep shot ...' So I blocked it. Job done.

After I'd blocked the final delivery of the over, the umpires got together for a chat and I walked past umpire Venkat at square leg and said: 'We can't play in this, it's crazy – I can't hold my bat properly!'

While they were deciding what to do, I looked up at the change room and became aware of the pandemonium going on. Arms were waving, heads were being held in hands, and Nicky Boje was sprinting towards us holding a piece of paper. I had no idea what to make of it, but I wasn't immediately worried because I knew the number was 13 runs ... What were they saying? There was a circus going on around me. Steve Bucknor, the senior umpire, was telling Nicky and Allan Donald to get off the ground.

Then I noticed Kumar Sangakkara and Atapattu unfolding a piece of paper in the rain and trying to read it. What? The fielding side had the D/L calculation and the batsmen didn't? What sort of an arrangement was that? Then I realised it had just been delivered to them from the boundary, but Nicky wasn't allowed to come and give us the sheet of paper. Bucknor said: 'You must get off, you are wasting time.'

I looked back up at the change room and could see everybody frantically waving at us to stay on the field. But the umpires had reached the conclusion that enough was enough and called the ground staff on with the covers. It was only after we were walking off that Nicky got the message through loud and clear: 'We need one more run, we have actually tied with them!' But at that stage there was nothing we could do. All we could do was hope and pray that the weather would lift and we would get a chance to carry on.

By the time Lance and I returned to the change room I was feeling sick. I was shouting and demanding an explanation, which really didn't help – but emotions were running high. I wasn't looking to make anyone the scapegoat; I just wanted to know what the hell had happened. Reading a number off a sheet of A4 paper seemed like a fairly simple job, and it was. The number *had been* read correctly. It was the small print at the top of the page that had escaped everyone's attention: 'Duckworth/ Lewis par score'. Why would they do that? Who is interested in a tie? The anger was made so much worse by the fact that I would have backed myself 19 out of 20 times to have scored a single off that last ball.

A little while later, the Sri Lankans claimed that they'd known what was going on all along. What absolute rubbish. You only had to see how their shoulders slumped when I hit the six. And if they were aware that we only needed a single off that final delivery, why didn't they change the field? Why was Atapattu basically giving me a run by standing so deep at mid-wicket?

It was a dreadful time. As the minutes ticked away and the rain stayed heavy, we had longer than most teams to suffer the agony of elimination. There wasn't much said in the change room as we waited for the umpires to call the game off.

I was just too emotional to think straight. Then I looked over to Jacques, who always sat in the opposite corner of the change room at Kingsmead. He had tears in his eyes, but there was nothing else to indicate the anger and frustration the rest of us were all feeling. I walked over to him and asked whether everything was OK. It was unusual to see him crying. He's very in control of his emotions. The only thing that ever upset him in defeat was if he felt somebody hadn't tried their hardest – or could have tried harder.

But I could sense straightaway that this wasn't about what happened that evening. 'My dad's just been diagnosed with cancer,' he said.

A few seconds earlier I thought I couldn't cope with not winning a cricket match; now it was the last thing on my mind. I put my arm around him and said: 'Buddy, I am so sorry to hear that. You know I'll do whatever I can for you.'

There isn't much you can say to a person, even your best friend, in that situation. We'd just been eliminated from our home World Cup – before the semifinals. That sense of destiny that so many people had talked about was gone. We were not untouchable, after all. But all I cared about right then and there was looking after Jacques.

Ali Bacher

The disaster at Kingsmead was undoubtedly the fault of the ICC and of the World Cup organising committee, of which I was a member. Spectators should be fully informed of exactly what is going on at all times, and the players even more so. It was a desperate mistake not to have the D/L information displayed on the scoreboard ... but we all learn from our mistakes.

One of his first serious coaches, Richard Pybus, told me when Mark was a teenager that he had national captaincy potential. He read the game remarkably well for a young man of his age. Fortunately he never went that route. It's too much to keep wicket, bat in an important position and be vice-captain.

He was a phenomenal all-round sportsman. His rugby skills were incredible. I heard many people say he could have been a South African scrum-half.

West Indies, 2007

South Africa showed some imperious form in the group matches and reached the semifinal with few difficulties. It was played on 25 April against Australia on the beautiful island of St Lucia. The Proteas won the toss and chose to bat first. They were 27-5 before the 10th over was complete. A series of uncharacteristic, overly aggressive shots by the top order contributed to their demise.

We were playing against a very good side at the top of their game and we knew we were going to have to do something very special to beat them. And that was the problem. Perhaps we thought too much about them and not enough about ourselves. We were also playing well, but we forgot to back ourselves. We'd come second too many times to a great team and we were just too anxious to put it right – a case of playing the man rather than the ball. We should have concentrated on doing the simple things right and playing as we had been playing, just better.

Although I was never motivated by records or statistics, I wasn't quite as grumpy as I might look after taking my 367th catch against Pakistan at Centurion (11 January 2007). This took me past Ian Healy's world record. The batsman was Faisal Iqbal. LEE WARREN/GALLO IMAGES

St Lucia, West Indies, 2007. There's a lot of hard work that goes on behind the scenes that is disguised by photographs like this. But that doesn't mean to say we didn't have a great time as well! DUIF DU TOIT/GALLO IMAGES

The 2007 tour of Pakistan was the beginning of South Africa's four-year rise to the pinnacle of Test cricket. To combat the tedium of 'hotel arrest' between matches, we grew beards. Jacques won! Jacques, Graeme and me – best mates. LEE WARREN/GALLO IMAGES

Umar Gul becomes my 396th Test dismissal, at Karachi on 3 October 007; as a result, I surpassed Ian Healy's world record. Adam Gilchrist overtook me a few weeks later, but I was in front again just a month later on our tour of Bangladesh. Records are just numbers. Play long enough and you will collect records! LEE WARREN/GALLO IMAGES

Despite all the wonderful years with the Proteas, I never lost my love of playing domestic cricket. The Warriors were a great team to play for. GALLO IMAGES

It's a fine line. This one gets away from me at the MCG in 2005. GETTY IMAGES/TOUCHLINE PHOTO

Third Test at Edgbaston, 2 August 2008. Pictures tell a thousand words, and this one will always remind me of the emotion after winning the series in England in 2008. Graeme, though, was the real hero.
TOM SHAW/GETTY IMAGES

The famous Sydney Cricket Ground. The victim is Shaun Marsh, my 400th dismissal in ODI cricket. Just another number that brought me level with Adam Gilchrist, but a good pic! MIKE BOWERS/GALLO IMAGES

The memories I will always cherish: the first South African team to win a Test series in Australia. Ever. GRAEME SMITH

And more of the same: Jacques, me, Morne Morkel and the captain with his broken hand. But not too broken to hold a beer! GRAEME SMITH

One more for the memorabilia collection. Gary Kirsten presents me with a long-service award at the 2012 CSA Annual Awards. It occupies a prominent place in my bar. LEE WARREN/GALLO IMAGES

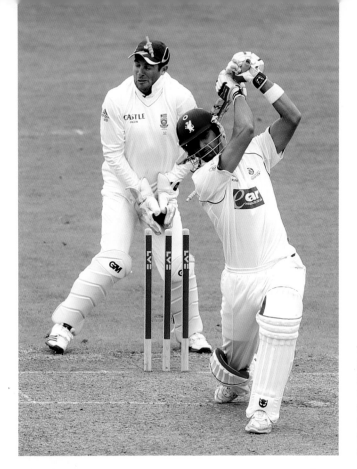

The day it all ended. The ball that pushed the bail into my eye is out of shot. One part of my life ended at this moment, but another began. Gemaal Hussain is the unfortunate batsman. GALLO IMAGES

Team physiotherapist Brandon Jackson takes charge in the immediate aftermath. You can tell from the players' body language that they have no idea yet how serious the injury is. GALLO IMAGES

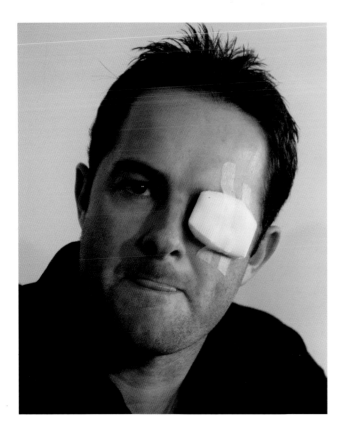

I have come to terms with the immediate physical damage, but not yet the long-term consequences. GALLO IMAGES

Meeting up with Mike Horn in Cape Town soon after the accident. As always, he is bullish and encouraging. DONNÉ COMMINS

On a rhino expedition with Mike Horn. Here we are removing the dart before taking a horn sample to extract the DNA.
HAYDEN PHIPPS

Dale, Kempy, me and Harro on one of our first rhino expeditions.
DONNÉ COMMINS

Rhinos don't say thank you, but sometimes you think they want to.
WILDCON

The deeper you can take a game towards its 100th over, the more chance you have of winning. But, instead of doing that, we walked out there and tried for the jackpot from the first ball. It was completely out of character. Then, when we tried to rebuild and consolidate, it was like quicksand; the more we struggled, the deeper we sank. We just wanted it too much. As any top sportsman will tell you, in most professional sports you need to be able to relax to perform at your best. If you're tense and suffering from 'white-knuckle' syndrome, you'll never achieve your potential. Our mindset was poor and, from a preparation perspective, we were in a bad space. Of course we were nervous. We did the usual things, but a team meeting before a normal game is different to a team meeting before a game against Australia.

That was to be expected. So the feeling that something wasn't quite right was normal. I just put it down to the occasion. We hadn't experienced a match like this for eight years. There were only a couple of us who had played at Edgbaston in the 1999 semifinal against Australia. The fact that they were playing so well was on our minds, too. That's one of my biggest regrets, that we became so fixated on having to play out of our socks to beat them.

Hindsight can be a cruel thing, but, if I could have that team meeting again, I would have emphasised how important it was to forget about them as individuals and focus on how good we could be as individuals and as a team. I would probably have suggested that we forget the video analysis session. What was the point in watching Adam Gilchrist and Matthew Hayden smashing boundaries all over the Caribbean? What was that doing for our bowlers' confidence? I would simply have said: 'Guys, we know they're good. Let's accept that they are going to score runs against us, but let's limit them as best we can and then score more than them. We are good enough.'

Instead, on the morning of the match, we were looking for that 'perfect game of cricket'. It was a crazy gamble. We opted for odds of about 40-1 rather than the 2-1 or 3-1 we could have had if we had just given ourselves a chance. Instead of scoring 300 or 350, we were bowled out for 149 and it was game over. Horrible.

The only other regret I have about the three World Cups I was involved in was our failure to make full use of home advantage in 2003, especially with regard to players relaxing between matches and the night before matches. In 2003 we all stayed together in the official team hotel instead of at home with our partners or families. I understood why – logistics, security, that sort of thing – but it was frustrating being a few kilometres from home and not being able to sleep in your own bed. I'm not suggesting it made a difference to the result, but it irked me at the time.

Mickey Arthur saw the logic in that. He was criticised for not placing a curfew and an alcohol ban on the guys in the Caribbean in 2007. There was the usual agreement that nobody would drink any alcohol the night before a game, but one night Hersch went to the coach and said: 'Can I have one banana daiquiri?' – or whatever the hell it was! Mickey knew that Hersch was nervous and probably wouldn't get to sleep without something to calm him down and relax him. So he said: 'OK, you take responsibility.'

I always had an early supper and early night before any game, but there were times when I knew one glass of wine with supper would make the difference between going to sleep easily or not. Changing something like that is a big decision. You have to trust the player. Unfortunately, not all players are trustworthy. It's a difficult one.

Chapter 16

Dropped – for the second time

During the 2010 tour of the West Indies, Proteas coach Corrie van Zyl opted for AB de Villiers as wicket-keeper for the five-match ODI series. Boucher took it as a clear indicator of how the coach saw the one-day side shaping up for the 2011 World Cup. Boucher was on tour in the Caribbean as the Test keeper. It was only the second time he would be dropped in his career. Van Zyl said publicly at the time, however, that it was his 'duty to explore all options', and that using De Villiers behind the stumps was an attempt to give the team another batting or bowling option, rather than a reflection on Boucher's ability.

T hings came to a head after the game against Pakistan during the ICC World Twenty20 in England. The lower middle order had felt that we weren't being given the best chance to win games because the asking rate was 10 runs an over by the time we came to the crease.

The team strategy was a legacy of when we had four or five power hitters, from number 6 right down to number 10, and we could 'load our bases' and keep going. But times had changed. Many of those players had retired, and without the likes of Klusener, Pollock and Kemp, we were struggling to score at that rate.

In the Pakistan game we were chasing 148, and we were 56-3 after 11 overs. We finished on 137-7, lost the game and failed to reach the semifinals. It was a deeply disappointing time for all of us.

I can't blame anyone, and never wanted to. That was the strategy. It just seemed a bit flawed to us. We knew Pakistan's spinners would be bowling in the middle and at the end of the innings in conditions which suited them perfectly in St Lucia, and we were supposed to hit them out of the park. We wondered why it wasn't preferable to attack the seamers a bit harder up front. It seemed reasonable to us. And, to be fair, that's exactly how the team's tactics moved, a short time later, when our tour of the West Indies followed on straight after the T20 World Cup.

That tactic had also formed the basis of our ODI game: cautious, low-risk beginning, high-risk, explosive batting at the end, whether we batted first or second. It was a problem for much of my career. Just because we had Klusener, Pollock, Kemp, Morkel and me – among others – the assumption seemed to be that we could produce fireworks every time, in any conditions. We didn't enjoy that planning, or think it was fair. Maybe we had Lance to blame. Just because he could do it more often than most, we all fell into the 'genius' category. We weren't geniuses. We had more chance of pulling it off through strength in numbers, but, by the time I was dropped, it felt largely down to me and Albie Morkel.

It had been a poor build-up to the tournament because many of the players had come straight from the IPL and Corrie had almost no time to prepare as a squad.

We had a serious meeting after the game. It was billed as an 'honesty session' and that's what it turned out to be. Corrie had a bit of a go at Jacques. He alluded to the IPL and said: 'Maybe you guys are more interested in the money; maybe you should concentrate on playing for your country.' If it was designed to hurt, it did. It was the first time I had ever seen Corrie behave anything like that. He was hurt, naturally, and frustrated, but I had only ever seen him in complete control of his emotions. He probably felt his reputation as a coach was on the line. He had been part of premature World Cup exits before, and I'm sure he felt he could make a difference this time. It felt like a no-win situation for everyone.

To ask a cricketer to give up a million dollars for a tournament that lasts seven weeks so he can rest for his international commitments is a big call. But he was serious. Jacques and Dale were targeted on the issue. Dale actually considered it, momentarily. He said that playing for his country was his greatest goal, and perhaps they could limit their IPL time. Perhaps just play half a season, or whatever. But he was trying to keep the peace. That's Dale. He knew he could never turn down the opportunity to change his life and that of his family.

As a senior player in the autumn of my career, I knew without a doubt that it would have been irresponsible to turn down a salary that could make a material difference to me and, more importantly, the family I might have in the future. Sport is sport, but it is also our career.

Then Jacques said: 'Perhaps we're looking at things which aren't actually relevant here. Perhaps we should be talking about having a batting coach in the squad.' Corrie didn't seem to enjoy that. As head coach with an expertise in bowling, he appeared to take Jacques's comment personally. He was obviously upset and frustrated. The subject changed.

The question of travelling in 'number ones' had been brought up a number of times in previous years, and it was raised again in that honesty meeting. The senior players had raised an issue that upset us, about travelling to the ground in our blazers and ties. We believed that not only was it uncomfortable but also it was impractical. We loved the idea of arriving in a new country or city wearing our number ones, but the first day of a Test was always awkward and uncomfortable. Everything ended up crumpled, and wearing a collar and tie in the heat was impractical. We had made a similar proposal to Graham Ford when he was coach and Corrie was assistant, and we had some great shorts and golf shirts designed which looked really smart. We loved them. So we didn't think Corrie would have a problem with our suggestion. I was actually in charge of clothing for the squad at that stage, so it was my responsibility to speak on behalf of everyone about our proposal.

Corrie obviously enjoyed the sight of a squad wearing number ones and I understood that. He said it was important that we travelled in number ones. I suggested a compromise: maybe number one pants and a smart golf shirt, with the added benefit of showing another of our sponsors' logos on the shirt. (Number one shirts had no logo on them.)

It was a difficult conversation for Corrie, and for the rest of us. He thought we were messing with tradition. I was genuinely hurt that he might have thought we were not showing sufficient respect to the Proteas blazer, when all we were trying to do was feel comfortable and look respectable. He may have underestimated just how much it meant to us. Maybe we didn't show it to him enough. Or maybe it was just bad timing.

Jacques and I discussed things after the meeting and asked ourselves whether we had gone over the top or been unreasonable. To us it seemed that Corrie had lost his temper, but we knew he was usually well-balanced and calm, so perhaps we'd pushed a few wrong buttons. We knew there was a backlash caused by the disappointment of the T20 World Cup. We asked ourselves, again, whether our suggestions or requests had been unreasonable. We honestly believed they were not.

I had been told by my father and by a number of other people that Corrie felt the clique of senior players needed to be broken up. I wondered whether that was the start of it. Certain administrators had said there was a problem with senior players having too much influence in the team, and my name was one of five mentioned. I had only heard the whispers second-hand, which angered me.

One-dayers, May–June 2010

Soon after we arrived at the Jolly Beach Resort in Antigua for the first of the five one-dayers, selection convenor Andrew Hudson called and asked me to meet him for a coffee in the breakfast area. He told me I was being dropped from the team. I asked why and he said it was because I hadn't performed. He said that he and the coach wanted to 'move forward' with the ODI team and felt AB could do a better job and give the team more options as keeper.

I explained my disappointment with regard to team tactics and the expectation on the lower middle order, and I pointed out that Albie, too, had paid the price for not being able to score at 10 runs per over every game. He had been dropped, too. Roelof van der Merwe was another who couldn't live up to those expectations.

Soon after returning to my room I received another call, this time from Corrie. He asked if I could go and see him in his villa. On my way, I saw Jacques heading in the same direction. I was confused. I couldn't understand why Jacques would be going to the same room as well. They certainly weren't about to drop him!

I think Corrie wanted to soften the blow by having Jacques along as he broke the news to me. I didn't enjoy that at all. It felt a little patronising. I felt it should have been just the two of us, or perhaps three with the selection convenor. I understand now how much pressure he was under. He needed to find the best combination for the World Cup. I was one of the players under examination. But at the time, it was painful and I was confused and hurt by the reasons given. I was convinced things would have been different if the tactics had been more balanced. Maybe I just wasn't absorbing it.

He confirmed that I was not in the T20 squad, at all, or in the ODI starting XI, although I was in the squad. He asked whether I wanted to attend team meetings or the T20 matches, but it transpired that, actually, I wasn't required at either. I was in the West Indies because the Test matches were at the end of the tour and I was still the Test keeper.

It wasn't Corrie's intention, but, given the stage of my career, I felt as though I wasn't just being dropped; I was being isolated. It was a tricky situation. Initially I was more stunned than angry. Surely I could still contribute on some level? I knew I still had a lot of value to add.

Jacques Kallis

Corrie wanted to play an extra specialist batsman. I didn't agree with the decision because I knew what Mark still had to offer, but it was the coach's call. They had been very close at one stage, but that incident caused a lot of friction and drove a wedge between them. Bouch was very, very down.

I'm not sure why I was there. Just to mediate, I suppose, but it felt strange. Mark thought Corrie had a non-cricketing agenda, and maybe there was a bit of that, but my recollection of the conversation was of Corrie saying he didn't think Mark could do the number 7 'finisher' role – and of Bouch saying he believed he could. It seemed quite open and honest to me. It was tough to sit there and listen to the coach's point of view because I disagreed with him and didn't think it was the right move.

Apparently Corrie had plans to take Bouch to the World Cup all along, but then why leave him out leading up to it? It didn't make sense to me.

That period hit Bouch hard. For him to say that he didn't have a lot of confidence, and that he was 'lost'... you must realise how tough it was for him. He was the most resilient guy in the game; he bounced back from everything. I spent a lot of time with him then, trying to help him along, being positive and encouraging. I knew he would grab the opportunity if he were given a chance – he's that type of character. I told him he had to believe in that opportunity. It would come if he just hung in there.

So I watched the team bus leave for the T20 matches and stayed in the resort. Later, it was confirmed that I was an ODI squad member but wouldn't be playing. So I went to the games and tried hard to contribute, but mostly I felt like a spare part. I tried to keep myself busy and wasn't afraid of taking my turn with the 12th-man duties. The TV cameras made quite a big thing about me wearing the bib and carrying the drinks during a break. It didn't feel great, but if that's the way I could serve the team then I had no problem with doing it.

It was a bleak and miserable time for me, to be perfectly honest. My sense of self-worth and confidence hit an all-time low. I felt I deserved better treatment, not in an arrogant way, but, after devoting so many years of my life to the game, and to the team, suddenly to be pushed to one side with no role to play was hard to take. I was too proud and stubborn to say anything, though. What could I have said? Corrie had made up his mind and that was that.

Maybe I should have seen it coming. Who knows? I never wanted to acknowledge that there was an end – that was the hardest thing for me to comprehend. I just didn't see it.

It was no consolation when I heard myself being quoted – virtually – in the first team meeting before the ODI series began. Corrie said the game plan from now on would be to attack harder up front and not leave too much for the lower middle order to do. So that was the new game plan.

I ended up playing the last game when one of the batsmen was injured, but I didn't keep. I understood that they were trying to get AB up to scratch and I didn't have a problem with that at all. I always believed AB had the ability and potential to become a great keeper, and, of course, his batting talent meant he would always bat in the top five, which allowed an extra bowler or all-rounder to be selected.

One who could and, in my opinion, should have benefited was Roelof. A 100 per-center and a fighter, he gave everything but wasn't given the backing of the coach or selectors. I felt he was the victim of the tactics – the entire lower middle order was, to a degree. I couldn't help feeling that we might not have 'failed' so often if the top order had left us with 8 an over to chase rather than 10.

Test Series, June 2010

Corrie decided that the use of cellphones should be banned during all practices before the Test series, and approached some of the 'junior' players to gain their support before he announced the new measure. He asked them to speak up in support of him if there was an objection raised. His decision had nothing to do with the ICC's anti-corruption code, because it wasn't an international fixture, just net sessions.

The senior players accepted his decision, but it came with unnecessary resentment because we felt he had imposed something on us rather than asking us to buy in to the regulation ourselves. We understood that it irritated him when he saw players on their phones between nets, and he had a good point, but the most effective and disciplined squads are usually self-regulating.

Seeing players texting at the nets is not appropriate. But there are always problems with the one-rule-for-all' approach. Some players practise for three hours before a Test match, others for half an hour. It wasn't necessary for a guy like Jacques to have to wait two hours before he could use his phone, even though he had completed his preparation and was simply waiting around for the others to finish. How many times are players criticised for not responding to requests for their time?

Corrie may have been expecting another fight, however, because he'd forewarned certain members of the squad. I don't believe anybody used their cellphones excessively, but Corrie was always conscious of portraying the right image.

Perhaps he didn't quite realise how strong the relationships were between the players as a result of the culture of honesty that had been grown by Mickey. So when anybody started feeling uncomfortable about anything, we spoke about it. If anybody had a problem or an issue with another squad member, either a player or one of the management team, they had been empowered to speak out.

Dale Steyn is a proper, proper team man in every respect. He is a natural peacemaker who just wants everyone to get along and respect each other. But he was caught in a quandary. Desperate not to go against his coach, he was still confused and a bit upset by the atmosphere that seemed to have been created among the players. He took me aside and asked me what the hell was going on. He didn't know what to do.

I felt Corrie misunderstood the situation. In retrospect I'm sure he would have tried to work with our strengths rather than focus on our perceived weaknesses. It felt like he was threatening the strong bonds which had been formed between us all. So we handed our phones to the manager for safekeeping at the start of net sessions and waited to be given them back when we'd finished. It just felt slightly over the top in my opinion.

I thought I knew what was happening beneath the surface. There had been more talk on various magazine forums about the clique, again. They had named the 'big five' – Graeme, Jacques, Kempy, AB and me. So was this Corrie's chance to break us up? That's the way it felt to me. It must be hard for coaches to come and go while a core group of players stays the same. We were always going to be tight, and we still are. Rightly or wrongly, I can be outspoken and determined in my ways, and I was invariably nominated as team spokesman in the event of fallouts.

But I didn't fight back. None of us did. What would have been the point of that? The team came first, not us. Or any individuals. Ultimately, we all had to take responsibility for our performances and mine hadn't been good enough. If you perform, you stay in the team. If you don't, you get dropped, like I was. Sure, I felt our strategy was flawed, but I could still have done a better job of chasing 10 an over than I did, so I had no problem being dropped for AB. I would have enjoyed the opportunity to play with the new game plan, but so be it.

AB de Villiers

When Mark was dropped from the ODI team in the West Indies it was one of the most difficult weeks of my cricketing life. It was also one of the darkest periods of his career. It was the first time since his very first tour that he was a 'reserve', just there for moral support. He still did it amazingly well but I could see that he was hurting. It was difficult for him to accept that he was moving on. None of us wanted to believe it but he went through a bad patch and the coach and selectors wanted to try something new. I felt it was a bit unfair – he'd lost a bit of form but that was normal. With his experience and fighting ability we knew he would bounce back.

We could see he had his bad days but he was the most professional of all of us. He helped me with my keeping drills. He has always been one of my biggest supporters and I'll always salute him for that. To help me as he did, with his career being cut short, was nothing less than amazing.

Mark was the 'tough guy' in the side, the 'hard man'. Other team members wanted that. When trouble was brewing, they lined up behind him. So it was difficult for him to be more sensitive when it was suddenly required. It wasn't up to him to change his personality. The guys who clashed with him were, possibly, guilty of the same thing as him – they were also too proud to change. But Mark has a huge soft and sensitive side to his personality. I have seen him dig very deep to help people in need. People needed to fit in and prove themselves as team players before they saw that side of him. He had a great sense of the balance required between work and play. He partied hard but he worked harder.

2011 World Cup

I was desperately clinging to the faint hope that I might be included in the World Cup squad, even if it was as the second keeper to AB. I was absolutely convinced that I could prove my worth and fight my way back into the team on merit. And if I couldn't, then I was equally certain that I could add massive value as an experienced campaigner in subcontinental conditions. AB might need to rest his back or just concentrate on his batting.

The irony is that Corrie had, apparently, turned 180 degrees in his view on me – or, at least, on the value I could provide. In the weeks before the squad announcement he was actually campaigning for me to be included. I didn't know that at the time, but was told after the tournament. What I was told at the time was that Andrew Hudson did not want me in the squad. He felt it would be a step backwards.

My hopes were still high, however, because almost everyone else close to the squad – players, management, coaches – had suggested that the convenor would be persuaded by the weight of opinion.

I was watching a game at Newlands in a crowded room when the squad was announced on the public address system and displayed on the big screen. I was devastated. That was how I found out. I looked at my phone and saw that I had a missed call a few minutes earlier from Hudson. That feeling of emptiness was not something I was accustomed to. I felt short of breath and helpless when I looked at the names again and mine wasn't there. I had a reputation for fighting hard and for making things happen, but there was absolutely nothing I could do about this.

I was equally unprepared for the inclusion of Morné van Wyk. He was an opening batsman for the Eagles, but he certainly wasn't going to open at the World Cup – there were plenty of guys to fill that role. I was expecting to see a reserve keeper who batted at number 7 and had a reputation as a finisher, because that's what the squad needed. A finisher, a guy with heaps of experience in those conditions and with a solid temperament on the big occasion. (Me!)

But disappointments happen in life, so I made peace with it. Sort of. I moved on and got on with my life. Sort of.

It was tough watching that tournament from my armchair. I thoroughly enjoy Morné, both as a person and as a cricketer, and he had enjoyed a successful domestic season. As an opening batsman. I watched him struggle batting down the order at number 6 or 7 and I felt a mixture of sympathy for him and fury at the fact that he had been placed in that position. Going from opening the batting on South African pitches to batting at number 7 on Indian pitches? From the top of the innings against new balls to the bottom of the innings against reverse swing? What?

If you have any cricket knowledge at all, which our selectors obviously do, then you would never make a selection call like that. Rather let AB keep and pick a proven match-winner like Albie Morkel who has played in the IPL and who has batted in those positions at the death.

Most of the guys were close friends of mine, among my closest mates, and I was as desperate for them to win as I had been to be a part of the squad. I shared their pain when they lost the quarter-final to New Zealand in Dhaka. I was still hurting many days later.

The next time I saw Corrie was sometime after the tournament when we were all in our Proteas blazers for the annual awards dinner. Corrie obviously knew I was upset with him. When he'd been assistant coach under Graham Ford, we'd been close, genuinely good friends, and had worked really well together.

He approached me a bit tentatively and said: 'Are we OK now?' I said: 'Corrie, with due respect, no, we're not and I'm not sure we'll ever be quite like we were.' I told him that I thought he had it in for me, and that would have been fine if it had been based on cricket reasons. But I felt like it had been a manhunt. I knew it and I thought he knew it.

It just made it worse when he told me that he had actually asked to have me included in the squad in the final days. You take the wrong guy, get knocked out in the quarter-final, and then come and tell me you wanted me there all along? I would have preferred him to wait a bit longer before he told me that. I was still too sore.

I have genuinely moved on now and the hard feelings are long dead. If only Corrie had been straightforward with me about the 'other' reasons all along. That's all I have ever wanted and asked for. If he thought I was a bad influence on the team, if I was too big for my boots, become stale – whatever. He just needed to tell me. I could have changed. I would have done anything for the team.

Strangely enough, I was reselected for the next ODI tour after the World Cup, against Australia.

Chapter 17

Looking back

I was called 'Guinness' for a while but, fortunately, it didn't catch on. Many of my records were largely meaningless – fastest to 50 dismissals, fastest to 100, 150, etc. They confirmed that I was lucky enough to be keeping to a very good bowling attack on wickets like the Wanderers. Even the record I'm most proud of from the early days, the world-record ninth-wicket stand with Pat Symcox against Pakistan in 1998, didn't mean much to me at the time.

The media love records, and they usually make headlines and a TV interview, otherwise we would be none the wiser in the change room. There were two unwritten rules in every team I ever played in: don't celebrate records too much (if at all), and don't let your team-mates celebrate them either!

Lance was the master enforcer of the second rule, but with great humour. He was hilarious with the one-liners that brought you back, too. If you ever tried to chirp him he was quick as a flash in response: 'Focus on your own piece of paper and then focus on mine,' was one of his favourites. 'Oh, someone scored runs today, did they?' he would say if anybody was a bit too cocky. He'd give you a boost, too. He was just as good at that. Sometimes I wondered if he gave you a boost just so he could bring you back down again!

If the records had really meant anything to me, then the guys would have known. Batsmen are paid to score runs and bowlers are paid to take wickets. I was paid to catch the ball, finish run-outs and make stumpings. If you do your job well, and for long enough, you will break records. If you chase them, you are missing the point entirely. The only record to be chased is victories.

My hero in this regard, and for many other reasons, was Jonty. He had a complete lack of interest in personal records. He would play shots from ball one, if that's what the team needed, and never gave his personal scores anything but the briefest thought. There were times when I could swear he had no idea how many runs he had scored after an innings. I chatted about his record, after he'd retired, and he conceded that, perhaps, he could have averaged a few more, but he said he wouldn't have enjoyed the game as much. 'I played the way I did because I enjoyed playing like that,' he said. 'And there's no point in playing if you don't enjoy it.'

During a tour of the West Indies I suffered one of my worst dips in form. I couldn't buy a run. Even when I was hitting it well, I'd play a perfect pull shot and square leg would dive and take a ridiculous, one-handed catch just above the ground. I couldn't do a thing right. I chatted to Jo about it and he said: 'You're getting it all wrong, Bouch. When you go out to bat you should only look at the total on the scoreboard. Don't even look at your individual score. Bat for the team. If the team are 200-5 when you bat, and 250-6 when you're out, then you've advanced the cause and helped create a winning platform. It doesn't matter if you've scored 15 or 20. Give it a try and see what a difference it makes.'

Inevitably, just because it was Jonty, the advice worked immediately. I didn't think so much about my own innings and didn't bother with all the usual thoughts – am I hitting it well enough to hook, how are my feet doing, should I take a few more risks? I relied on instinct and concentrated on the team score. The runs started flowing again and we won games.

That helped me throughout my career. There were other times when I struggled for form, and I would think: 'Do what Jo did.' He was probably the ultimate team man, and he would do whatever his team-mates needed. I could not have had a better role model.

When I look back on my career, I can say the same as Jo. I probably could have pushed my average up by four or five runs in Test cricket, even in one-day cricket, but I can say, in all honesty, that I never quit on what I was trying to do for my side, and I never put my own score ahead of the team goal. That is so important for me. I'd rather get out playing a big shot because my team-mates needed me to than finish not out and play for my average.

Adam Gilchrist and Ian Healy

There was a long period in my career when Gilly and I seemed to be trading records from series to series, whether it was Tests or one-dayers. 'Most dismissals' was the common one but it also included 'most in an innings' and 'most in a match'. The media enjoyed it, and did their best to make it look like an even contest, which was kind.

Adam Gilchrist was in a different league to me. We may have had a similar ability to catch a ball, and maybe even to read the game and assist our captains and bowlers, but as a cricketer he made history. For over a century the wicket-keeper's role had remained largely unchanged. He batted at 7 or 8 in Tests and was expected to make gritty 20s and 30s. When ODI cricket started, the keeper's role remained largely the same. Adam Gilchrist changed all of that.

Only two keepers have played more than 100 Test matches – Ian Healy (119) and me. When I broke his record for the most Test dismissals, he sent me a handwritten letter. That was true class. Heals also took the trouble to have a couple of sessions with me in Morocco, of all places. Nothing nationalistic or patriotic, just keeper to keeper, for the sake of the art of the gloveman. My hero was Dave Richardson, but Ian Healy and Adam Gilchrist came very close to the top of the list. Great men, both.

For a time I felt awkward that I was placed in the same class. Gradually I accepted that it was OK to be mentioned in their company. I had done

197

a good job for a long period of time, and the numbers certainly placed me in the top few.

Technique, injuries and 'biltong finger'

In terms of technique, I was probably one of the worst in international cricket when I first arrived on the scene. I didn't have a technique at all. Bob Woolmer helped me with that, and Ray Jennings did a huge amount later. I relied on my natural ball skills to get me through. My positioning was poor and my skills needed a lot of work. The one aspect of my game I never denied, and was happy to pat myself on the back for, was my fitness and dedication. Nobody could ever criticise me for not working hard. In 15 years I never turned down an extra session. Often it was me asking for more. There was no aspect of my game I wasn't prepared to work on, and no aspect I ever thought was perfect. I would rather have been dead on my feet at the end of training than worry that I'd left something behind. I never had an injury I couldn't play through – at least, not a cricketing injury.

One injury was purely down to my stupidity. We were playing a three-match ODI series against Australia in the Colonial Stadium in Melbourne. It still brings a smile to my face. Real, proper, international cricket under a roof, with real boundaries. We could hardly contain our excitement. At our first practice we took it in turns to try and hit a ball into the roof. It was a natural obsession for a group of guys who had played every game of their lives in the open air. That was a great series. We hoped and believed it might change the game forever, and perhaps it still might. But indoor cricket has stalled since then.

Mom and Dad had decided to travel for the series, as much for the novelty as the fact that it was against Australia. Dad asked me if I wanted anything brought over, and I said: 'Some biltong would be nice.' Then I told him I was kidding. You weren't allowed to bring biltong into Australia; the sniffer dogs at Customs would catch you.

Dad can be stubborn and determined. I can't think where I get it from.

So he put some biltong in his hand luggage and handed it straight over as soon as the beagles started sniffing. The rest was in his suitcase. He was very proud of himself when he gave it to me on the day before the third game

I took a thick piece, which looked fantastic, but it had a chunky piece of fat at the end. I tried to cut it off, but managed to slit my whole finger, right through the tendons. I immediately stuck my finger in my mouth, as you do, but there was blood squirting out of my mouth. It was horrible. Then I put it under the tap, which was, apparently, the worst thing I could have done. I was making a bit of noise by then, mostly swearing.

Jacques came running into my room, wondering what the hell was going on. He called our long-serving physio, Craig Smith, who immediately said: 'Hospital – *now*.' At that point I was still convinced I would be able to play. I said to Craig: 'I'll be OK, right? It's just a cut.' He replied: 'Yeh, maybe ... no, I don't think so.'

I couldn't straighten my finger. At the hospital I said to the surgeon: 'Please, you have to get me right, I have got to play in the last game.' I had no idea how serious the injury was.

The following day, once the plasters were off, Craig asked me to perform a couple of basic functions, starting with bending the finger. I couldn't do it, and that was the end of the fitness test. Andrew Hall took the gloves and had an unbelievable game. He opened the batting, kept wicket and then took the pads and gloves off to bowl the 47th over of the innings while Gary kept wicket. We won the game by eight runs to square the series. Amazing.

When we returned home I had to have the operation all over again because I'd made a mess of it by trying to bend my finger too soon after surgery. It should have been kept straight for weeks. I was so keen to play in that third game. Professor Sydney Biddulph, our hand and finger specialist, did the best he could to sort out the mess. Fortunately we had a lengthy break and there was time for it to heal. But I could never straighten the finger after that. It was a reminder of why you shouldn't mess with Australian Customs.

The wicket

Boucher's total of 555 dismissals in Test cricket remains the record ahead of Adam Gilchrist (416) and Ian Healy (395). Added to his ODI dismissals (425) and T20 Internationals (19), he appeared to have fallen agonisingly short of a landmark which may never be surpassed, with 999 dismissals in international cricket. But he also claimed a solitary wicket as a bowler, giving him the perfect 1000. It belonged to West Indian allrounder Dwayne Bravo and came at the end of the 4th Test on the tour of the Caribbean in 2005.

Antigua was one of the flattest wickets I have ever played on – there were a world-record eight hundreds in that game. Chris Gayle made a triple. There was no chance of a result, the bowlers were tired and understandably grumpy, and AB had taken the gloves from me so I could run around and stretch my legs. AB had bowled before he took over behind the stumps and had taken two wickets, which put a smile on his face and made the bowlers even grumpier.

After a few overs AB started getting a bit sore. So now all the bowlers were stiff and tired and the batsmen were going the same way. Graeme looked around and his gaze settled on me. 'Everyone has had a bowl except for you and Hersch,' he said. 'Fine,' I replied, 'give me the ball.' A little while later Hersch bowled, too.

I wasn't nervous; I just didn't know what I was going to bowl – off spin or seam-up medium pace. AB said I should definitely bowl seam-up because the ball was reversing a little bit and he reckoned I had good seam position the last time I bowled in the nets!

It was fitting that Dwayne Bravo was on strike, as we'd had a bit of an altercation earlier on tour. A couple, actually. First he'd accused Graeme of making a racist comment, which infuriated all of us. To this day we still don't know what Bravo thought he heard, but it must have been something in Afrikaans, because that's how we communicate on the field when we don't want the opposition to understand. He was batting when Graeme shouted something to the bowler about moving deep square leg out for the hook shot, or something like that. Dwayne thought he heard something derogatory and the next thing he's making an official complaint. It was a hell of an accusation, and we were furious. Graeme handled it well in the circumstances.

The second came a little later, after we'd won the series. We were having a drinks party in my room with some of the wives and girlfriends. The bathroom was occupied, and I was in considerable need of relief, so I went outside onto the first-floor balcony, looked up at the stars, checked there was nobody below (which was a team room anyway) and relieved myself. Nobody could see me – there was absolutely nobody around. Except Dwayne Bravo! He told me I was an animal, or something. I didn't think it was such a terrible thing to do. It was dark and I was desperate.

So there I was, marking out my run-up in a Test match. With Dwayne Bravo on strike. My aim was to bowl a yorker right up in the blockhole, and I hoped to get some reverse swing into the batsman's toes. But my aim was the problem – it came out about chest high! The umpire, Simon Taufel, said: 'Bouch, please keep the next one a bit lower.' I reminded him I was bowling at about 100kph, not fast enough to hurt a child, and that it wasn't deliberate.

Embarrassingly, the second one came out just the same and Taufel was forced to give me an official warning. I apologised to him and the batsmen, and promised I wasn't trying to bowl beamers on purpose. But I was a bit rusty. It had been about ten years since my last bowl in a competitive match. (I bowled three overs at a cost of 20 on my first-class debut for Border 'B' against Natal 'B' in 1995, although my memories of that are hazy, to say the least.)

The second ball of my second over was even worse. I was so scared of bowling another beamer that I almost pitched it on my toes. It floated down gently towards Bravo, who could have hit it off the island. He had so much time to decide where to hit it. He decided to hit me over mid off, off the back foot – typically Caribbean. But he mishit it completely and Ashwell Prince took the catch.

It was one of the biggest moments of my life on the cricket field. For all the irrelevance of the wicket, I loved it – especially after what had transpired between us. I didn't even abuse him. There was absolutely nothing I could say or do to make that moment better. I just put my arms in the air and smiled. Dwayne Bravo would forever be in my pocket. I would never bowl again, but he belonged to me.

When we walked off the field, Polly signed the ball for me. A little while later, when I looked at the scoreboard which showed the West Indies with about 800 runs, I noticed that Polly, Nicky Boje and Jacques hadn't taken a wicket between them in 100 overs. AB and I had picked up three between us, although AB had worked a lot harder for his, bowling 21 overs compared to my eight balls. I couldn't resist it. I stood up in the change room and made a little speech: 'To the bowlers, I'd just like to say I don't know what you've been complaining about all these years. You always say bowling in Test cricket is hard work. Well, a couple of wicket-keepers didn't find it so hard today.' Then I tied my boots together and hung them on my locker. 'Graeme, I'm done with bowling, thank you. Please don't ask me to bowl again.'

I believe I still have the best bowling average in South African Test history. Somebody might pass my total of dismissals one day, but I bet nobody ever has a lower bowling average than 6!

But the very best thing about that wicket came well after I had retired. Richemont and Remgro chairman Johann Rupert is a great supporter of the Proteas, and his promise to Jacques of lifetime membership at Leopard Creek Country Club in Mpumalanga if he scored a double century had received plenty of coverage. When Jacques finally reached the landmark he made the gesture of swinging a golf club to show his excitement and appreciation. Every time I saw Johann after that I asked what I had to do to earn membership at Leopard Creek. But it wasn't to be.

After my accident, he was a giant in his support of me. Most things were already organised but he offered to put me in touch with surgeons, rehab people, ophthalmic experts, anything. He invited me to play on the Alfred Dunhill Links in Scotland, which I would have loved to accept, but the injury was still too recent for me to fly. I hope to accept a similar offer in future.

Then Johann finally relented – and gave me a chance. It was only a couple of months after the accident and the Test team were about to play the third and final match against England at Lord's, the home of cricket. They were 1-0 up in the series and victory would confirm them as world Test champions. Johann loves to see South African success, and was very excited, as we all were. He told me on the morning of the match that if Jacques scored a hundred, and got his name on the most famous honours board in the game, I would receive honorary life membership at Leopard Creek.

Not only was fate out of my hands (which I have always hated), but it was also too late to get a message to Jacques. The players were warming up already and their phones would be off for the rest of the day. I sat in a darkened lounge watching more nervously than if I had been playing. Jacques was looking good. He had scored a huge hundred in the first Test and was batting as well as ever. By the time he reached 30 I knew he was really 'in'. It would take a great delivery to get him now, and I knew he was very unlikely to make a mistake. His was the hardest wicket to earn in world cricket.

Early in his first innings he played a leg glance against Steven Finn, which brushed his thigh pad. He was given out. It was robbery. Even with one eye I could see it wasn't out. In the second he moved effortlessly into the 30s, and I started dreaming of Leopard Creek. Then Finn trapped him again, on 31, and that was that.

The next time I saw Johann was on a visit to his house at Leopard Creek. (Fortunately I had a good friend who was a life member so I was able to play as his guest!) We had a sundowner and admired the stunning views; then he said: 'You know, I would have given you membership if you had reached 1000 international dismissals.' I told him immediately that I had! He replied: 'No, you didn't, I checked the stats. You were stuck on 999 when you retired.' I replied: 'My wicket – what about my wicket? Did you forget about that?' Johann looked at Jacques and asked him whether it was true. Jacques confirmed it.

Then Johann said: 'Well, I have the ball with which Shane Warne took his 300th Test wicket. I'm sure Jacques remembers that. So if he will sign it for me, then I will arrange membership for you.' Jacques remained straight-faced. Warne's 300th wicket was Jacques's, bowled by a googly between bat and pad. 'I'm not signing any bloody ball,' he said. 'You will sign it, Jacques, or I will kill you,' I said.

It's not just the golf course that makes Leopard Creek so special. It's the bush and the surrounds, that excite me so much. I look forward to visiting many times in the future, and I will doubtless be grateful to be a member of such an exclusive club.

I should probably invite Dwayne Bravo for a visit.

Criticism and the media

In February 2010, while we were on tour in India, my back went into spasm. I was off the field getting treatment, and JP went on as the sub. He had single-handedly won us the Melbourne Test only months earlier, and played the major role in winning us the series against Australia. But then he went through a bad patch where he didn't score many runs, as we all do. During the Kolkata Test, Kepler Wessels, who was assistant coach to Corrie at the time, went to go throw balls to Johan Botha. JP had just got onto the field when Virender Sehwag nicked one to first slip. JP put it down.

I was on the treatment table when Kepler and Johan returned to the change room. Kepler said: 'What's happened?' The 12th man said: 'Sehwag nicked one and was dropped.' Kepler said: 'Let me guess, JP Duminy at first slip.' I thought that was pretty sharp from a guy who wasn't even watching. I looked at our physiotherapist, Brandon Jackson, who was massaging me and wondered what was going on. Then Kepler said: 'He can't bat, he can't bowl and now he can't catch!'

I said to Brandon: 'Jeez, Jacko, this is supposed to be our batting coach, and he's meant to be helping this guy get back into form. Yet he's saying things like that!' It was just a joke. I'd heard a lot of people talking about Kepler as a coach, that he was hard and uncompromising, but that was bit harsh. JP's confidence was down. As a batting coach, it was surely

Kepler's job to get him back into form again? I'm sure it wasn't meant as harshly as it sounded, but it did occur to me that Kepler wouldn't have enjoyed hearing that during his own playing days, as hard as he was.

Criticism can be useful. But when I hear some of it these days, I'm inclined to throw stuff at the TV. It's not about me; I'm retired. What sometimes upsets me is the lack of qualifications the commentators have to say what they say. And the effect it can have. To listen to a number 11 batsman talking about technique against the short ball, with such authority, makes me shudder. He probably got hit with every second bouncer he faced, and he was probably on his backside for the other ones. Who is he to comment on a top-order player playing the short ball? He may discuss his knowledge of technique, but to imply that the player he is talking about is deficient or careless – that upsets me. Broadcasters should know their limitations – and the limitations of their experience. They should understand the consequences of what they say.

I used to get irritated when someone who used to open the batting, or bowl, started talking about wicket-keeping. What the hell do they know about foot movement and glovework? If Ian Healy, Dave Richardson or Ray Jennings commented, then it was a different story.

I enjoyed listening to guys like Robin Jackman. He was always respectful. He played first-class cricket for over two decades (almost three, probably!) and knew how much effort it took and what sacrifices are required. He instinctively knew that players don't mess up on purpose. He coached, too, so he was aware of players' sensitivities. When Jackers criticised, players would, more often than not, say: 'You know what, he's actually right. I could have done better, it wasn't a great shot.'

There was a stage in Australia's history when they were beating everyone and winning 16 consecutive Test matches. I'll never forget a conversation with Tony Greig (he loved the Eastern Cape connection we had) during which he told me that Channel Nine had specifically told the commentary team that they were forbidden from saying anything negative about the Australian team. Everything had to be positive. I asked him: 'How can you always be positive? What happens if Ricky Ponting plays a bad shot – walks across his stumps, and tries to work one through the leg side?' He said: 'There are easy ways to do it. You don't always have to criticise. You can praise the bowler.' I listened to his commentary when Ponting was out – he played across the line to a delivery and was lbw. Greigy was: 'Ah, great bowling! He knows Ponting moves across his stumps and that shot is his strength. On another day he would have whipped that through mid-wicket for four!'

Commentary is not about having a personal dig at a player you don't enjoy. You must rise above that, but it does happen. Craig Marais was a wicket-keeper/batsman for Boland and Griquas before he became a radio commentator. He was pointedly vocal about me at most opportunities, no matter what was happening or what I was doing. I'd learnt not to accept second-hand opinion towards the end of my career, but people would record what he said about me and replay it to me. If commentators or journalists feel strongly about an issue, like me being replaced in the team, then they should stand up for that point of view in all forums – including talking to me, face to face. But he was always smiley-happy whenever we met. He didn't say anything to me directly.

I know how difficult it is. When I did a little commentating stint for the IPL, I wasn't the greatest. I admit I found it difficult to comment on Graeme, for example, because he was my captain. I was trying to imagine Robin Jackman's style all the time. The bowler gave Graeme a long-hop and he pulled it straight to mid-wicket. It wasn't a great shot and it was a soft dismissal. It was such a poor delivery it probably surprised Graeme – he didn't know whether to hit it for four or six, or where to hit it. All I could say was: 'When he gets back to the change room I'm pretty sure he'll want to throw his bat at the TV.' The television business knows its product, and I'm sure the directors and producers have a clear idea of what they want from commentators, but I can't understand the point of stating the obvious and being critical for its own sake.

Cricketers need to have the confidence and ability to approach commentators and journalists if they are upset about something that has been said or written about them, even if it is just to correct a fact or a perception about something. Too many players feel that they can only make the situation worse. Sometimes that's true, but many other times both parties can be pleasantly surprised at the mutual benefits of building a relationship. Not a friendship necessarily, but a working relationship with a bit of trust and respect. I certainly never held back from having a chat. Sometimes my team-mates held me back, which was probably a good thing from time to time.

I was brought up in the same part of East London as journalist Telford Vice. For years and years he was always pretty good, I thought, and then one day he wrote an article about me that was a personal attack on my character, nothing to do with cricket. He questioned what I would do with my life after cricket. It was belittling and, in my opinion, unwarranted. It came from nowhere. I wanted to tackle him about it, but I realised it was pointless. The relationship was ruined from that point. He was suggesting I would be a nobody after cricket, that I wouldn't be able to function in the real world. Maybe he was right. Perhaps I won't be able to function. He was right about one thing, though. I will be a nobody. We are all nobodies after our 15 minutes of fame. I'm not worried about that. If he'd wanted to write that article, why wouldn't he have spoken to me first? Or even offered me the chance to comment once he'd written it? Perhaps he was just having a bad day. If he was, he should have realised how much of an impact he could have.

Respect comes from understanding, and unfortunately there isn't enough of either between the players and the media. Players don't understand the various demands placed on journalists, who, in turn, probably make many assumptions about the players that are unfair or uninformed. There are bridges to be built. It can only benefit the game if there is respect. Players are there to be criticised; it's part of being on stage. But casual comments and throwaway lines can have consequences.

Some players don't answer their phones, and others are guilty of neglecting their responsibilities. Their attitude might be: 'I'll do this amount of media and no more.' I was there once. I treated it as a chore. I had no real understanding of how important it was in the big picture. I focused on small, irritating but irrelevant things, like one reporter who would ask silly questions in a press conference. So what? Move on. It doesn't matter. There were other people asking decent questions.

I also had a very bad experience right at the beginning of my career. I come from a small town, so I was a bit wet behind the ears when it came to promotion and marketing. Instinctively I shied away from anything I felt was self-promotion, but somehow I was talked into doing an interview with *You* magazine. It involved a photoshoot, in which I was asked to take off my shirt. I still shudder when I think about it. I was sledged for about ten years about that article, and rightly so. When people say, 'Any regrets in your career?', I usually say no but the real answer is: 'Yes, just one little one.' But it happened. I can't change it.

The more players and the media understand how effectively they can both market the game by talking to each other, the more everyone will benefit. It still amazes me how much the players are gagged by the same people who are supposed to be trying to sell the game. The list of things we're not allowed to say or talk about is ridiculous. Once again, anybody can say whatever they like about the players, but the players can't even say 'umpire' without somebody in authority getting twitchy.

There's no doubt that young players don't realise the amount of harm and good they can do themselves, never mind the game, by their dealings with the media. There's no substitute for experience on the field, and there's no substitute for it off the field either! After a decade in the spotlight you realise how much truth there is in the old British saying: 'Today's news is tomorrow's fish and chip paper.' It's gone and forgotten.

'Marketing' can be a misleading term. For me, marketing yourself is about taking some responsibility for the perception that people have of you. You are taking a big chance if you allow people to form an opinion of who and what you are based on what they see of you as a cricketer on the field. Donné was brilliant at that. Where did I want my Christian faith to fit into my 'profile'? Which charitable organisations was I involved with, and how private did I want my private life to be – were there any exceptions? It is extremely important to take charge. If I hear a young player complaining about a perception that people have of him, the first thing I'll do is ask: 'How did it get there? What have you done to create that perception, and what can you do to change it?'

Sponsors

I've seen too many examples of how not to treat sponsors and sponsorship. No matter who you are, or think you are, or who your parents or agents think you are, you deserve nothing. You are owed nothing until you earn it. Sponsors are approached all the time by people who say: 'This boy is going to be future of South African cricket [or rugby], so give him R10 million over the next three years and he's yours – he'll promote your brand.' That's not how it works.

Sponsors are just like any other consumer: they need to know what they are getting for their money. They need to know that there will be a relationship built on trust and loyalty. My advice to young sportspeople and their representatives would be: 'Don't place yourself under pressure. Start slowly, build a relationship, ask yourself what you can do for a potential sponsor first before you ask them for anything.' I have sponsors who are still looking after me now because of the strength of the relationship we built over the course of my career.

I've met many sponsors who have been burned by the attitude of arrogance and sense of entitlement of young sportsmen, who expect to be given cars and even cash just because they have potential. Instead of approaching Mercedes-Benz and saying: 'It would be an honour to represent you. If you are interested in sponsoring me then I will do whatever I can to promote your brand. I'll drive whatever car you would like me to drive,' the attitude can sometimes be: 'I want an SLK 500, and I want it now!'

Faith

I have never deliberately hidden my faith. There are certain people who will show it publicly in a physical way, like crossing themselves when they score a hundred. I've got no problem with that, but I'm not that sort of person. I prefer to keep that private. That is my own relationship with God, and I don't want this book to be about God or religion. For me, it's more about what's on the inside than the outside. I know I've got a personal relationship with Him, and I'm happy with that.

Some people might ask how, as a Christian, I could be such a hard cricketer, play the game so competitively and be such an in your face character. I don't feel the need to explain or justify anything. God would understand my character and my frustrations at times, so he wouldn't have a problem with me getting the 'white-line fever' and trying my best. I'd like to think that every time I've played the game, I've played it nice and hard. But when I walk off the field, I'll be the first to have a beer with the person I've been abusing. There were only one or two occasions in my life where I haven't done that, and that's because certain things were said that crossed the line.

The Indian fast bowler Sreesanth started making comments about my mother while I was batting with Jacques at Newlands. I thought: 'This is going a bit far.' I didn't respond for a while but eventually I said: 'You can say whatever you like out here, but when the day is finished I'm going to come to your change room and we are going to have a little chat in private, just you and me.'

I wanted to hurt him! But it was one of those things; the guys calmed me down when we returned to the change rooms and Sreesanth visited me later to apologise. The next day he carried on at me again! It wasn't as personal, so I guess it was fine. But I wouldn't put him at my table for an ideal dinner party.

In retrospect, he just didn't get it. He was trying so hard to be hard, to be competitive, but he didn't know how! Effective sledging isn't about being filthy and foul-mouthed. If he'd said, 'I hear your place in the team is under threat, Bouch, I hear your coach doesn't back you,' now *that* would have been a good sledge!

Good times at the Sandton Sun

There were many reasons we enjoyed playing at the Wanderers and Centurion, but the one that was common to both was the Sandton Sun.

Everyone enjoyed the comfort and convenience of the place, and being able to walk into Sandton City under cover was a favourite with the guys who enjoyed a bit of shopping. Staying there two or three times per season meant we got to know many of the staff on a personal level, and they always made the effort to reserve the rooms we preferred – close to the lifts or the end of the corridor, depending on how lightly you slept or how late you got up.

Manager Shelley Mallet presided over much of our time there, and she proved to be one of the most amusing and persistent characters Jacques and I ever met. I can't be certain who started the pranks between us, but I recall the day she told Jacques and me that we were being assigned different rooms – despite having been roommates for a decade or more.

We fell for the bait, hook line and sinker. We were asking all the questions that Shelley wanted us to: 'Why have you sent us to different rooms?' 'What's the problem?' 'Is there a misunderstanding?' She thought it was hilarious, and didn't mind sharing her thoughts with us. We'd known her for several years by then, so we certainly felt comfortable enough to pop into her office when she wasn't there. There were papers all over her desk so we tidied them up for her and put them into the various filing cabinets. The desk itself was a bit heavy but the chairs, pot plants and other pieces of furniture all found themselves in new places. We felt quite pleased with ourselves and assumed that would be that. Now she would know who she was dealing with.

A couple of days later, during the Test match, we returned to the hotel and ordered some chicken from room service for dinner. We were surprised when it arrived covered in a large silver dome. We thought it was the wrong order. It looked like it should have been heading to a banquet. The waiter didn't take it off; he just put the tray down and left.

When we took the dome off we saw a freshly slaughtered rooster, head still on, all its feathers in place, and just a neat slit in its throat. We thought that that was going a bit further than just tidying up someone's office for them. We wondered what we could do with the rooster. Sending it back would give Shelley too much pleasure, but it wasn't a straightforward job getting rid of it. So we decided to make it somebody else's problem. We wrapped it up and set off looking for a suitable recipient for our gift.

While we were walking down the corridor we noticed that Hansie's door was open, as the hotel cleaner was just finishing her work in his room. It was too good an opportunity to miss. She was a little suspicious and asked what we wanted, but she recognised us, and Jacques smooth-talked her, so she left us alone. We laid the bird neatly in Hansie's bed, with its head resting on his pillow.

Once again, we felt very pleased with ourselves. But, a few minutes later, Jacques had a horrible thought: 'Wasn't Hansie out for a duck today?' he asked. Oh heck.

Now we had no idea what to do. As always, we couldn't be sure how Hansie would take it. His reaction to practical jokes was unpredictable, so we decided to play it by ear. If he laughed and asked who'd done it, we would own up. If he was fuming about it, then we'd keep a diplomatic silence. As it turned out, there was no reaction. For days we waited, but there was nothing. Our curiosity was burning, but we didn't think it was worth the risk of asking. Only much later did we pluck up the courage to ask him about the rooster. He laughed long and hard and said he thought it had been a sick joke – but he hadn't wanted to give anyone the pleasure of asking about it. I have no idea what he did with it.

It was our move next. Shelley would be expecting something and we didn't want to disappoint her. It had to be fun, hopefully inconvenient, preferably a little embarrassing, but not dangerous and not a problem for other guests. Those were our rough criteria.

So we bought an inflatable, life-size doll of the variety that lonely men use to keep themselves company. We managed to hang the doll from one of the chandeliers in the lobby of the hotel. When Shelley was alerted to the development, I imagine she spent the next 15 minutes talking to everyone in the lobby to make sure they didn't look up. She had to call the maintenance guys, who needed scaffolding to get that thing down.

It was barely a couple of days later that we arrived back from training to find our room completely empty – literally stripped bare, apart from the wallpaper. No beds, desks or chairs, no towels in the bathroom – nothing. All our clothes were gone, too. Nothing in the minibar. No kettle. We tried to call downstairs, but the phone was dead. So we waited. And waited. It was three hours before there was a knock on the door from housekeeping, and the room was slowly put back together ... with Shelley supervising operations with a big smile on her face.

We had to come up with something special to top that. Again, we applied our minds using our criteria. We bought a pile of stink bombs but decided against using them because of the other guests. Besides, it wasn't very original. So went shopping and bought the largest bottle of bubble bath we could find in the whole of Sandton City. I think it was three litres.

There is a large water fountain just inside the entrance to the hotel. You can't miss it – especially when it's pumping out perfumed foam into the lobby.

After that Test match, we went out for dinner and a few glasses of wine. When we returned, we couldn't turn any of the lights on, or even the TV. The electricity to the room had been cut. I needed a pee and decided to use the bathroom 'blind' before tackling the situation. I located the toilet without any difficulty, but failed to identify the clingfilm stretched over the bowl. My jeans were soaked.

On another occasion, Jacques and I ordered lamb curry for supper and we fell for Shelley's silver dome trick, again. This time there was the head of a lamb on a platter, eyes still wide open, and with fresh blood still oozing from the neck. Jacques is squeamish at the best of times, so that wasn't his best moment.

After that we conceded defeat. She was the devil woman. We had given her a good run for her money, but we realised we were minor league – and she was playing on home turf.

Jacques decided to dispose of the stink bombs in the kitbag of the England physio, Dean Conway, with whom he had become good mates when he played county cricket for Glamorgan. The England team were leaving South Africa for a short tour of Zimbabwe. A couple of days later Jacques received a call from a furious Conway demanding an explanation. The stink bombs had burst all over the bandages and flexi-grips he used for the England players, who were moaning about having to wear them. That put a smile on our faces.

The Sandton Sun was our home away from home, and Shelley was our 'Joburg Mom', although we did get up to a bit more mischief than the average mother and her sons.

Shelley Mallet

To the '1820 Settlers',

Many years have passed since we first met at the Sandton Sun, even though it feels like yesterday. Together we experienced many coaches, captains and team-mates. We certainly had many great times and celebrated many team successes as well as individual successes. A few disappointments, as well, but there were fewer of those. The young men I met about 16 years ago were quiet and reserved, yet showed a fierce determination and hunger for success on and off the pitch. But I think we'll call our 'match' an honourable draw. I was never sure what each stay with the Proteas was going to bring. I recall our meetings on the day of the team's arrival, and the first question was always: 'Shelley, what are you planning this time?' Bouch and Jakes have given us all great memories on the pitch, but they've left me with some of the best memories off it, too. Thank you!

Oh, and by the way, the room wasn't completely empty. Don't you recall the voodoo doll hanging from the ceiling?

Joburg Mom

Chapter 18

The IPL and the future of cricket

The Indian Cricket League (ICL) was the first game-breaker. The people behind it, including Kapil Dev and Tony Greig, got wind of the formation of the Indian Premier League (IPL) and jumped in first. For a lot of cricketers, it seemed like the way forward. They were either approaching the end of their careers or, perhaps, weren't as confident about having a long or reliable international career.

A lot of guys had been informally or even formally approached about the IPL as much as a year before the first season, and there was huge excitement. It was hard to imagine earning so much money, but it was also the thought of all the world's best players being involved in the same tournament. The franchise system existed in South African cricket, but it was still very regionally based and made up almost exclusively of local players. I was offered an ICL contract right at the beginning, but it was made very clear to us by the IPL that theirs would be an officially endorsed tournament, whereas the ICL would be unofficial and would almost certainly jeopardise, if not completely end, our international careers. I told them immediately that I had every intention of carrying on playing for my country and they should not bother contacting me again.

The reality of the ICL hit us in the change room after the 438 game against Australia in March 2006. Johan van der Wath had just played a spectacular role in winning that game, and yet he was wondering whether it might be his last game. He had been offered a lot of money, and, although he was only 28, he was leaning strongly towards taking it.

I watched a couple of ICL games on TV. There were some star players, but the standard was pretty average. There were plenty of guys who probably weren't bursting with enthusiasm and commitment and were really there for a cheque to bolster their retirement plans. Andrew Hall was another who probably thought his international days were over, although, along with Hally, at least you could be sure he was giving 100 per cent in every game. Many guys didn't get paid for the second season, which was a shocking thing for them to go through. I had a similar although much less costly experience once my ODI days were over. I was invited to play for a 'World XI' against an 'Asia XI' at the Rogers Centre in Toronto. I was offered US$8 000 for the match, but it was more the experience that persuaded me to go. I ended up carrying many of my own expenses and the fee never materialised. There is a lot of money in international cricket and there are a lot of people trying to cash in on it. Many of them are either unscrupulous or incompetent, and I won't be the last player to get burned.

Indian Premier League

The IPL was inaugurated in 2008. During that first season there were times when I'd pinch myself and think: 'Is this really happening?' Whether it was playing two or three times a week in front of crowds of 45 000, travelling those hectic itineraries, being required to attend an after-party at 1:00 am or just playing with and against so many of the world's best players – it was everything. There was also the knowledge that the game had changed forever. We weren't sure where it would go, but the opportunities for players were immense.

I was fortunate at the Bangalore Royal Challengers because there were three other South Africans: Jacques Kallis, Roelof van der Merwe and Dale Steyn. Many people assumed that Jacques and I had been 'bundled' together at the first player auction, while others asked me how we managed to wangle it so we ended up on the same team. I have no idea. We weren't the only ones, though. Mahela Jayawardene and Kumar Sangakkara were also signed by the same team; it made obvious cricketing sense to try and have a couple of team-mates together. It was a great bonus to be with Jacques. I just wish they'd paid the same for me as they did for him!

My fee of US$450 000 was life-changing in many ways. It was income I was able to invest to help secure my future life after cricket. It's very difficult to say no to the money on offer. For a player to turn down a contract, he must have family money, a wealthy personal sponsor or a national board with enough cash to compensate him for not playing. Anybody who says they're not interested in earning a contract is either lying or not good enough.

The players who went with the right attitude are the ones who have done best. First of all, you have to *want* to play. There have been a couple of guys who have signed up and travelled to India with the desire to have a holiday and collect a fat cheque. They have been found out. Not only do you need to have the desire to play, but also you should be open to learning and sharing your own knowledge. The IPL is also a cultural experience and a valuable opportunity for networking, which can be so valuable later in life.

Some people haven't been able to handle the money, and that's not entirely surprising. The players who are most vulnerable are those who have never cracked it at international level and have little or no exposure to big crowds and large pay cheques, and there have been a few in the first half-dozen years of the IPL – mostly young guys who produce a couple of eye-catching performances in their domestic tournaments, and suddenly they're in the limelight. Franchises know and understand that it's a gamble paying big money for a player with no proven track record, but they can't afford to take the chance that he may become the next Chris Gayle and he's playing for someone else.

It's up to the national boards and coaches to look after those players and to make sure they're going in the right direction and that they don't lose their heads. If I am ever given the opportunity, either with SACA or in a private capacity, to work with players in that situation, I believe I could make a valuable difference.

Dale Steyn

Some of the best cricket conversations I have had have been at Mark's house, either at his bar or in the Jacuzzi. Similarly, during the early years of the IPL, there was quite a bit of downtime in Bangalore and we spoke a lot about real issues like banking, buying a house, appointing an agent, investing, paying tax ... He gave me a lot of good advice and important information which I couldn't have asked many other people for. I couldn't ask my parents – they'd never had any money!

Lalit Modi

Of all the larger-than-life figures the IPL has thrown up, none exceeds the first commissioner, Lalit Modi. I arrived in Bangalore on a Thursday afternoon and our first game was the following night. By the time I had unpacked in the hotel room, I was thinking about ordering room service and preparing for an early night with a movie. Lalit telephoned my room and told me to come down to the bar for a drink and a chat.

He was there with a couple of other big guys from the IPL. I was thinking a cold beer would be quite nice. He asked if I liked tequila and ordered a bottle before I could reply. A bottle. He poured a drink and passed it to me. He introduced me to the others at the table and we had a fascinating conversation about the magnitude, impact and reach of the IPL. He poured another tequila. We chatted some more, and he poured another. After three or four, or maybe five, I politely excused myself and said I needed to go to bed. There was still plenty of time for an early night. But Lalit was having none of it and insisted that I sit down and have another drink. I became equally insistent: 'Lalit, I'm not going to mess up the night before any game, never mind my first one. I'm excited and I want to be 100 per cent.'

He replied: 'Bouch, I understand that this tournament is about cricket, and I'm pleased to see you are so committed. But it's also about a little bit more than that. It's my dream, and it's also about networking and meeting people.' So I sat down again and carried on chatting but I didn't drink much more. Lalit wanted me to be there – the other gentlemen were interested in my thoughts and it wasn't right for me to be leaving. They could have been paying my salary, for all I knew at that stage.

Lalit was very good with the players. A lot of issues emerged later on about the nature of his business dealings, but I never saw anything untoward. Our relationship was purely as employer/employee, and, trust me, I've worked for many, many less desirable bosses. He had a strong, personal relationship, even friendship, with many of the top players, both foreign and Indian. He made you feel special, and he made you feel a part of the whole concept of the IPL, which was important in bringing out the best in the players.

I am speaking now mostly as an observer, although I still have many friends and colleagues in the tournament. But it does seem to have lost a lot of the unique flavour that made it so special to play in and watch. The governing body that took over from Lalit in 2010 doesn't seem to have his flair and energy. The IPL was a mixture of cricket and entertainment. When people tell me it isn't 'real' cricket, I say 'yes and no'. It is T20 cricket, and it is the IPL, so there is a lot that is very different to more traditional cricket. But that doesn't make it any easier to execute the skills that make it so exciting to watch

Who runs world cricket?

India and the BCCI run world cricket. I may have strong words and opinions about things that I know and understand, but I'm not one to make judgements and pronouncements about things that are beyond my expertise. Cricket politics is one of those areas.

The infighting and power struggles at the BCCI are serious and have direct consequences for the ICC and the rest of the world, so that makes me concerned. I follow Lalit Modi on Twitter and it seems ironic that he has such a fertile resentment and hostility towards many of his former colleagues. I shouldn't laugh – but sometimes it's hard not to.

I've heard from too many well-connected people how the BCCI manipulates the boards of other countries and indirectly controls the destiny of so many players, and that concerns me. It was no secret that they objected to CSA appointing Haroon Lorgat as its CEO and made some strong suggestions that it would not be in South Africa's interests to employ him. That can't be right. The independence of each country, and their right to make their own decisions, should be protected.

But nothing I do or say is going to change that. Ultimately, they have the money, and with money comes control and power. People may deny it, or resent it, but that doesn't change anything. The BCCI makes the decisions and, ultimately, everybody else is going to have to abide by those decisions more often than not. That's the way it is. Life isn't always fair.

In a perfect world, organisations like the ICC, SACA and FICA (Federation of International Cricketers' Associations) would be able to coordinate a democratic agreement on most issues and we'd be able to move forward in a way that would benefit the majority, but I've been to India many times now and I know that is not going to happen. So what do you do? You make the best of it and move on. Making the best of it from the players' perspective is still working towards an IPL contract and then justifying it by playing to the best of your ability. It is still a great concept and a way for players to be rewarded in a way that justifies dedicating the very best years of your life to the game.

SACA

Early in my career I knew Dave Richardson had started working on a players' association, but nothing really solid had materialised. The foundations were laid but much work needed to be done. Dave had put together a structure aimed at protecting the commercial rights of players, but it was only for the top Proteas, and the initial payments were small. My friendship with Jonty, who was the first president of the South African Cricketers' Association (SACA), and various other players, led to my involvement in the early stages. Despite my concerns that I might be out of my depth, I threw myself into it.

When Dave left to join the ICC in early 2002, Jonty asked Tony Irish to take over the running of SACA and also asked me to become involved in benefiting all of South Africa's professional players, not just the elite. By June 2002, we represented approximately 250 players under the old provincial system. From 2004 to 2006 I served as president.

I'll never forget the first meeting of the 20 senior players. It was held under great secrecy at the Inanda Club in Johannesburg because the guys were worried that the administrators would try to stop it. Percy Sonn was president of the UCBSA at the time and could be quite an aggressive bloke when he felt he was being challenged.

We were all made aware of the fact that there would be tough times ahead, especially if we wanted to be represented on the board, because that was ultimately what we wanted. We needed to stand together. We needed to have a say in what happened in what was then the United Cricket Board of South Africa (UCBSA). We knew that there would be opposition, but we had no doubt it was the right thing to do. We had help from Tim May, who had already led the way with the formation of the Australian Cricketers' Association.

The first thing Tony did at SACA was to meet Tim and get SACA affiliated to FICA. At times it was harder than we had ever imagined. SACA was a union, after all, and many administrators felt threatened by it. Luckily, the guy we chose to run the organisation, Tony Irish, was an experienced and tough lawyer, and he was prepared to work without being paid for the first year or two to get it going.

Before the 2003 World Cup, we had to take a stand on a huge issue. It's complicated, but essentially the ICC had sold the players' commercial and image rights to its sponsors, but they did not own those rights. Neither the ICC nor the national boards owned those rights – the players did.

If we had agreed to proceed on that basis, a precedent would have been set. Of course, we were concerned about the public perception, about our threatening not to play in any World Cup, never mind on home soil, but the stakes for the players were too high to ignore.

The players owned their image rights. A lot of money was being made from those rights, but the players weren't getting anything from them. Tony asked the players to sign their image rights into a trust, of which they were to be the beneficiaries. Then he went to the UCB and told them that they had to pay the trust if they wanted to use the players' image rights for the World Cup. Percy flew into a rage and told Tony that the players wouldn't get a cent. Tony met with the players and told them they needed to stand together on the issue and not to sign the World Cup contracts unless a fair deal was given.

As the deadline for the contracts got closer, the players stood firm under SACA. It was a tense time. At one stage, Tony was summoned to a meeting with Percy at a coffee shop in Durbanville. Tony thought Percy was now ready to start negotiating, but, when he got there, Percy wanted to fight. A few expletives were used and it was even suggested that the whole team would be dropped – a couple of weeks before the tournament started.

Tony told him, however, that the players wouldn't sign until they got a fair deal. With two or three days before the deadline for signing the contracts, it was a case of who was going to blink first: UCB or SACA and the players. The players stood firm, as we knew we were in the right. Finally, the day before the deadline Tony, Jonty and Polly were asked to meet at Durban airport and a deal was reached to pay the players for their rights. It was such an important day for the players. We learnt that, if we stood together under our players' association, the administrators had to listen to us and to deal with us fairly. Similar commercial deals have been in place for all ICC events ever since.

So much work went into the agreement. We went to every franchise and asked if the players were interested in getting involved. The over-whelming majority of players said they were fully behind the associa-tion. There was always a concern that the administrators would say:

'Fine, we'll employ other players.' But when Tony explained that all but one or two professional players in the entire country were signed-up members of SACA, it was clear how the land lay.

The long-term consequence is that the players are guaranteed a percentage (just less than 20 per cent) of CSA's annual revenue. It makes the players genuine stakeholders, in the literal sense. It is in our interests to see the game grow and thrive.

Looking back, it seems incredible that Percy actually threatened to replace the entire squad. Errol Stewart, also a pretty tough lawyer as well as a former Protea, was on the SACA board, and he travelled around talking to the franchise players, asking them to support the national squad and to say no if they were asked to replace one of them.

After the 2003 World Cup SACA signed up all the provincial players. It was tough at first, because there was no obvious change in their circumstances, no extra money. But they had seen what could happen when players stood together. Within a year or so, just about all the players had become members, and that's how it has been ever since.

The earning potential for the players has increased far beyond what it had been before SACA. Player trust funds were set up to organise payments to players for various things like appearances at sponsorship events and the use of image rights. In 2006 SACA concluded a major collective bargaining agreement for players, which guaranteed that certain percentages of cricket revenues went to players and were distributed according to grade. All the professional players – not just the Proteas – benefited from this and, from that time onwards, players started to get paid fairly for the value that they added to the game.

It all started from that one major standoff between the fledgling SACA and Percy Sonn.

It's not just about money; it's about security. SACA is the players' voice on all of CSA's committees that deal with things affecting players. SACA is also heavily involved in FICA, the global body that deals with the ICC on player issues, including safety and security. There have been certain tours where safety was a genuine and legitimate concern but, fortunately, SACA and FICA took over the negotiations and even commissioned their own security reports, if necessary, leaving the players to concentrate on cricket in the knowledge that their safety was in good hands. I'm sorry to say that that wasn't necessarily the case with the administrators, who saw their job as generating income. Short cuts were sometimes taken.

I know Percy wasn't the only UCB member who was against the players having any meaningful power. They were old school; they believed that players play and administrators administer. But, ultimately, the players are the product and they need to have a say.

Tony would brief the players on every meeting he had with the UCB board or potential SACA sponsors – any meeting that was relevant to the game and our involvement in it. As professionals, I believe it was important for us to have knowledge and an understanding of the game beyond just what happened on the field. I became increasingly aware that it was no accident that players were kept in the dark about the business side of the game.

Today SACA is an established and integral part of cricket. The organisation has considerable power, but it uses that influence constructively and has a good working relationship with CSA. The wellbeing of the players, both short-term and long-term, is SACA's most important objective. I'm a big supporter of the player education programme, which provides grants and support for cricketers to study at the same time as having a cricket career.

I am only too aware of how things were when cricketers retired a few decades back. All too often, they gave the best years of their lives to the game only to look around at the age of 35, when they weren't needed any longer, to see that they were left with very little to show for their efforts. Even today there are too many great cricketers from the 1980s who are struggling to make ends meet.

SACA has set up medical aid schemes, pension funds and other savings schemes which most young players don't have a clue about when they are starting out. They offer expert advice on everything from tax to buying a house. If a player has a contractual problem, or has a breakdown in relations with a coach or franchise administrator, he can turn to SACA for free legal and personal advice, even mediation if that's necessary. That was never the case in the past. Contract meetings were a nightmare for most players. You would be told X, Y and Z by the chief executive and then presented with a 'yes or no' type scenario. It was intimidating – deliberately so, in some cases. Now players can say: 'Thank you very much, I'll have a chat to my representative to make sure I understand everything. Can I get back to you in a day or two?'

The CSA bonus scandal

I was saddened and angered by the demise of Gerald Majola as CSA chief executive. I was disillusioned that he was paying bonuses that hadn't been approved, and angered because it came on top of the Diteko Modise affair. Modise, as CSA chief financial officer, had skimmed a percentage off the national players' salaries for years, and he ended up being convicted and imprisoned. We used to call him 'De Taker'. Who knows if he would ever have been caught had it not been for the sharp eyes of Shaun Pollock and Tony Irish? I hate to admit it, but I wasn't surprised to hear about the bonus scandal. The way I felt about the administration at that stage, it could have been anyone. There were a lot of good people working very hard for the good of South African cricket, but in every business you are going to get a couple of bad apples.

Fortunately SACA uncovered the Modise theft and many of us were repaid a lot of money by CSA. Our monthly remuneration packages are complex, to say the least. The division of prize money, win bonuses and payments from trust-fund activities are extremely hard for most cricketers to follow. I know and understand what each payment is for, but working out the exact figures requires an expert. We had no choice but to trust the system. Polly is sharper than most when it comes to figures, but even he only had a gut feel that something was wrong. But he raised the red flag and eventually it was uncovered. The sad part about the bonus scandal was that it dragged on for two years and CSA's reputation was badly affected. Only now are we really feeling the effects and paying the price for it.

We made a collective decision as a team that the best way to salvage the reputation of South African cricket was to perform better than ever on the field and to win games. We knew all about the sponsors who had pulled out and about those who were threatening to leave the game. With respect, sponsors gain most of their value from players, not administrators, so they talk to us. We knew exactly what was going on. As tempting as it was to make statements asking our bosses to get their act together, the best course of action was to maintain our dignity and integrity, and to do what we do best.

My view on Gerald's disciplinary hearing was based on natural justice. I believe in karma. I thought he had let me down badly during my own disciplinary process, and I thought he would see the results of that with his own.

The most important point about SACA is that its foremost goal should be to work *with* CSA rather than against it. Everything possible should be done to avoid conflict. There are many levels of mediation, and even arbitration, stipulated in the memorandum of understanding between the two bodies that are designed to avoid conflict. In recent years CSA has benefited massively from the organisation and structure of SACA. The attitude of the players, which saw them rise above the crap during the bonus scandal, would have been impossible with the reassuring safety of SACA.

The future of cricket

I'm a purist, so naturally I worry about the future of Test cricket. Only an idiot could ignore the evidence that suggests that the greatest form of the game is under pressure everywhere but England and Australia. It irritates me to see young players emerging and being given respect and recognition as T20 'specialists'. I'm not suggesting that there aren't specialist skills required to succeed in T20 cricket, but you can also hide in that format. You can disguise the skills you don't have.

Test cricket needs to have more of a fuss made of it, and to be treated by the game's administrators as the head of the family. A lot of it comes down to finance. Prize money and match fees need to improve. Look at the IPL – it tells you everything you need to know about the state of the international game. I enjoy the IPL, but it is a domestic tournament. Young Indian players already aspire to land an IPL contract above anything else; they don't aspire to play Test cricket. The same thing will soon apply to young players all over the world.

Do a comparison. You have one form of the game that lasts five days, 450 overs and exhausts you, physically and mentally, while examining every aspect of your character and technique. Only the strongest survive. Then you have another form that lasts 40 overs and three hours. You need to think on your feet, but the results are quickly forgotten and you can recover quickly. A good eye and physical strength can cover any number of technical deficiencies. You can earn anywhere from 10 to 20 times more playing the second format, and your career will last considerably longer.

I would completely marginalise 50-over cricket, and make it the most exclusive of the formats: just one or two ODIs per tour, keep the World Cup at 50 overs but spend the rest of the money usually invested in 50-over cricket on Test cricket. I fully understand the financial implications of marginalising ODI cricket, but aren't we just making excuses for the marketers who haven't found the best and most effective way to market Test cricket? Everybody I have ever spoken to tells me they prefer Test cricket to 50-over cricket, unless it's a World Cup or something really meaningful, so why is it less lucrative? I include myself in that list, too. I can't watch a 50-over match; it's far too boring. I could watch a T20 match or a Test match at any time. So that's my answer. Give Test cricket the status that has been metaphorically conferred on it. Make it a bigger event. If Test matches can attract full houses in Australia and England, and if Newlands is full more often than not for Test cricket, then it must be possible.

The players are doing their bit. The quality of the entertainment provided in Test cricket over the last decade has been outstanding. Players are prepared to take more risks, run rates have increased, and bowlers will spend a few runs to buy a wicket if necessary. The percentage of drawn games is tiny compared to what it used to be. Test cricket is a highly marketable commodity; T20 cricket is a decoration, an exhibition of the game.

It's a weak excuse to say that people no longer have the time or inclination to come to the stadium for a whole day. I agree that the pace of everyday life has changed, so let's work with that. Target the people who only have two or three hours to spare. Pull them in for a session: 'Lunch at the Test Match', or 'Sundowners at the Test Match'. Don't ask people to go for the whole day; just ask them to go! T20 cricket has attracted a whole new audience to cricket and I've heard that many of them are now asking what the 'real thing' is like. So let's cash in. Let's be creative.

Limited-overs cricket has undergone countless face-lifts and make-overs, and that's inevitable because the game is ... limited, by name and nature. That's not a criticism; it's just a fact. If a bowler gets on top of a batsman, he has only a few overs to dismiss him. The battles and personal confrontations are limited, and a captain can hide his players. The same applies on an even greater scale in T20 cricket. The changes and adaptations will start soon with 20-over cricket. People will get bored of it. The ICC are doing their best to keep the game fresh and interesting, but there's a lot of competition out there for the world's sporting audience. So use T20 cricket to take the game to as many places as possible. Make ODI cricket special again by changing it to the elite limited-overs format. And cherish Test cricket – really cherish it.

Gary Kirsten is a proponent of a Test Championship that would run along the lines of any other league, on a basis that everyone can understand: in other words, one game against everyone else, home and away. You can't get simpler and more appealing than that. I'm all for that, I really am. One Test, home and away, against every other Test-playing nation in a two-year period. I'm sure the players would buy into the concept; there's no room for preciousness now.

It would not mean an end to traditional tours – not at all. Tours are still critical to the fabric of international cricket and why we dream of playing the game. The visiting team could nominate which Test in a series would count as the 'Test Championship' fixture. And the other games could, literally, be one-match tours. Forget warm-up games. Two or three days, that's all, then play the Test and come home. Let's stop whining about quality preparation time. Take the rough with the smooth. Each team will face difficulties and suffer bad luck. It would even out over the course of 18 Tests in 24 months.

At the moment, the two best teams in the world might not play each other for three years. It's ridiculous. The more Test cricket we play, the better. It would make sense of the rankings, but, even better, you'd have a straightforward, simple league table on which everyone plays the same number of games against the same opposition.

Fresh ideas

I was convinced for many years that the marketing strategies used by cricket boards were a little predictable and unimaginative. Many good people have been involved over the years, but there needs to be an injection of fresh ideas. That may sound strange to the marketers I worked with, because I wasn't always the most enthusiastic player when it came to marketing, but that was because I was tired of the same things.

A good example is a signing session after a game. I know and understand that youngsters want to collect signatures, and that is good, but it's become a bit stale. The players sit at a table and just sign ... Couldn't we take a leaf out of the Americans' book? Anyone who has been there can't fail to be impressed by the way footballers and basketball players, and their sports in general, get promoted. They make it fun, and a whole-day event. The youngsters get to see the players when they are fresh and at their best, not cramping, smelly and perhaps a bit grumpy after seven hours in the field.

I have ideas – many ideas. I see golf tournaments reinventing themselves, building little stadiums around par-threes, thinking out of the box, challenging the accepted norms. Cricket is doing it but we need to do more, especially in South Africa.

In American sports, the players' locker room is almost open house after a game. Some fans are allowed in and the media are allowed a certain amount of time to talk to players. In cricket the change room is a hallowed space; nobody is allowed in. Many people will smile at the suggestion that I would be open to a change in policy, because I was at the forefront of protecting our space during my career, but I see things differently now. One advantage would be, hopefully, that you could have a full and frank exchange of views with a member of the media without being fined for it! I would have enjoyed that.

It is not easy. I'm not suggesting it is. It will involve a lot of give and take, but there's definitely room for a change. Not so much in the game itself, but in attitudes around it. We've got to keep the game alive. Cricket is in decent health at the moment, but we cannot rest on our laurels. And there's a lot we can do to make it even better for future generations.

Chapter 19

Heading for the exit

J acques and I had made a pledge in 2007 to win a Test series in England and in Australia and to win the World Cup. We'd achieved the first two parts and I felt helpless and desperate that the third part was out of my control. The wind went out of my sails when I wasn't selected for the 2011 World Cup. I knew there was no way back into the ODI or T20 sides and it was a bleak feeling. My confidence was broken at that stage and I knew I needed something fresh to inspire me and make me want to work to get back to my best.

Gary Kirsten was a breath of fresh air when he took over from Corrie van Zyl as coach in June 2011. He organised a two-day camp for all of the contracted players, and another ten or so of the 'A' side, at the Arabella Country Estate, near Hermanus, and the vibe was fantastic. If you had something on your mind, you could speak to him over a coffee or a beer without fear of recrimination. I didn't feel that with Corrie. Perhaps it was my issue. I don't know.

I had a lot to deal with. For a couple of years I'd felt I was being questioned all the time, at practice and in matches. I wondered constantly whether it might be my last game. When I was left out of the World Cup team, I felt abandoned. 'Cheers, see you. We've got someone else now.' I wondered whether someone might say: 'Thank you for the last 250 games you've played and for everything you've done for the ODI team. This is the direction we are thinking of taking; what do you reckon?' It felt very sudden, like being cut off at the legs.

I never, ever minded playing for my place in the team. I had learnt how to do that. For most of my career I felt there were people knocking at the door. Perhaps, for two or three years out of 13 or 14, I felt I was sufficiently on top of my game to be the natural first choice. I knew there was nobody good enough to take my place – provided I stayed at that level, and continued to improve. But I never, ever took my place in the national team for granted. I know that wasn't the impression some people had, but I was on my guard at all times and I worked harder than most people can imagine to make sure I stayed there.

But when the end of my time was approaching, I believe I was extremely fortunate to have Gary as my coach. I don't know how it would have ended if Corrie or Andrew Hudson had been left in charge. I was told that Gary had asked Andrew to leave my career situation to him. He felt very strongly that a player with over a decade of service and more than a hundred caps deserved to leave with pride and dignity, and he knew he would do that.

We had always related well and he understood what I was going through. He had been in a similar place a few years earlier. He was honest with me, and asked how long I wanted to play for. I said: 'I'd love to play for another year – and I'm certain I can.' I knew I was still good enough. It wasn't an emotional decision. I had faced the reality of life without cricket; although it scared me, I hated even more the thought of carrying on beyond my sell-by date. He said: 'Why don't we set a date, to give you clarity on the whole thing? I want to see you go out on a high. Please don't wait for someone else to tell you that you're finished. You deserve better than that.'

When he asked me about the future, I said: 'England, one more time. I want to go out as number one.' He said: 'You deserve that. You have earned the right.' I felt an enormous weight lift off my shoulders. The thought of bowing out with my head held high was an incredible relief. Having a coach who backs you is essential to success.

Gary Kirsten

He was in desperate need of a plan for the end of his career. He needed direction and, ultimately, an exit strategy. Fortunately I had just had experience with helping a couple of senior Indian players manage their departure from the game with plenty of honour and pride. It was a matter of gauging the sentiment in the country, so that everyone could enjoy Mark's last couple of tours. I suggested he might call it a day after the England tour, but he made the decision and took ownership of it. Instantly he had a sense of direction and control over his own destiny. Once he made the decision to cut the cord, he lived every day as if it was his last in the game.

My focus turned to the 2012 Test series in England. The bad memories started fading away. I thought of Corrie van Zyl throwing to me in the nets and looking up at the heavens when I punched a half-volley through mid-wicket instead of cover-driving it, and it didn't matter any more. I was no longer being judged.

I don't blame Corrie, or anyone else. It was merely the emotional state I was in at the time. I needed my self-talk to get me back to the state of mental fitness that I needed to be in to perform. I know some people find me intimidating, but that's just my demand for honesty. I give honest opinions and I expect them in return. I took full responsibility for my lack of form but I felt it was being caused, at least partly, by the lack of clarity and honesty from the coach and selection convenor.

Gary also asked me about my form, and I told him I was certain I could still perform at the highest level but that the atmosphere hadn't been conducive to playing at my best. Then he asked me about my back. Typical Gary. I didn't know he was aware of a problem with my back, but I guess all wicket-keepers have bad backs. I told him the truth. It was sore. Bloody sore. Sometimes it was sore enough to wake me up in the middle of the night and prevent me going back to sleep. But I could manage the pain until the end of the England tour. I assured him of that. It was only pain.

Sri Lanka in South Africa, 2011–2012

I didn't enjoy the series at all. I wasn't keeping well and my confidence was pretty shattered. I dropped simple catches, catches I had never dropped before. I couldn't get over the fact that people were talking about my retirement, incessantly. It was awful being booed and abused by your own fans. I was devastated. I was playing my backside off, and 'Time to go, Boucher' and 'Your time's up' were not what I needed to hear. Despite all the emotion, I was convinced I could be honest about my form and ability, regardless of coming to the end of my career. I really wanted to go to England one more time. And I knew I still had the ability.

For the first time I paid attention to comment in newspapers and on radio and TV. I wasn't aware of *wanting* to hear it, but I couldn't get away from it. If I missed it first time around, there was always someone to call me up and tell me about it. I suppose it's inevitable at the end of your career. I spoke to other players who'd been through it, notably Polly, and he also said he heard voices he'd never heard in the prime of his career.

I arrived home after a day's play at Newlands, which had been my all-time favourite venue, and spoke to my folks on the phone that evening. 'I hated that, I absolutely hated it,' I told them. 'I can't believe I'm saying it, but I didn't enjoy playing Test cricket at Newlands.'

I hadn't played well, and it's hard to enjoy yourself when you're playing poorly. I had a lot on my mind and, probably for the first time in my life, I couldn't control it. I dropped a straightforward catch, I was chirped from the crowd, and I felt uncomfortable.

There was talk of me being dropped after the Sri Lanka series. The tour to New Zealand in March was to be Gary's first overseas tour as coach, and he was adamant that I should be the Test keeper – provided I still wanted to play and was up for it.

New Zealand tour, 2012

As soon as I arrived in Wellington and Auckland, I became aware of media previews in which I was mentioned alongside Jacques and Graeme as stalwarts of 'one of the best teams to visit New Zealand.' The Kiwi commentators were building me up rather than knocking me down. Once again I found myself looking at newspapers and watching TV bulletins, but this time they were talking me up as a 'street-fighter' and as someone who comes good under pressure rather than as someone who should be retiring! My confidence began to return and I was reminded of how long I had played and how much I had achieved. I knew I was still that player. I knew it didn't have to end just yet.

My talk with Gary about career planning and creating an exit strategy had done me the world of good. The road ahead was clear to me and, thanks to the New Zealanders, my confidence was restored before we'd even started playing. I felt like a completely different player to the one who had struggled through the Sri Lanka series. I had two more series left and I was going to make the best of them – New Zealand and England, a great way to bow out. Two of my favourite tours, though for different reasons.

As far as form was concerned, New Zealand was certainly among my best tours. As for enjoyment, it may well have been top of the list. Gary's philosophy is that there's not much point just getting from A to B unless you can enjoy the journey. What's the point in winning lots of cricket matches and becoming a great cricketer if you only have runs and wickets to show for it? Happy cricketers are more likely to play winning cricket than those who are merely hard-working.

I thought I'd seen a fair bit of New Zealand on our previous tour, eight years earlier. But we'd barely strayed from the beaten track. This time I was able to see just why so many people rave about the country's beauty. Instead of flying, we hired cars and drove for two days to the next venue – like real tourists! We stayed in the most amazing little hotels and guesthouses, visited vineyards, went fishing and played golf on courses that take your breath away.

We took the second Test in Hamilton (15-17 March) with a convincing win in three days, and moved on to Wellington. I was playing good cricket again, I was part of the team, and I knew the guys were all pulling for me and grateful to see me back. I was happy.

When we returned home, the reality that I had only one more tour hit me hard from time to time. In between I was calm and quite certain that I had made the right decision, but, now and then, I would have little panic attacks.

I had it in my mind that I would go out on a real high. The England tour was the perfect scenario: the world number one playing the world number two – effectively a World Test Championship. I wanted so badly to be number one. I wanted to be able to say that I was part of the team that became the best in the world. I was convinced we would do it, and that the team would stay there for a long time after I'd finished.

I was convinced we would win in England, but equally certain that it would be as hard a series as we'd ever played. There would be many, many pressure moments when the Test or series would be at stake. I knew I could make a difference in those moments. I trained like never before. I was a man possessed, not just with fitness but also with catching thousands of balls and working on my keeping drills. I had never really batted in nets for a long time before a tour because I wanted, or needed, a bit of a break and valuable time away from the game. This time, however, I was going to have the break of a lifetime after the tour, and so I batted for hours and hours.

Switzerland

When I boarded the plane for the last time in a Proteas blazer, I was like a kid going on my first overseas holiday. Never mind the previous 15 years; this was it. We were going to play for the Test Championship of the world.

The tour would be preceded by a five-day camp in the Swiss Alps with legendary explorer Mike Horn. I had met Mike a couple of times before, once in Cape Town and another time in Kolkata. I knew what sort of character he was and I'd heard about his exploits. Mike has pushed himself to extremes that are beyond the imagination of most people. All we knew was that we would be challenged by tasks and situations we had never encountered before.

The day we arrived, Mike told us we would be going for 'a little run and cycle ride'. It was more of a climb than a run. The scenery was incredible, with snow-tipped peaks all around us, although most of us kept our eyes on the path. Eventually we reached the top and there was a bit of high-fiving because we were proud of ourselves for getting there. We were exhausted but exhilarated at the same time.

We were admiring the view when Mike pointed to the mountain next to us and said: 'Now we're going up there, on bikes.' I honestly thought he was joking. The mountain was enormous. The peak was in cloud. I tried to see if there were contour paths where you might be able to zig-zag up, but Mike said there was only one path, and it went straight up.

I knew I was one of the fittest in the squad, and I was in the best shape of my life. But halfway up that mountain I stopped and thought: 'This is ridiculous. Someone's going to die.' I couldn't breathe. We had started on a rocky path but now we were pushing our bikes through snow. If I was struggling, how were some of the other guys doing? I looked around at them and they were in pain. I don't think a single member of the squad had any previous experience of conditions like that, but no one showed any sign of quitting. It was a powerful moment for me, seeing the determination (and pain) on their faces.

When we did finally reach the top we would have high-fived each other again but we couldn't breathe, never mind lift our arms up.

But we still had to get down.

The single track led down the mountain into a beautiful valley – stunning and scary in equal measure. For the big guys, like Graeme and Jacques, it was terrifying. Graeme had cycled a bit, but Jacques had never spent any meaningful time on a bike. I heard the crazy squeal of locked brakes and much swearing as guys went arse over tit. But there was also the sound of perseverance. Everybody got back on their bikes. It was the only way down. Again, I was moved by their guts and determination.

Eventually we made it to the bottom. Most of us will remember that day for the rest of our lives. A little later, we listened to Mike recount some of his adventures and our lives changed even more, and that's no exaggeration. The inspiration you draw from hearing about those kinds of life experiences is extraordinary. Whether it was in the Arctic or the Amazon, whether freezing or boiling, Mike has stared death in the face and smiled. But as crazy and death-defying as his expeditions seemed to be, the secret of his success was in the level and detail of his physical and mental preparation. Every night in Switzerland I was the last guy sitting and chatting to Mike. I was like a sponge absorbing his life lessons. I couldn't hear enough about how he approached things, before and during his expeditions.

In 2001 he circumnavigated the world around the equator, solo, using only non-motorised transport, mostly his own feet. At one stage he was travelling through the Amazon rainforest, fighting his way through thick jungle and so covered in cuts and scratches that they hid the snakebite he had suffered on his right hand. It was only when his hand started swelling and his vision became blurred that he realised he was in trouble.

He had to cut his vein and insert a block, and then remain still and hope for the best. He lay in the jungle for three days, but nothing improved. He had a small radio transmitter so he could be traced in an emergency. It only sent five basic messages, and couldn't be used for two-way communication. Number 1 meant: 'Everything is fine, I'm going well.' Number 5 meant: 'I will be dead by the time you receive this. Don't waste time and money looking for me.' By the end of the third day he was seriously considering sending message number 5.

But he thought of his wife and children and decided to wait one more night. The following morning, despite terrible dehydration and various illnesses and wounds, his vision started to clear and he felt an improvement. He managed to crawl to some water and started the slow battle to recovery. But never did he consider quitting. He had thousands of miles to go but he finished the journey.

In 2002 he and Børge Ousland undertook to walk 965km to the North

Pole. It had been done before, but never in the 24-hour darkness of winter. They were the first men ever to achieve that. One aspect of the expedition that fascinated me was the relationship between the two men. They really didn't get on – at all. They were completely dependent on each other, yet they barely spoke unless it was necessary. Mike said: 'What would I have said to Børge? I am hungry? I am cold? He was also hungry and cold for months on end. We knew how we were feeling but we were not friends. We kept each other alive because if one died the other would have followed him very quickly. By keeping one another alive we were keeping ourselves alive. But we didn't have anything to speak about.'

It was a great lesson about team spirit and what it really means. You don't need to be friends with your team-mates, but you do need to respect their strengths and recognise that you cannot achieve your goals without them.

All his stories hit home with me. We really did get along very well as a squad, but the point about respect and trust being more important than friendship when you set out to achieve something as a team wasn't lost on me. Our mission was to become number one, and Mike's mission was to help us reach a point where we knew that we would help a team-mate at whatever risk or cost.

Glacier crossing

The crossing of the glacier was an experience that affected all of us. It was highly symbolic that we were roped together in two eight-man teams, but it was for a genuine and very practical reason – to stay alive. If one man slipped or fell into a crevasse, hopefully the weight and traction of the other seven would hold him up. At that time of year there were sections of the ice that were soft and prone to collapse. While we were being briefed it dawned on a few of us that this was a life-and-death situation. It was one thing riding down the side of a mountain, but this was a situation beyond our control. We needed to be a team in every sense of the word.

239

Hashim can run between the wickets all day, for days at a time if necessary, as we all saw a few weeks later at The Oval when he made 311. But he was definitely out of his comfort zone in Switzerland, as we all were. It was on the glacier that Hashim struggled most and, at one point, became a bit stuck. To see Graeme lift him up and carry him to the next step was a sight I'll never forget. It was purely practical, of course, but like the rope it was impossible to ignore how symbolic it was. At times we all need lifting and we can't get to the end of the journey without a helping hand somewhere along the way.

This was a genuine situation we were getting into, it wasn't a rah-rah team-building bit of fun. It was no laughing matter being a metre away from a 50m drop. The safety briefing was lengthy and thorough. Just as Mike did everything possible to prepare himself before an expedition, he was making certain we had the best chance of making it off the glacier in one piece. So at the shout of 'man down' the other seven (hopefully!) would hit the ground immediately to try and prevent the man down from disappearing. They would then call out which man was 'down' and position themselves to pull him back up.

There was plenty of genuine fear among the guys. We trusted Mike and his brother, Martin, but they were honest about the dangers. I'm not certain whether any of the squad had second thoughts but if they did, they didn't voice them. There was so much adrenaline pumping around amongst us it was hard to escape it. Adrenaline can lead to wild and excitable behaviour, but that would have been asking for disaster to strike. It was a great lesson in learning how to think clearly and control your emotions under pressure. Which is exactly what you need to do playing a high-pressure Test match.

Somebody asked Gary one evening whether he was worried about injuries and he said: 'No, not at all. I don't care if anyone gets injured – I just want you all to get to England alive.' There were a few bumps and bruises but everyone wore them as badges of honour after that experience. Perhaps there was a greater power looking after us.

Jacques has had a fear of heights all his life so Mike's own, home-made adventure – canyoning – was his worst nightmare. You basically slide down a foefie slide hundreds of feet in the air, down a canyon before letting go just before the bottom and splashing down in an icy mountain pool. The water is freezing but we wore wetsuits as well as life jackets and helmets. We never put any pressure on Jacques but we all knew how much he was struggling with the idea of doing it. You only had to look at his face. So we went first and told him we'd be at the bottom to support him. We left it open for him to opt out. But nobody was opting out of anything on that trip. I took a video of him when he climbed out of the water and he was shaking, but it wasn't from the water. He kept saying: 'I can't believe I did that, I can't believe...' Jacques wouldn't even climb a ladder before that trip.

A few minutes later and the next challenge was even greater. An 8m jump into the next pool from a narrow ledge on the side of the mountain. Once again, Jacques dug deep to overcome the fear that he'd lived with his whole life. It was very moving seeing how much it meant to everyone else, never mind Jacques, that he had confronted this fear head on and overcome it, even if it was just for a few minutes. Everybody congratulated him afterwards in the hut where we changed into something a lot warmer and drier.

He said the fear would always be there but now he knew he could live with it and manage it, if he had to. Previously it had controlled him.

I will never forget that Switzerland trip. Many people said it was no way to prepare for a cricket tour. I think the preparation was far too good just for a cricket tour. It was good enough to prepare for a whole lifetime after cricket. The greatest compliment I can pay to Gary and Mike for organising it is to say that it contributed significantly to the Test series win. Several times during the series I saw a player rise to the occasion and produce a critical performance to win a key moment. I thought of Mike every time.

AB de Villiers

He always did lead from the front. Switzerland was a special few days because of what happened soon after, so we'll always remember the impact he had on the team. It was nothing new to me, to see him leading from the front, motivating, encouraging. That was him. He was in his element. He was the first to tap you on the shoulder when nobody else was watching and say: 'I know you're sore, I know that hurt, but you did it for the team. Well done.'

Dale Steyn

I saw a huge change in Mark in the months before we set off on that England tour. Many of the other guys thought he changed during the Switzerland camp, when he spent so much time with Mike Horn, but it had actually started before that.

I think Bouch sometimes allowed the lines between Mark the cricketer and Mark the person to become blurred, so he would say to me: 'Dale, just be who you are at all times.' Mike Horn's stories of his adventures gave us a great perspective on life. Fame and money will fade, so be a real person during your time on Earth. Cricket is your job; it should not be who you are.

Mike Horn

On the veranda of Pipo's chalet at an altitude of 1 600m I saw all of them look out into the distance over the mountains as if the others around them did not exist. It was an intense moment of silence. Everyone present, management and team, was promising themselves that they would give better than their best.

To be number one in the world, the whole team needed to make the decision first of all individually, and then together as a team. There couldn't be any weak links and no backing out!

If you are afraid of losing you will never win. The will to win must become bigger than the fear to lose.

During those couple of seconds of silence each team member needed to make the right decision. Nothing more needed to be said. The decision was made to write history and become the number 1 team in the world!

I spent four days with an amazing team of talented individuals. I took them through their paces, making them discover their weaknesses and strengths, making them overcome their fears, getting to know each other better and to know what to expect from each other. This team had a great leader, experienced senior players, great human qualities, dedication, determination, commitment and their biggest asset was that they were humble. These where all the ingredients they needed to be a winning team. The team that left Switzerland was not the same team that arrived there four days earlier.

Coming home

When we left Switzerland I had never, ever been so keen to get on to a cricket tour. Our mental state was stronger than ever. Many aspects of our approach to playing international cricket had changed, but probably the most important was that nobody felt daunted by the challenge ahead. The trouble was, when we landed in London, everybody was still talking about glaciers and survival rather than cricket! Gary was funny, trying to get everyone's attention: 'OK, guys, we need to move on to the cricket side of things now.'

We had discussed our attitude towards the media, which presents a greater and more persistent challenge in England than anywhere else. But just as you can suffer from a negative attitude, you can also benefit from being positive and understanding the reporters' jobs. We were as well prepared in that department as we had been arriving in Australia four years earlier. We knew exactly where we were as a team and what message we wanted to convey. Humility was a key factor once again. It wasn't hard to respect the opposition – it was a damn good England team.

There was an awful lot of criticism and speculation about how little cricket we were going to play before the first Test. Two extremely low-key, almost non-competitive county matches – that was it. Michael Vaughan wrote a full-page column in the *Daily Telegraph* saying how undercooked we would be and that it would be a near-miracle if we managed to be competitive in the first Test.

It sounds a bit wise after the event, but we genuinely weren't worried about the itinerary before the tour. After the Swiss camp, everything about preparation made sense. Gary always said that it was impossible to recreate the physicality and intensity of a Test match, so what was the point in trying? Of course, there is value in hitting balls and bowling overs, but the major preparation has to be done in the head. And we had just prepared in a life-changing way. We were ready.

Spirits were very high as we drove to Taunton for the first game. The first two days there were spent in the indoor nets because it was raining. We put in long hours – four or five hours of intensive, quality work. It was clear that this was a team on a mission. After the first day, Jacques shocked everyone by calling for extra shuttle work. That really isn't his thing. As an all-rounder, he believes in conserving energy for when it is needed most, not spending it all on training that doesn't even involve batting or bowling. Normally it would have been Graeme, AB or me suggesting an extra set of sprints – never Jacques. But he was serious. So I didn't say another word.

Our thinking was so clear the night before that game. Everybody knew what he wanted to achieve. The focus was beginning to come together. I wouldn't say we were over Switzerland, because many of us will never be over it – or want to be – but the cricket journey had well and truly begun and the build-up to becoming the best in the world had started. It was my last tour and it was going to be my best. I was certain of that.

AB de Villiers

I was the first guy to reach him. I'd only ever seen him keep with a helmet to the spinners. I was horrified that I hadn't noticed him without the helmet that day. I instinctively felt guilty. But it was a warm-up game and I was standing at cover minding my own business. On any other day I might have said: 'Listen, Bouch, there is a bit of bounce here, why don't you put a helmet on?' But I didn't.

He didn't get up right away, so I knew something wasn't right. I ran over to him and he looked confused, then really shocked. I didn't say a word. I couldn't get anything out. I expected to see blood. That would have been much better than seeing white stuff on his cheek, and a bit of blue. When he collapsed the second time, I went into shock myself. I knew it was terribly serious. Mark Boucher doesn't collapse.

I didn't want to go to the hospital, initially. I wanted him to have his space, not to be pestered by us and to think he had to talk to us. Then Graeme and Doc Moose said they were going and it would be good to have my support. I got changed in about two minutes. When I saw him I realised he wanted us there, he needed us – his cricket family. I felt silly thinking he wouldn't have wanted us hanging around.

Chapter 20

Aftermath

When I arrived back at Cape Town International there was a wheelchair waiting for me. Even through the pain and drugs, I found that disturbing. But I was tired and still a bit numb, so I just sat in it. There were cameras and reporters in the arrivals hall, which I really didn't want to face. I just wanted to put my head down and go. I felt like I'd done something wrong.

Then I saw my folks – well, my mom, at least – Justin Kemp and Doug Worth, my closest mates, my girlfriend, Carmen, and my manager, Donné Commins. Dr Shuaib Manjra, CSA's lead physician, was also there. Jaques Faul, CSA's acting chief executive, had flown from Joburg to be there, which was extremely good of him. They wheeled me towards a private exit and we climbed into a car.

My mates who saw me coming through in the wheelchair said: 'No, this is not him.' Then they saw my face and realised it was pretty bad. They had no idea what I had been through – not only the injury but also the mental and emotional impact. I was drained and probably still in a bit of shock. I was able to appreciate their support, but unable to express it. They wanted to talk to me and reassure me, but I wasn't in a position to reciprocate.

They took me back to my house and I climbed into bed for a few hours, but that afternoon I had my first appointment with ophthalmologist Dr Raoul Scholtz. He was so calm and soothing. He told me exactly, with no emotion, what the prognosis was. It was great to hear the truth – just the plain, honest truth. He spoke softly and gently, but with no sweeteners. My mother and girlfriend were there, but not my father. He couldn't see me. I knew how much he cared, but he couldn't see me injured like that. He couldn't cope. I respected him for being honest about that. Oddly, he was revealing a weakness in himself, which was touching.

The following morning at the hospital, Doc Scholtz told me he wanted to take an MRI scan of my eye. He explained that this would determine how badly the eye was damaged and whether there was any chance of regaining sight. After viewing the images, he said: 'Good news, I think we can save the eye cosmetically, but I'm not sure you will get any vision back.'

Much as I appreciated the truth, this was not the news I was hoping for. I didn't really care what the eye looked like cosmetically; I just wanted some sight in it. But my greatest fear had been that the eye would have to be removed.

Thee days later, I went in for the first operation. It was scheduled for an hour and a half but lasted five hours. When I woke up and realised what time it was I had a bit of a panic attack. Why had it taken so long? Was it bad news? Doc Scholtz came to see me. I couldn't pick up much from his expression or the tone of his voice, so I had to listen carefully: 'The damage isn't as bad as we had all feared. It is still very serious, but I believe there is a chance we can regain some sight in the eye.' I felt like throwing my arms around him and thanking him, but that wouldn't have been appropriate. Besides, with the general anaesthetic still wearing off, I would probably have missed.

Even when he explained that it would be a two-year process, maybe longer, I didn't care. I could survive that. I would do whatever I had to do in order to regain some sight. I kept hearing the voice of Mike Horn in the back of my head. Calm, determined, prepared, self-belief. Fortunately I had my self-talk to fall back on.

That night, after the operation, I experienced real pain for the first time. It was as though sandpaper was being rubbed on my eyeball. I kept ringing the night bell to ask the nurse for more morphine. When she said I'd had enough, I begged. It was that bad. I didn't sleep for about eight hours. I couldn't; it was just too painful.

Doc Scholtz arrived in the morning and asked, in his usual calm way, how I was. I said: 'Fine. A bit sore.' He did a couple of basic tests, and then said I could go home.

I was put on strong painkillers, which I had to take every three hours. I was grateful for Carmen's help and support; she went through the whole process with me, especially putting the drops and cream in my eye, which made me a little queasy.

The healing process takes a long time because the eye, and especially the retina, heals very slowly. Once the eyeball itself has been stitched up, scar tissue is created, which takes four or five months to heal. When the scar tissue is removed it requires another four or five months to heal again. The eyeball is filled with oil to help it retain its shape, and the doctors wait for the eye to start producing its own fluid again. But if the pressure in the eyeball isn't high enough, there is a danger that it will shrink and pull away from the retina wall. If that happens, you may lose any chance of sight. You can never be certain of the prognosis, only of the process. If all goes well and my eye is able to start producing its own fluid again, the pupil and iris are inserted without problems, I'm hopeful of gaining about 50 per cent vision. For the 15 months since the injury it has, at best, been only peripheral.

Dr Raoul Scholtz

The media knew about Mark's appointment with me before I had been notified. They were waiting at the front gate and we let him in through the back door. I had watched Ali Bacher's interview on TV and was well aware of Mark's achievements. With all the hype in the press and the public concern about his wellbeing, I knew that I had to focus on my patient and respect his privacy. I decided then and there that I would not be involved in press interviews, and would leave that to his professional team. For this assistance, I would like to thank Dr Shuaib Manjra of CSA for his advice and for the very professional way in which he handled the situation. He was later assisted by Mark's friend, GP and previous team doctor, Dr Peter Sandell. Mark's manager, Donné Commins, was extremely friendly, approachable and helpful in providing my staff with the logistics of appointments to fit in with his busy schedule.

Prior to surgery I sought advice and encouragement from experienced colleagues, namely, Professor Ferenc Kuhn, a world expert on trauma surgery, who had recently imparted some of his extensive knowledge to many South African surgeons during a lecture tour here. I thank him for responding promptly to my emails. I also thank Dr Jonathan Rossiter for a job well done during what must have been an extremely difficult primary repair of the injury, and for his extensive notes and description about the injury. Drs Louis Kruger and Kelvin Rivett fielded my phone calls, and Drs Kendrew Suttle and James Rice (what would the Groote Schuur retinal service be without these two surgeons!) provided expert and patient assistance during the prolonged surgeries. Thanks to the Medical Protection Society for important advice about patient confidentiality issues. Most importantly, I thank Mark, his family and team of assistants, for putting their trust in me.

As retinal surgeons all know, the issues and difficulties would be insurmountable without trust, adequate preparation, patient determination and, in this case, the expectation of prolonged follow-up and guidance through difficult times ahead. The surgery is perhaps the easiest part of it all! Patient and family expectations have to be dealt with up front, and have to be revisited many times. An approach to severe eye injuries and/or illness has to be dealt with in a methodical way, and our patients need to understand the importance of the issues at hand, namely, to repair the injury, to save the eye, to ensure the eye is cosmetically acceptable and comfortable, and to optimise useful vision. It is also important to build trust. How many times have Mark and I discussed these issues?

During Mark's first visit to me he, was accompanied by family, friends, Dr Manjra and Donné Commins. It was a room full of people, with a very quiet, slightly abrupt, concerned and anxious patient. My first question to him was for his need for privacy, but he requested that all remain for the examination and discussions. I was also aware that he had many pressures on him, including advice from many people concerned about him, to seek many opinions. I had to guide him through this, and offered my full support and assistance for follow-up were he to receive surgery elsewhere. We had to discuss his injury, his loss and the need for support in whatever form that might take.

After three major surgeries with him, I have come to know a man who has a lot more than cricket in him. He is of good Eastern Cape stock, with a supportive family and network of friends. He rarely arrives on his own for appointments – always with Carmen, a friend or family member by his side. In good Xhosa tradition, we always discuss family, fishing and rhino poaching before attending to the business at hand. A patient rarely accepts his or her loss fully, but Mark has persevered through a difficult period of repeated surgeries, interviews and pressures, and has nurtured a passion for our wildlife preservation.

With respect to achieving the goals of saving his eye and hopefully some vision, I think he has done remarkably well. All is not lost, and I think Mark now appreciates the complexities of the problem and has learnt the need to be patient with the healing process, whatever form that may take. To quote the writer Abraham H de Vries (also a patient of mine): *'Elke reisiger bly homself, en reis kan dit nie genees nie, het ek eers gedink. En dis waar. Maar soms op 'n reis belewe 'n mens iets gevaarliks en iets waaragtig moois, en daarna is jy nooit weer dieselfde mens nie.'*

For a long time after my return home, driving was the last thing I felt like doing, but I didn't even know I was allowed to. I imagined that I would need to sit another test and qualify for a disability licence. I didn't even ask anyone for about a month. One day I said to Raoul: 'Doc, will I ever be able to drive?' He looked a little surprised: 'Of course you can – you can drive now. You'll just need to learn a few new skills.'

I think the Doc saw me parking one day before a check-up and decided to have a chat about one-eyed techniques. He gave me a few tips on what I could and couldn't do and the situations I might find tricky. Fortunately, thanks to Mercedes-Benz, I now have sensors on my car that alert me if I'm parking too close to anything. There were times, in the beginning, when I parked the usual 30cm from the curb and got out to discover I was still in the middle of the road.

By this time all my mates were having a ball – or throwing one. They would lob apples or tennis balls at me. I learnt the best way to catch a ball is to turn sideways. It is particularly difficult if you are face-on to an object, but if you are side-on you can pick out the flight path of an object.

One day, when I was feeling better about life and had grown physically stronger, I invited some close mates for dinner at one of my favourite five-star restaurants. I ordered a bottle of red wine, intending to pour them each a glass to say thank you for their help, support and friendship. I poured it all over the tablecloth. Wasn't even close. I missed the glass by several centimetres, much to the hilarity of my mates. You need to hold the glass with one hand and the bottle with the other, and then your brain can locate them without a problem. It's just one of the little things I've had to learn along the way.

Golf

Jacques organised a golf day at Steenberg with a four-ball comprising Hein van der Venter, Grant Veenstra, himself and me. I was very reluctant. I love playing golf so much, and I think I was probably fearful of how playing with one eye would affect me. I didn't want to face it yet; I preferred to be in denial. But he said: 'Come on, don't worry – you won't be alone.' So Jacques handed out three eye patches on the first tee and declared that everyone was equal, so official handicaps applied. I was touched by the thought, but I insisted they didn't start like that. Jacques loves his golf as much as me, and, whenever he gets on the course, he loves to perform at his best.

Perhaps for the first time in my entire life, I wasn't feeling competitive. Not to start with, anyway. I just wanted to feel what it was like. I was a little scared, in truth. I'd been dreaming of playing more golf throughout my cricket career. What if I couldn't hit the ball?

My first drive went straight down the middle – and far, too. It was a great feeling. The chipping was a little different, though. I hit the first couple flush in the teeth. The bunkers were the worst. Doc Scholtz and a few other people had warned me about the difficulties of depth perception, especially with the sun shining on white sand and a white ball.

Jacques had obviously been tipped off and was watching carefully the first time I went into a bunker. Sure enough, I grounded the club almost immediately and he was there, right behind me, chuckling away: 'Two-shot penalty,' he said. 'Give your mate a break here, will you – Jeez!' But there was no mercy shown. 'We gave you an extra four shots on your handicap; that's it,' said Jacques. 'And you've just used up two of them.' That was when my competitive streak kicked straight back into top gear. I thought losing an eye was worth more than four shots, but I didn't say anything.

On the next tee I insisted they wore their eye patches. Grant is a professional golfer who has played in the British Open. He slapped his shot straight out of bounds. Jacques drop-kicked his, but Hein hit it perfectly down the middle. We were barely 200m down the fairway before they were moaning about getting headaches and stumbling over their feet, so off came the eye patches. 'I don't know how you do it,' Hein said. I told him things were a bit different when you don't have a choice! At least they knew a little of what I was going through. It's harder in the beginning but, very gradually, the good eye starts to compensate for the loss of the injured one.

Raoul Scholtz has seen thousands of eye injuries – from car crashes, golf balls, wood splinters, and many other freak accidents. He's seen some pretty nasty things in his time, but only two or three with as much damage as I sustained. Fifteen months after the accident I still didn't have a lens, pupil or iris. Someone had wiped my original iris off my cheek in Taunton, and I think the pupil was left behind, too. Doc Scholtz has had the replacement iris in a jar in his office for months. It was made in the Netherlands using a scan of the good eye, so it should be a good match! If the accident had happened 10 or 15 years ago, the injured eye would have been removed and probably closed. That's how recent and advanced the surgical techniques are.

The vision I have without the lens and pupil is very blurred, like looking through completely unfocused binoculars. When I do look through binoculars and close the good eye, I can feel the injured one trying to improve. So that gives me hope for the future. Even my eyes are determined.

My admiration for Raoul Scholtz grows every time we meet. He has operated on me for three hours and I'm the third or fourth patient that day. He even calls Mom after every operation and gives her a full run-down. And that isn't just because I am well known. He does that for every patient. He treats people as individuals and tailors the treatment to suit them. You're supposed to take it easy after surgery, but he could see that I was desperate to run after being cooped up. He's always done what he could to allow me to exercise as soon as possible. He said it wouldn't make any difference if he told me to stay in bed, so he might as well work with me.

Best mates

I have many friends now who didn't know me when I was a young-ster, and when I tell them stories of Dad and his discipline they don't believe me. They just see this gentle giant with a big heart who cares for everyone and is lovely with kids. He was firm but always fair with me.

I'm happy to say he treated me differently, as the son! There was equality in some things, but not everything. Certainly not when it came to handing out discipline. I got plenty more of that than my sisters.

A few people were surprised that he didn't want to see me when I arrived back from England, but I wasn't. And I wasn't disappointed. He would have been upset and uncomfortable – why would I want my father to feel like that? When his dad was lying in a hospital bed with cancer, he said he could not see his father like that. His father was not a frail person who needed washing and feeding; he was a strong man. Dad wanted that to be his lasting memory, so he excused himself from watching my grandfather die. It was a similar, although less tragic, situation with my eye. He knew I was strong and fit, so to see me cooped up in a darkened room, drugged and in pain, unable to look after myself – he couldn't handle it. It takes courage to face discomfort, but just as much to admit that you have to look the other way.

As a professional sportsman you are not alone in your career, no matter how lonely it may feel. Plenty of family and friends live every moment with you, but nobody more than your parents. So as much as I wasn't ready for retirement, neither was my dad! It's impossible for most people to imagine how your parents get caught up in the rhythm and routine of the game. Mom and Dad were on the roller-coaster, they lived for the high moments and they shared my pain during the low moments. They could see when I was hurting. I didn't need to say anything.

They would have loved to see me finish in different circumstances. My father would have been the proudest man in the world if I'd played my 150th Test match at Lord's and been part of the side that became number one. But you can't always get what you want. It was sad for him.

For the first few days in Cape Town there was a lot of emotion, confusion even. I was physically injured, of course, but there was emotional and psychological damage, too. Most of it was related to the uncertainty of the future, and the shock of what had happened. There was a bit of anger and probably moments of depression. It was unsettling for everyone.

My mother was by my side all the time. I needed looking after in many ways. After a couple of days, maybe a week, once I was up and about and able to walk around the house, Dad was there, encouraging me. The funny thing is, I could feel his pain. I was very aware of it. He didn't need to say anything.

One day, after about a week, we were watching some of the first Test at The Oval, he said: 'Don't worry about things. I know you; in a couple of weeks' time you'll be running again. Just take it easy for a couple of weeks, get all the shit done with the surgery, and you'll be kicking and screaming again because I know that is the person you are. I know you are a fighter, you always were and you always will be. Nothing has beaten you before, and you will win this little battle.'

That was all I needed from him. Just to be there. I didn't need him to come and hold my hand. I had my mother there to do that – and to feed me! As hard a person as he is, and as hard as he was on me as a youngster, there is an understanding and love between us that doesn't need words. It is based on mutual respect. He is one of my best mates.

Schalk Burger

I thought I had moved to a nice suburb of Cape Town until I discovered that Mark was my neighbour! Actually it was very exciting for me because I am a cricket fanatic, so we were soon having many braais together and discussing the Proteas and the Springboks. We are both sponsored by South African Breweries, so we travelled to and from many functions together.

Sunday afternoons were often our best time together. It took me a long time to convert him from a Sharks to a Stormers fan, but the trick was a good quantity of quality red wine.

We are similar personalities, although he is more intense and I am much more relaxed – which is probably the wrong way around for our sports! He is a straight shooter and wears his heart on his sleeve, which is a quality I have always admired. He doesn't back down from anything, even when he is wrong, and he is a bugger to try and beat on the golf course. But he does pay up if you manage to sneak a win against him.

I was so excited before the England tour. I saw first-hand how hard Mark had worked for that series and I had many parties and celebrations in mind for when he returned, having played 150 tests. When the accident happened I was devastated for him, but when he came back the only tears were from me and his other friends. He was the strong one, as usual.

Stuart Webber

Mark and I were both schooled in the Eastern Cape, both of the matric class of 1994, he at Selborne and me at Grey. I first met him at an inter-school squash tournament; he was playing as Selborne's number one and was only in Standard 7! Mark's name was a painful one to hear when you were on the opposing team. He excelled in most sports and caused many an unhappy day for the Grey 1st XI.

We reconnected years later when some mates and I went to the West Indies in 2001 to support the Proteas tour. Mark remembered me immediately and responded very kindly to a request from me for a shirt signed by the team for my younger brother. I have lost count of the number of random acts of kindness I've seen from him since then.

I was developing a cluster of houses in Cape Town, and one morning Mark and Jacques arrived on site for an impromptu inspection. Mark was interested, but he gave nothing away. He is shrewd and careful in his business life. He has worked hard for everything he has achieved.

The upshot was that not only did we become neighbours, as I was buying one of the houses, but I also landed the job of finishing Mark's house to his personal specs. With Mark away so much of the time, it wasn't the easiest job. Despite his head for business, Mark has an allergy to admin. I mostly relied on Donné, but when I did speak to Mark, he said: 'Keep it neutral, nothing too "out there". Finish it like your own home.' This we achieved, with the exception of Mark's critical 'three B's' – his bedroom, bar and braai area.

The spec for the bedroom was to add a lounge area. That way, it felt more like a hotel room – and that was what he was used to! The braai area is a specialist's dream: a built-in patio braai, a freestanding SAB-keg braai, a Weber, a pizza oven and a fire pit for the more social braai/potjie evenings. Evenings around his fire pit with good friends are the ones Mark loves the most. He's pretty useful with an oxtail potjie, too.

The bar had to incorporate his Castle Lager beer fridge, presented for his 100th Test, and to have enough space for his beloved red wine collection, a decent-sized TV and a pool table. When it was all finally finished I said to Donné: 'It looks quite the party house.' She rolled her eyes and said: 'Yes, you'll know when the cricket season has finished!'

Moving on

Many years before my career ended I had dreamt of taking a full year off when I stopped playing. You spend nine or ten months of the year devoted to the game, and there are so many things you miss out on: friends and family, parties, weddings, anniversaries. Mostly what you miss is just *time* – time that is your own, time when you aren't thinking about the next tour, or the next camp. Time when you don't have to worry too much about staying fit, flexible and ready for action.

One of the few, great positives of the time I had during the recovery period was the quality time I spent with Mom and Dad. I had left home as a wet-behind-the-ears young man all those years ago and somehow never really caught up for more than a few days. When they came to stay with me in Cape Town, we had the conversations that a normal life would have allowed in the previous decade.

I watched the Test matches throughout my recovery. And I shared my views with the boys, even when I knew they couldn't read my messages

257

because they were on the field or had their phones turned off. When Jacques scored his hundred at The Oval, and he pointed to his eye, it was impossible not to be a little overcome with emotion. In all the commitment to the team cause, in all the determination to win the Test match, it would have been easy to forget me at home. I wouldn't have cared if he had. I expected him to call me after the game, but not that – not on the field. Tears were good for my eye, apparently, so I didn't mind.

Jacques Kallis

I probably had six or seven messages on my phone after every day's play – most players did! He wasn't on the tour but it felt like he was – his presence was there. It was particularly emotional scoring the hundred at The Oval because we had discussed long and hard about me carrying on the tour, and that century was definitely for him. I touched my eye just to make sure he knew I was thinking of him. I was proud to score that for him. I was so used to him being on the change room balcony, or in the middle with me.

I was aware that there was a picture up of me in the back of the change room the whole time. The guys sent me pictures and messages every day. I really did feel like I was a part of it. Gary had said: 'If you have any ideas, let me know.' The only guy allowed to keep his phone on during the match is Doc Moosajee, so I did send the odd message through to him saying: 'What about this or that, what about coming around the wicket?' One of the ideas I suggested actually worked. It was Imran Tahir bowling over the wicket to Strauss; I think he top-edged it. Graeme probably would have done that anyway, but it made me feel that I had sent the message, it had gone out there, and they had done it.

Johann Rupert asked me if I wanted to go over for the last Test, at Lord's. He said it would be fabulous to have me in the box, no media, just private and quiet. He would look after me. I was desperately keen; I would have loved it. But Doc Scholtz asked me how I would feel if it jeopardised my chances of regaining my sight, and that was that. He was concerned about the pressure in my eyeball after flying for 12 hours. I was seeing him every second day at that stage, as he needed to drain the blood, sticking a needle in the eye to take it out. There were still many intricate procedures that I had to go through, so the trip was impossible. I was tempted to ignore doctor's order, as I had a few times before, but this was different, and I knew it.

When England were nine wickets down at Lord's, I sent a tweet: 'Is it time to crack the champagne yet?' Someone replied: 'Watch out the cork doesn't pop into your eye.' I just laughed at him. How sad. The response on Twitter was amazing. It wasn't just from fans, but also my team-mates. Jacques was very outspoken about the whole thing and wanted to find this guy. I just moved on, didn't give it a second thought. I think my priorities and what was important to me had shifted.

The last hour of the Lord's Test was uncomfortably tense. England had seemed dead and buried, but they notoriously have three number 8 batsmen and a number 9 rather than a 'tail'. Led by wicket-keeper Matt Prior, they started smashing it all over the ground. I thought: 'This won't last.' Half an hour later I was thinking: 'This *can't* last.' Then Morne had Prior brilliantly caught by Hashim at deep mid-wicket and I thought: 'This has ended!' I was having my first beer since the operation with Doug Worth, and I jumped in the air with such force that the beer hit the ceiling. But it was a no ball. It was agonising.

But the new ball was due and Vernon made great use of it, nicking Prior off to Graeme low at first slip. That was a phenomenal catch in the circumstances. I don't know how long it took before the pictures and texts started arriving from the change room. It felt like just a few minutes … photographs of the guys holding my picture and saying: 'This one's for you, Bouch – number one in the world.' It was a very special feeling. Naturally I would rather have been there, and playing, but there was no sadness. So much had happened, and I had probably moved on a lot further down life's road than I realised. But it still felt fantastic to be involved, to feel a part of the joy and celebration.

When Graeme went up for the presentation wearing the shirt with my name on it, I probably dropped another couple of tears. Jacques had my name on his shirt, too. They gave them to me when they came back and they are in a safe place. I'll hang on to them for a while. Someone will have to pay a lot of money and save a lot of rhinos to buy either of them.

They phoned quite often from the fines meeting after the game. I think they even fined me a couple of times and made me have a sip of beer. Later that night, long after I'd gone to bed, I received a couple more drunken messages on my phone. It was a huge day and night for me. I finally had closure on my career and on playing for the Proteas. The team had kept me involved throughout the tour and made me feel like I was still part of the squad. I knew what was going on and what the strategies were – everything. Then, when we won, I knew that I had finally retired. I was finished when I was injured, but it wasn't quite over. But that night, when I went to sleep, I said: 'It's done now, Mark. It's cool. Now it's time to move on.'

AB de Villiers

He had a huge impact on my career from the very beginning. There were times when I would probably have been dropped if it hadn't been for him. I didn't have much experience of keeping in England and he gave me a lot of tips; he was right on the money. I am sure he was still traumatised after the surgery but he was on the phone within days, helping me out, giving me support – 'watch the ball', little tips that were invaluable. At the end of every day there were a few text messages waiting for me. I looked forward to them, couldn't wait to turn my phone on. Especially when they said: 'Great day – you were excellent!'

Chapter 21

A new beginning

Donné had been advising me for several years to get involved in things that might lead to a future career once cricket had finished. She said I was fortunate to be in a position where I could choose something I was passionate about and that really interested me rather than getting an office job or selling something I didn't know anything about.

I thought long and hard about it and reached the conclusion that I wasn't good enough to be a professional golfer. My greatest passion has always been wildlife and the bush. I had no idea what I might be able to do, but Donné encouraged me just to keep an open mind. Something would come up.

About a year before the final tour to England, I met a man who changed my life. Frik Rossouw heads up the anti-poaching intelligence operation in the Kruger National Park. Albie Morkel happened to be good friends with Frik's son, Jean, and they had organised a tiger-fishing trip to the lower Sabie River. The expedition included brothers Albie and Morne, as well as Jean and two other brothers, Ludwig and Jaco Sevenster.

It was going to be a three- or four-day trip, with fishing in the morning and game drives in the evening. We slept in tents and made camp every night – it was bliss. On the final day we pushed deeper into the park, found a large water hole and made camp near it for the night.

We had a fantastic braai that night, but Albie was a bit careless with his bones. After a couple of lamb chops he chucked the remains into the bush, much to our surprise. One of the boys said: 'Are you chumming?' He looked a little embarrassed. It wasn't as dangerous for the Morkels and the other guys because they were sleeping in army tents made of thick canvas. But I was in a pop-up tent that more suited to a kiddies' birthday party. I set it up in between the proper tents and hoped for the best. Poor old Jacques Rudolph had to share it with me.

It had been a superb day. We had seen seven or eight rhinos and we could hear elephants drinking at the water hole and lions roaring in the distance. But the bones from the braai were making the hyenas go crazy. We had a couple of mugs of red wine to celebrate the day and help us get to sleep.

At about one o'clock in the morning, long after we'd got to sleep, the fire was going down and the hyenas were – we thought – at a safe distance. I was woken by quite a commotion. I heard a voice yelling: 'F*** off, f*** off, *VOETSAK!*' Jacques and I were suddenly very aware that our tent was about as thick as clingfilm.

We looked nervously out of the entrance and there was Albie, standing up and shining a torch about frantically. I asked what the problem was and he said something had just tried to bite his head through the tent. I thought he was joking but he insisted something had just tried to bite his head. We took the torch and went round the back of the tent and there was a pack of about 15 hyenas just staring at us. So we clapped and shouted '*Voetsak!*' and they reluctantly slunk away. Albie's head had been lying right up against the back of the tent but the canvas was pulled tight, so, fortunately, the hyena hadn't been able to get a proper bite. We still weren't sure whether to believe him until we saw all the slobber and saliva on the canvas. Needless to say, we didn't get much sleep that night.

We had been talking to oom Frik about the plague of rhino poaching and asking how we might be able to get involved in the fight against it. He told us about the DNA recording programme, in which small samples of rhino horn are sent to the lab at Onderstepoort Veterinary Institute to be recorded on a database. It allows the authorities to prosecute anybody buying, selling or just in possession of rhino horn with a match to any sample on the database. There is still much that needs to happen to make prosecutions more successful, but the DNA database allows investigators to make the link between a poached rhino and the poachers.

Frik suggested that the DNA programme might be the best way to get involved. He said he knew Dr Cindy Harper, the director of the Veterinary Genetics Laboratory, and that there were a few sponsors involved. One of them was South African Breweries. The link between cricket and SAB was obvious, with Castle Lager having been a sponsor of the national cricket team for over 20 years. Suddenly I could see the beginnings of an opening for me. My mind was racing, but one thing was clear. If there was a chance, I would give it everything I had.

After the trip, Albie was busy playing T20 in England, so I said I would go to Joburg and talk to SAB. I arranged a meeting with brand manager Rob Fleming, a great friend, and asked him to put me in touch with the right people. He contacted Andre Fourie, who heads up SAB's sustainability arm. Dale Steyn is the 'water ambassador' for SAB, so, after a couple more meetings, they suggested that I become their 'anti-rhino poaching' ambassador. I was more excited than I can describe. Here was something I was passionate about that would give me something to look forward to after cricket.

There were so many things to set up before we could get under way but I gave SAB and everyone else my commitment that, as soon as the England tour was complete, I would give them every spare minute I had. The injury left me incapacitated for five weeks, but in my clearer moments, rhinos were all I thought of. I had made commitments to meet companies and clients of SAB and I couldn't wait to start.

Albie Morkel

Albie is a great cricketer. South Africa never made the most of his talent, and that should always be a source of regret. When a cricketer of his talent fails to produce his best form for his country, the responsibility has to be shared. You can't just blame the player. There are circumstances that have to be taken into consideration; any time a player is given an ultimatum to perform, he will become tense and will struggle to produce his best performances when they are needed most.

I know that Albie's problems started when Corrie was national coach. Albie took the pressure placed on the lower order too personally. He believed he should be the leader at the back end of the run chase, and the weight of expectation was never lessened by Corrie. I suspected that Albie lacked confidence during Corrie's reign as coach, and he confirmed that when he retired from international cricket in 2012.

Cricketers are confidence players, and that is especially so with Albie. We all need to know that we have the support and confidence of our bosses and team-mates. Nobody can be a match-winner all the time, but it certainly doesn't help if you feel you are on trial and having to prove yourself. That's why Albie has performed so consistently well in the IPL with the Chennai Super Kings; he knows the main men there believe in him. MS Dhoni and Stephen Fleming understand people. Some cricketers can be 'rocks' and can be left alone to sort themselves out; others need plenty of encouragement and support.

Some people may argue that Albie had his chances and didn't take them, but he did. In Australia in 2009, he put in incredible performances in two ODIs, winning games in which nobody thought we had a chance. In Melbourne, the first game of the series, we were chasing a target of 272, and it is notoriously difficult batting second under lights. We were in trouble at 221-7, but Albie launched into the last couple of overs and finished with an unbeaten 40 from just 18 balls. We won with three balls to spare.

It was more convincing in Sydney, where we needed 270 batting second. Nobody gave us a chance because no team had ever chased that many at the SCG, where it turns a lot in the second innings. Like the MCG, the team batting first generally has the advantage. I'll never forget that game because Shaun Tait broke my toe with a yorker, but I wasn't going to give him the pleasure. So I pretended it didn't hurt.

Albie joined me at 209-6 and it was likely to be touch and go. Or, at least, that's what most people thought. We took the score to 265, with Albie dominating the partnership with 40 from 22 balls. It was a deeply satisfying win and, even afterwards, the pain in my toe felt irrelevant. I loved batting with him. He has the power and talent to take the pressure off you, and most opposition bowlers find him intimidating. He was similar to Lance in that way. He talked, too. Not frantic, adrenaline-fuelled banter, but clear, calm and rational decision-making.

You always feel that nothing really bad can happen when you're with Albie. He has that calming effect. Albie is as passionate as I am about the rhino project and I can't wait for him to join up full-time once his playing career has finished. He will become a vital member of the team and his passion and enthusiasm will comfortably match mine.

Albie Morkel

Mark, my brother and I bought a little house together at a place called Ntsiri, in the Timbavati, part of the greater Kruger. We share a passion for nature and love relaxing there. When he is there, Mark turns into a different person, switches off from day-to-day concerns and gets in touch with his inner self. You see the softer side of him. The chats around the campfire are rarely about cricket. He is driven by conservation at the moment. I believe Mark still carries the tough guy front when he is at home in Cape Town because he has to. He has built up that image over his 15-year cricket career, but when he swaps the city for the bush that all changes.

So he says the hyena story was funny, does he? Maybe now, but at the time I thought it was the end. I was the chef for the evening and in charge of the braai. I went to the cooler box and found that all the chicken had gone off. It stank, so I threw it into the bush. Not very clever.

After the braai, a few glasses of red and many stories, we decided to call it a night. Morne, my dad and I shared a tent, the ranger and his son were in another and Mark and Jacques Rudolph shared a small pop-up tent that they had bought for R99. Now that thing was funny.

Once the ranger chased the hyena off, along with the rest of the pack, I returned to our three-man tent to discover it had become a five-man tent. Boucher and Rudolph had no intention of returning to their children's wigwam. The next three hours until first light involved no sleep. I think someone found another bottle of red.

Mark would like young cricketers to realise that much of their life as professionals will be 'false'. The more successful they are, the more false their lives might become. It is very good advice. Unfortunately, most cricketers will not realise that until very late in their careers. To play for your country is the ultimate – you make many sacrifices, but you also live life in the fast lane, with everything done for you. Once that privilege is taken away and you are exposed to how things are done in the real world, you soon realise that you have a lot of growing up to do. Some sportsmen do it easily, others struggle a bit more, and some, sadly, never make it.

In the second ODI against Australia, we were chasing 270, a record score. When I got to the crease we needed about 60 and Shaun Tait wasn't bowling anything under 150kph. He had just hit Mark on the big toe. He could barely walk, or talk. I looked down and saw blood oozing from his boot. He was a bit pale. He snarled through gritted teeth: 'Albie, we are not losing to these f***ing guys tonight, you understand!' He ran singles for the rest of the partnership; I don't even know how. His toe was broken. That was his last game on tour.

There was a trend in world cricket towards the end of his career for one or two batsmen to be kept back for power plays and death overs, and that was the only place you batted. It made it very hard for us. If the better batsmen before you struggled to score runs fluently, how were we supposed to score at nine or ten runs per over? Confidence was definitely a problem. Most innings were played under immense pressure and there was rarely a chance to play yourself in. But that was my role in the team and I'm deeply grateful and happy for the opportunities I was given to represent the Proteas.

Rhinos, funding and conservation

Raising funds for rhino conservation has become my major job; that is where I can make the greatest difference. Much as I love being in the bush and close to the animals, I understand my role. And I do it unpaid. I realise there may be scepticism about this, but absolutely no money from donors or sponsors comes to me. This is a passion for me.

It is fascinating to see the DNA lab at Onderstepoort. It is far too small and the equipment they have is outdated, but the team does a heroic job. It takes a long time to record each DNA sample; the last time I was there they had a backlog of approximately 600 cases.

One of the most potent ways of raising both money and awareness is by taking sponsors, or clients, on DNA darting trips with us. The helicopter flights and the darting are an adventure at first, and then comes the personal touch. It's an opportunity for people to experience a rhino up close: to touch and feel the animal, and to be involved with the process of checking its temperature while the animal is tranquillised, to water it and stop the bleeding from the notch in the ear. As well as notching the ear, we drill a hole in the horn and implant a transmitter. On private game reserves they have names for their rhinos. They'll say: 'We've notched Romeo and Juliet like this.' But in the Kruger you can't have names for the 15 000 rhinos that live in the park.

Clients and sponsors are usually blown away by their first experience of a darting expedition. Just being so close to a rhino, to touch one, put your hand in its mouth, touch the horn, feel how loose it is in the skull. It's usually pretty emotional. It's hard to imagine becoming so moved by a tough-looking beast like the rhino, but people routinely are. It's also hard not to realise that you've done something good and meaningful by trying to protect them.

Naturally we tell those people to tell their friends, colleagues and bosses, and hopefully we spread the word. If a company sponsors a rhino-darting expedition then they pay for the helicopter and the DNA kit and we get more information for the database.

Once the rhino is darted, it takes approximately five minutes before you can approach it. The first thing is to place a blanket over its eyes and socks in its ears to try and keep the animal as calm as possible. The rhino goes down for about 25 minutes while the work is done. You need to care for the animal while it's under anaesthetic, making sure its breathing is OK, its eyes are protected and its temperature is stable. The reversal is then applied and you stay with the rhino, holding a towel or blanket over its eyes so it doesn't get scared or aggressive while it's coming round. Often, when they are waking up, they call out for other members of their crash to orient themselves. The sound is more like a low-pitched birdcall than the thunderous roar you might expect.

On my first darting expedition, we woke the rhino up after we'd done all the testing, and, when I was sure he was steady, I returned to the truck. I was in the middle truck of five. I was sitting at the back of the game-viewing platform with my foot on the bumper, about 30m away from the rhino. After about a minute, he started to move. He turned around and looked straight at the middle vehicle. Then he started to move towards me, not looking left or right. Just a gentle walk – not aggressive in any way. He walked right up to where I was sitting and put his horn where my foot had been. If I had not moved my foot he would have touched it. Then he turned and walked away. Donné was sitting next to me, with tears in her eyes. She said maybe there was a higher power at work.

It was very unusual behaviour for a rhino. I was nervous that he was going to try and hit the car, as he was still pretty drowsy. Nobody feels great after a general anaesthetic, so he had reason to be pissed off. Everybody knows rhinos have poor eyesight and a very good sense of smell, but there was another sense in action there as well. It was clear to me at that moment – and to many others watching – that he wanted to know whether I was a threat. After a few seconds, he turned away and stumbled back into the bush. I stood still the whole time. I felt as emotionally charged as when I hit the runs to win the 438 game. It was a different sort of emotion, but just as strong.

Dale Steyn, Paul Harris and Justin Kemp were all there that day. When the rhino finally disappeared into the bush, they suggested that conservation and I were meant for each other.

AB de Villiers

I was one of the first guys to introduce him to the bush. We spent some time at the Morkels' uncle's farm close to Thorny-bush game lodge in Hoedspruit. We had a few glasses of wine and were hitting glow-in-the-dark golf balls into the bush and running to fetch them. The game ranger told us about black mambas catching impalas there, and, a few days previously, a leopard that had dragged an impala into a tree across the river 100m away. We were young and stupid.

On another trip we went with Rob Walter and my singing partner, Ampie du Preez, to Pafuri in the north of the Kruger National Park. We stayed in a tent every night, 15-20km of walking in the bush each day – we saw the big five on foot. It was amazing. Every night we had a glass of wine, and I had my guitar, so we sang a few songs and reminisced.

We are all going to face huge changes when our playing careers finish. He went through a traumatic shock with his injury, but an equal shock would have been: 'What now?' But he will make a success of it; I have no doubt about that. Once again, he's helping out with things he feels he can have an impact on, to make situations better. That was always what he was about in the cricket team. He tried to improve other people's lives and now he is doing the same for wildlife. I am extremely grateful for his friendship, and we will always be part of a family.

The survival of a species

DNA sampling isn't going to stop the poacher, but, if you get transmitters in rhinos, you are giving them a better chance for survival. They might get poached, but you're still creating a deterrent for the poachers. It's about working towards a much bigger picture, trying to make a difference to something even more important than the saving of one individual rhino. It's the long-term security of the entire species that is at stake.

Right now, we feel passionate about the future. It's not just about individual animals. If you see a mutilated carcass, shot for the sake of a horn with no magical or medicinal qualities, you will struggle not to be angered. We believe we have to do something. I've been involved with recording approximately 80 rhinos. We can do four or five in one day. There have been, perhaps, one or two in particular that I had a personal association with, but overall I feel proud about my ability to keep the relationship professional.

Poachers have their price; they all do. The numbers are terrifying. The kingpins of the poaching operations approach poachers in Mozambique, Botswana or even South Africa, and they say: 'Here's R60 000, go shoot the rhino and take its horn off.' He can look after a family for a long time on that money. The risk, they believe, is worth it.

The bigger picture is to catch the kingpins and the sad, deluded wealthy people who believe that rhino horn will somehow improve their lives, or even sex lives. It is pathetic. There have been so many absurd claims about rhino horn. A cancer cure? Ridiculous. In China and other Asian countries, wealthy men mix rice wine with a bit of rhino horn and declare it a 'nobility' drink. It is a status symbol to them. Ostrich toes are about 96 per cent the same composition and they are commercially farmed. Why not use them?

The consumers are the ones to target. I'm not saying go easy on the poachers. They must always know what a risk they are taking and what the consequences could be, but it's easier to understand a man killing to feed his family than one paying for the slaughter so he can drink what he could getting from biting and eating his own fingernails. It's going to be difficult to educate people in the East. But that's no reason not to try. It was difficult educating the West that slavery wasn't a good idea 200 years ago.

I don't particularly like dehorning as an option. God gave the rhino a horn for a reason. They use it for fighting, for self-defence and for accessing food. However, I do understand why rhino farmers do it on small game reserves. Imagine the human fingernail. If you cut it too short, you bleed. If you cut a rhino horn too short, it will also bleed – to death. So you have to cut it about 10cm above the base, which leaves the thickest part of the horn intact. Poachers know that. It's still worth big money, and poachers will kill a dehorned rhino if that's all they can find.

The use of dye or poison is an option that has been explored. The dye would be picked up by X-ray machines at airports, enabling Customs officers to make an arrest. A problem with using poison is that it kills the bot fly larvae, a parasite vital to the health of the rhino. The bot fly eggs are laid on the horn and dissolve there before ending up in the stomach. The poison kills the bot fly eggs, which could create any number of problems down the line.

Like dehorning, dye and poison are not permanent solutions, because the rhino's horn grows back. In a large rhino population, keeping track of individuals is a never-ending job. Identifying from a helicopter which animals were due for an 'update' wouldn't always be straightforward either. A coloured tag on the ear is unlikely to last for four years.

The DNA database will depend on the support of governments and prosecuting authorities for its success. At the moment we are simply trying to record as many animals as we can – there's nothing controversial about it. The only unsatisfactory aspect is the way we have to bring the animal down. There is an urgent need for a reliable drop-out dart. That way, we could fire the dart from the helicopter and it would collect sufficient evidence from the rhino for us to record the DNA. The dart would drop out somewhere along the way and we could detect it for collection using a radio frequency. But how we would know which rhinos we had recorded and which still needed to be recorded? Unfortunately, it's not as simply as firing a splash of indelible ink or paint. Rhinos are mud dwellers; they sit in mud all day, so it is sod's law that we'd end up recording the same animals over and over. So, until a genius improves the system, we'll carry on the way we are now.

The 'drug'

Winning is like most other drugs, I suppose. The more you have it, the more you want it. When I think back to some of the best wins I still feel the rush, the 'high' you experience – the 438 game, the Mumbai Test in India, winning Test series at Edgbaston and the MCG. The antidote is losing, and I remember those days, too – the World Cup exits and the Test defeats to Australia in the early years.

I recall something Jonty said after he retired. The main difference, he said, was: 'The feeling when you win a hard, competitive game for your country – you'll never feel that again.' Strange as this may sound, I disagree with Jonty. I certainly never came close to feeling the drug for a while after the England tour. But I experienced it also when I went on the rhino-darting missions. The more I became involved, the more rewarding it became. It might be a farmer's rhino, or belong to a game park, but he feels like your boy when you're looking after him on the ground and drilling a little sample out of the precious horn that could be the cause of his death. It feels like you're making a difference. I hope we are.

My mates asked whether the adrenaline rush could possibly be the same. Well, I knew that Brett Lee couldn't charge me and run me over, so it was probably a greater rush with the rhino! But the sense of achievement is the same. Different, but definitely equal.

Chapter 22

Beyond the bubble

I am not a teacher, a life coach or even a great example. My major goal in writing this book is to record my experiences for the potential benefit of young cricketers starting out on their careers. I was extremely fortunate, in so many ways, that mine started so early and lasted so long, but it did mean that I had to learn as I went along – and to learn many lessons the hard way. I don't regret that. But if half a dozen people can skip one or two of the harder lessons of cricket life from reading this, I'll be happy and it will have been worth it.

Actually, it will have been worth it if you smiled and enjoyed the read.

Getting back to the bubble – the environment inhabited by the majority of professional cricketers – if I have a single piece of advice to professional cricketers, it would be this: 'Don't live your life in it.' At least, not all the time. It's not a healthy or normal place to be. Professional sportsmen have big egos. I guess we need them on the field. But don't be surprised or upset if your ego gets pricked from time to time. We do it to each on the field all the time, so why be upset if people do it off the field? Be stronger than that. Don't rely on your cricket personality to carry you through real life.

Adjusting to the real world has been a problem for cricketers for over a century. Cricket is an unnatural sport in so many ways; the demands it makes on your life and lifestyle are unmatched by any other sport. You end up becoming dependent on it, and then it can spit you out when it's had enough of you. My advice to cricketers would be not to underestimate what you are giving up to pursue your dreams and how difficult it can be to make the transition from cricket life back to real life.

You would be a fool not to acknowledge and then recognise the difficulties in balancing your real world with your cricket world, and also the importance of taking advice and professional help in making the adjustment. It isn't easy or straightforward. I have no problem in saying that I have sought professional help and guidance. I'm not suggesting that I needed my ego bursting. That happened when my eye burst, although it had started happening some time before that.

I respect what I achieved on the cricket field, and I'm proud of it. I'm also proud of what I'm doing now and what I hope to achieve in the future. It is so important that cricketers have a future, something to sustain their souls once they have finished playing. Pensions and savings are one thing, and extremely important, but they don't take care of your self-worth and personality.

While you're in the bubble, you protect yourself and justify it. You don't want to listen to anyone talking about it because you're thinking: 'I'm playing the game now, and I need to be like this.' Recently, I heard Polly talking about the selfish nature of cricket. It's a selfish lifestyle. I am not, and will never be, one to criticise anyone in the bubble, because I was there for so long. Maybe cricketers need to be in it to succeed? Perhaps it's the process of moving out of it that needs to be addressed? But my instinct says we need to help players not to live in the bubble full-time while they are playing.

All I know for certain is that you don't want to be trying to live in the bubble once you have finished, because nobody else from the real world lives there. When the bubble bursts, you may feel alone and awkward, unsure of what to do. That's OK. It's normal to feel that way. That's when you could benefit from help. These days, more players retire with something in the bank, but in days past players were faced with a bleak future. Too many sank into depression of some sort. I was stunned to read recently of how many cricketers have taken their lives over the last century. I don't want to be alarmist, but facts are facts.

Another thing that needs to be done is to address the people, family and friends who you've hurt in the past. No matter how much you may have let them down in the past, you have to try and sort those things out. Especially with regard to friends who were once so close. I let a lot of friends down in the past, and I wish I could take my behaviour back. But, unfortunately, some of those friendships may have been damaged beyond repair.

It's amazing how time flies in the bubble. Friends and family think: 'Can't you just find five minutes?' And you should be able to. Some people can, and they are the special ones who can stick their neck out of the bubble. It's not intentional; nobody I ever met said there were deliberately ignoring people and staying in the bubble. But time passes and passes, and then your career finishes. However, many years have passed and friends have married, had kids and divorced – even remarried, in some cases – and you've missed it all. Not that you didn't get the invites, but you were just too busy ... 'Jeez, I haven't heard from that guy in a while. What's he up to?' Then you see a message on Facebook, or something, which you haven't read in months, and you realise he's been trying to get hold of you for so long, and you've ignored him and put him off. You feel absolutely crap. How are you going to rescue that relationship? But you have to try.

Fortunately I do have friends who understand my situation, and who are always supportive of me. But there are always going to be one or two casualties, and I've certainly let down a couple of people in my career.

Leaving the safety of the bubble is difficult. Somtimes you feel down, or even depressed. You've got to be man enough to admit you have a problem. Maybe people will read this book and think: 'I've got a problem, too!' There's nothing wrong with having consequences from the decisions you make. You think you are invincible, but you learn that you are not. Who on earth are we, as international sportsmen, to think we are invincible? It doesn't matter who you are, you still need to treat people with respect.

I am *not* pointing fingers at anybody. If there is finger-pointing, it is at myself. As Polly said, maybe you need to be selfish to perform at your best. And if you're doing the job for your country, then your country is happy. Maybe they don't really care about the person you are. That's understandable.

It is not easy to admit to the difficulties in adjusting. That was an area in which Paddy Upton bridged the gap. He's a level-headed guy. He began his Proteas career as a biokinetics specialist and transformed himself from a trainer of the body to a trainer of the mind. Gary and Paddy concentrate on the big picture rather than just the cricketer. I had some great chats with Paddy towards the end of my career. He provided a different perspective for me, and it was something I needed at the time. I wanted to be a better person. It's a decision you make as a person, and as a player. You look in the mirror and say: 'Yeh, you're a good cricketer, but are you a nice person?'

You make the decision to go to Paddy, or to someone else, and ask for advice to make you a better person. To help you realise where you're going wrong, and to help realise what you're actually doing in life, and what you want to do.

Donné Commins

Some sportsmen are motivated by personal accolades, others by crowd and fan adoration, others by the money. In sport, as in life, athletes each have their own inspiration. It took me a while to work out what Mark's was, but I got there in the end.

For the first couple of years in the industry, when I was working with Dave Richardson at sports management company Octagon SA, Mark terrified me. He was abrupt, I felt, to the point of rudeness, had a mind of his own and was stubbornly difficult and reluctant to change. Whenever a phone call needed to be made to Mark, I would ask Dave to do it. It took a very long time before I became one of Mark's trusted people. But it was worth the wait!

And it is his trusted people that make him tick – his team, his group of friends, his advisers, his confidants. It may take a long time to become a member, but, once you are in, there is nothing in the world he won't do for you. Mark comes into his own when he is needed and valued by those closest to him, when he is doing something of importance for others – whether it's at the end of an innings with a couple more runs needed, or getting a team-mate to come clean about betting, or being with a friend when his father is terminally ill, acting as the team spokesman or, as now, fighting to save rhinos.

He is 100 per cent a team man. I honestly believe that it is very rare quality about him. He places the team above all individual concerns, certainly above any of his own.

In the months leading up to him being dropped in the Caribbean, I could see a struggle going on. He so badly wanted to stay part of the team, to contribute, to mentor, but he could see that the end was in sight. What appeared to be anger was the realisation that he was going to need to find another team, another group to be part of and to contribute to, and it was deeply sad for him, even traumatic. It presented itself as anger and frustration as he struggled to find his next team.

Another characteristic, rare for a professional sportsman who has spent so many years on the public stage, is that, because of his shyness and humility, Mark is not naturally comfortable being in the limelight. It was always a struggle to get Mark to do any PR or marketing, unless the focus was on something or somebody else.

More recently, the interviews he has been doing – albeit with a hefty push from me – have been outstanding, and the feedback has been amazing. Sometimes his reluctance has been interpreted as rudeness or a lack of appreciation, but nothing could be further from the truth. He just needs the spotlight shining somewhere else. When Mark is doing something for others, you won't find a more committed or generous person.

When my father was killed in a house robbery in January 2013, Mark called off his entire CSA tribute day during the Test match against New Zealand at Newlands. There was no way he was going to be presented with anything while one of his team was 'down' and hurt. It had been hard enough getting him to agree to the event in the first place. He also spoke to every policeman he knew, without telling me, and asked Rory Steyn to help with the investigation of the crime. He constantly checked in on me. He took me and my husband to his place in the bush with JP and his wife, Sue, just to get away from it all. And when he was there, he made sure everything was perfect and that we had the most incredible time.

He has a passion for the bush which I can see is similar to his passion on the field. He will drive for five hours looking for a leopard if he has seen some spoor; he will sit inches away from elephants just to experience the thrill (it wasn't very thrilling for me – I had my head under the seats). We all slept outside one night on the sleeping deck; there were no fences, and it was the greatest thrill for Mark when we woke up the next morning and spoke about our experiences. If we were happy, Mark was happy.

Mark is not afraid to stand up and be counted, to speak his mind, and that has sometimes backfired, but at least he is prepared to take a stand and have an opinion. It could be seen as inflexibility, but with too many flexible people in a team you won't get to the goal very quickly. He is also not afraid of dealing with issues head on. His intentions are always good, as he is motivated by a strong sense of justice.

He's a very special person. It has been a privilege working with him and to call him a friend.

Mike Horn

Mark was heading towards the most important period of his life so far, the transition from his playing days to the next stage. He was reflecting on his value and his legacy. He played and competed hard, in every sense, and was concerned that that might be the perception of him as a person. He knew there was a lot more to him than Mark Boucher the cricketer, and it was natural for him to think about that with his retirement around the corner.

He didn't want to be labelled as a 'hard guy'; he wanted to bring his own beers and meat to the braai of real life, and he knew he could. 'Hard men' aren't necessarily the most popular, and that troubled him a bit. He played a role for the benefit of the team and was suddenly feeling that he would be burdened with that when he left the game.

My own father was a sportsman; he played rugby for Transvaal. One day he was dropped from the squad and his career came to an end. I was devastated. I went to school and the boys teased me, saying my father was too old to play rugby anymore and that he was finished. I was only 9 but I got into a terrible fight with a 14- or 15-year-old. When I returned home I had a black eye, a split lip and a bloody nose. I was defending my father, after all. He looked at me and asked what had happened. I said: 'It's all your fault! If you were still playing rugby this would never have happened!'

He calmed me down and told me a story about the forest. He said there were trees of many shapes and sizes, tall ones and short ones, all trying to get their heads above the others. Some got there too quickly, and others didn't grow enough to get there. The first ones fell over when the wind blew and the others stayed short and never blossomed. He told me that the trees which grew to the top best were the ones with a firm base and a solid trunk.

I told Mark that he had the ability to withstand the storms

and the high winds, that he would not blow over. It was important to remind him that his true personality would be far, far more important in the rest of his life than what some people thought of him as a cricketer.

If he thought he was afraid of what the future held, I told him he wasn't afraid of the future – he was afraid of changing the environment he had lived in for 15 years. They are kids, these professional cricketers! They get everything done for them and they don't think for themselves. I reminded him, too, that he had risen to every challenge he had faced in his life so far.

Then his injury came, soon after the team left Switzerland. I contacted him, eventually, and reminded him about what we had spoken about. Everything that ends is, in fact, a new beginning. As an explorer I cannot afford to look behind me. I take the lessons I learn forward; I don't reflect on what didn't happen or the mistakes I made. I have not always lived up to my expectations, but that will not change my desire to make sure I do next time.

We should all appreciate and enjoy our achievements in life. I have done things no other men have done, and so has Mark. It is right that we should smile and enjoy those things, but not live on them. Move forward, onward to new, exciting and fresh challenges. Mark is doing that and I have no doubt that he will reinvent himself and live all of the next stages of his life with the same energy with which he played cricket. He has a greater perspective on life now, and on what's important, but, then, don't we all as the years roll by?

Afterword by Graeme Smith

Fundamentally, Mark hasn't changed in all the years I've known him. As this book shows, there have been many subtle and important changes as he's got older, but he's still the same guy at heart. That is a sign of someone who knew who he was, and what his values were, from a very early age.

My first Test match was in incredibly difficult circumstances. I was 12th man in the first Test against Australia in 2001-2002. Shaun Pollock was injured, so Mark captained. We were hammered. Allan Donald tore his hamstring and ended his Test career. Then we moved to Cape Town for the Newlands Test. Darryl Cullinan withdrew from the team because he wanted a CSA contract on his terms. It was a time of great uncertainty.

My overriding memory of that time was the way Mark rose above the distractions and plied me with information: how to bat against different bowlers, try this, don't do that, think about this. From the very start to the very end, he had a million thoughts on the game.

In my early years as captain, he was invaluable at providing insights and ideas when times were tough. Actually, he was always valuable in that regard, although I probably didn't need quite as much feedback as the years went by! He is a great thinker. Sometimes he would come up with ideas that really challenged my thinking.

He is the most competitive person I've ever met, even more than Polly. The only person who comes close is Ricky Ponting. They played the game as hard as it can be played. It was the same with everything, from a seven-a-side football game to a Test match. If you were partnering him in a game of golf and standing over a five-foot putt, not having played in two months, his presence made you feel that your life depended on it.

If we faced a particularly hard session of Test cricket, and I needed to think and watch, I would ask him to take charge of the intensity that we needed to make a move in the game. He did it, every time. He was extraordinary with bowlers' actions, detecting the tiniest variation or problem. The angles of the field placings were a special strength of his. He would nudge a fielder a few metres left or right, and I always knew it was for a good reason.

His perspectives on cricketing issues and contributions in team meetings were always outstanding, and I found him fascinating during video analysis sessions. He came up with specific plans to get Michael Vaughan and Rahul Dravid, and they often worked, too! After watching a couple of minutes of a new batsman on-screen Bouch could analyse his technique instantly: how he picked the bat up, where he planted his front foot and what angle to attack him in the first 20 balls. He was brilliant like that – such a sharp mind. Often, before a big series, I would organise a session with just me, the coach and Bouch. We would watch videos together and listen to what he thought.

It was tough for all of us when he was dropped from the squad for the first time. It felt like there was a lot of misunderstanding and too little inclination to deal with things openly. I can understand if Mark felt like a scapegoat. Being a selector is a hard job. Looking at statistics and making decisions on the basis of someone averaging 28 is a dangerous game. There are always other factors to consider, which the selectors can't understand because they are outside the team environment. It will always be the captain's struggle.

Jacques and Bouch are old school. They don't do 'touchy feely'. They are 'get on with it' guys. They grew up in strictly hierarchical systems. They did what they were told to do.

Mark is the most loyal person I know. If he knows you, and respects you, there is nothing he won't do for you. Mark's loyalty and commitment means he does get hurt and he takes things personally. There were times when he spoke his mind immediately, but there were other occasions when he would bite his tongue. If I knew something was wrong and it was on his mind, I knew I had to go and discuss it immediately. If it was an issue with someone else, then, naturally, he would bring it up with that person. But if it was something personal, he wouldn't necessarily approach anyone to talk.

Sometimes he could be overpowering. When Bouch really believes in something he commits to it 100 per cent; there is no other way. If you want to argue a point with him, you have to let him cool off for a couple of days. Then the discussion can be a bit more balanced!

The most important point about his personality, and virtually everyone knew this, was that he meant well and only ever wanted what was best for the team. He's probably reflecting on whether he always handled things in the best way, but we knew that he was coming from a good place. If his team-mates had ever felt his motives weren't sincere, then things could have been quite different!

The manner in which Bouch bowed out of the game must have given him a lot of time to reflect on the good and bad. When you are lying in pain in a hospital bed, I can imagine the things that go round in your head ... I was there, I saw it. You can't help reflecting on your life and career when it ends in a couple of seconds.

Retirement

Gary Kirsten's man-management skills are very good and he helped Bouch a lot with the decision to retire. All of us played a role, but Gary had many meetings and helped Mark build a vision for the future. He was able to figure it out himself, the where, what and how. He made the decision to retire after the England tour many months before we left for Switzerland.

Constantly having to prove himself after 140 Test matches was weighing him down. Every time he played he felt he was playing his first game – all eyes were on him and every mistake was pounced on. Not that there were many. But the feeling of playing for your place is unpleasant; it burdens your game.

Once he made the decision to retire, you could feel him relax. You could see it. He was incredible at training sessions and fitness camps. He was one of the top three at everything and always at the front of the pack. It was partly his competitive nature, but he always led by example. In Switzerland it was no different; he never moaned once, and was always the guy at the front, helping others, picking them up and pulling them along. He was a pillar of strength. A couple of times I thought: 'Bouch is going to have an unbelievable tour. He's going out with a bang. He's not going quietly.'

As devastating as his eye injury was, the depth of feeling and outpouring of love from the team – and so many thousands of other people – was an incredible thing for Mark. As appalling as the situation was, he was reminded of all the great joys and successes his career had encapsulated, and he knew, without doubt, that all the sacrifices had been worth it. Little bits of criticism here and there can get you down, but that made him realise what the wider body of opinion was about him. It was a great comfort.

Taunton

Warm-up games, especially in England, have long ceased to be about trying to win. The counties rest their main players, so the standard isn't high. We just try to get as much out of them as we can individually.

I threw the ball to Imran Tahir to have a bowl and went down to field at long on. When Bouch went down, I thought it was perhaps a cut under the eye. I had gone through my entire career, until that day, without ever thinking about injuring an eyeball. By the time I got to him, it was obvious that the injury was serious. I saw white goo coming out of his eye; there was no blood. I had never seen anything like it before, and my brain could not compute what might have happened. I took one side of him, and the physio, Brandon Jackson, took the other, and we started helping him off the field. Then he just collapsed. I looked down at him and was about to move something black from his cheek when I realised it was his iris. Everything had come out. I felt a bit weak myself at that moment.

I had to finish the day with the team on the field, although it was the last thing I felt like doing. After play ended, a couple of us went straight to the hospital and we stayed with him until he went into surgery. I returned to the hotel briefly to get changed and pack my bags, because we were leaving the following day, and then I returned to the hospital. We were in the waiting room for hours. Nobody expected the surgery to take that long. Eventually we persuaded the guys to go back to the hotel to get some rest. Me, Jacques and Doc Moosajee stayed behind and promised to keep them up to date with any news.

When Bouch finally emerged from surgery, you would have thought he'd been in for an open-heart operation. It was hectic. They were trying to control his pain with a mask, and there were wires and tubes every-where. It was frightening. You could see that he was in a bad place. We stayed with him for a while and, eventually, Jacques and I went back to the hotel and Doc Moosajee spent the night with him. Next morn-ing we went back to the hospital and brought him back to the hotel. Jacques and I didn't go to the ground that day – it was the second day of a two-day game. Given what had happened, I couldn't think of anything more inconsequential than that game. Instead, we helped Mark pack his bags, tried to cheer him up a bit, spend some decent time with him. Doc was trying to sort out a couple of flights back to Cape Town.

It was very emotional. My prime concern was who was going to take care of him. The sense of family that we shared in the team was never more obvious, and none of us was going to be there when he got home. At least Doc would be travelling back with him. Doc was incredible dur-ing the whole thing. I always had the greatest respect for him, but, if pos-sible, that respect increased even further when I saw the care he gave Bouch and how selfless he was.

It was a bleak moment when we heard the news after surgery that he probably wouldn't regain any sight in the injured eye. His eyeball had 12 stitches across it. At that stage, the surgeon's main concern was saving the eyeball so he wouldn't need an artificial, glass eye.

Jacques wanted to go back to South Africa with him, but Bouch gave him short shrift on that. His parents were going to stay in Cape Town and he had plenty of friends, who assured Jacques that Mark would be well looked after.

It was obvious that his career was over. Mark decided to deal with it immediately and announce his retirement. We worked on a statement together, and Paddy Upton wrote it up. Paddy was very switched on. He could see a scenario in which Bouch just quietly disappeared from the game and went underground.

Mark didn't want to make any public appearances but was more than happy for us to read the statement on his behalf. He walked away from the game with his dignity and pride intact, and that is exactly the way it should have been for a very special person and cricketer.

Graeme Smith
October 2013

Vital statistics *All details as at 31 July 2013*

Test career

By Series

Series	Venue	Venue	M	Inns	NO	Runs	HS	Avg	SR	100	50	Ct	St
v Pakistan	Pakistan	1997/98	1	1	0	6	6	6.00	50.00	0	0	0	0
v Pakistan	South Africa	1997/98	3	5	0	188	78	37.60	48.08	0	3	17	1
v Sri Lanka	South Africa	1997/98	2	3	0	56	33	18.66	28.42	0	0	13	0
v England	England	1998	5	6	0	84	35	14.00	48.00	0	0	25	1
v West Indies	South Africa	1998/99	5	8	2	168	100	28.00	51.06	1	0	14	0
v New Zealand	New Zealand	1998/99	3	1	0	8	8	8.00	16.32	0	0	10	0
v Zimbabwe	South Africa	1999/00	1	1	1	55	55*	–	56.12	0	1	5	0
v Zimbabwe	Zimbabwe	1999/00	1	1	0	125	125	125.00	52.96	1	0	4	0
v England	South Africa	1999/00	5	6	1	212	108	42.40	42.57	1	0	19	0
v India	India	1999/00	2	3	1	45	27*	22.50	49.45	0	0	10	0
v Sri Lanka	Sri Lanka	2000	3	6	0	111	60	18.50	50.68	0	1	6	1
v New Zealand	South Africa	2000/01	3	3	1	98	76	49.00	71.53	0	1	8	0
v Sri Lanka	South Africa	2000/01	3	4	0	157	92	39.25	71.68	0	1	14	1
v West Indies	West Indies	2000/01	5	9	0	126	52	14.00	41.44	0	1	18	0
v Zimbabwe	Zimbabwe	2001/02	2	1	0	14	14	14.00	73.68	0	0	2	1
v India	South Africa	2001/02	2	2	1	115	68*	115.00	74.19	0	1	11	0
v Australia	Australia	2001/02	3	6	0	169	64	28.16	52.81	0	1	7	0
v Australia	South Africa	2001/02	3	6	1	95	37	19.00	57.92	0	0	13	0
v Bangladesh	South Africa	2002/03	2	1	1	14	14*	–	82.35	0	0	9	0
v Sri Lanka	South Africa	2002/03	2	3	1	123	63	61.50	51.68	0	1	10	0
v Pakistan	South Africa	2002/03	2	2	0	62	55	31.00	50.00	0	1	7	1
v Bangladesh	Bangladesh	2002/03	2	1	0	71	71	71.00	52.98	0	1	9	2
v England	England	2003	5	8	1	271	68	38.71	54.63	0	2	17	1
v Pakistan	Pakistan	2003/04	2	4	0	114	72	28.50	67.85	0	1	3	1
v West Indies	South Africa	2003/04	4	5	1	192	122*	48.00	60.00	1	0	13	0
v New Zealand	New Zealand	2003/04	3	4	0	36	22	9.00	39.56	0	0	7	1
v Sri Lanka	Sri Lanka	2004	2	3	1	67	51	33.50	36.81	0	1	6	2
v England	South Africa	2004/05	2	4	0	95	64	23.75	58.28	0	1	8	0
v Zimbabwe	South Africa	2004/05	2	1	0	18	18	18.00	58.06	0	0	12	1
v West Indies	West Indies	2004/05	4	5	2	112	41	37.33	31.37	0	0	12	0

Abbreviations

M = matches played; Inns = innings; NO = times not out; HS = high score;
Avg = average run rate; SR = strike rate; 100 = centuries scored; 50 = fifties scored
Ct = caught; St = stumped; Dis = dismissals; Wkt = wickets.

Series	Venue	Venue	M	Inns	NO	Runs	HS	Avg	SR	100	50	Ct	St
Wld XI v Aus	Australia	2005/06	1	2	0	17	17	8.50	37.77	0	0	2	0
v Australia	Australia	2005/06	3	6	1	119	62	23.80	56.66	0	1	12	0
v Australia	South Africa	2005/06	3	6	1	175	63	35.00	45.10	0	2	11	0
v New Zealand	South Africa	2005/06	3	5	0	78	33	15.60	38.80	0	0	12	0
v Sri Lanka	Sri Lanka	2006	2	4	0	186	85	46.50	59.61	0	2	4	0
v India	South Africa	2006/07	3	5	0	139	53	27.80	55.37	0	2	15	1
v Pakistan	South Africa	2006/07	3	4	1	123	46	41.00	63.40	0	0	11	1
v Pakistan	Pakistan	2007/08	2	3	0	84	54	28.00	40.77	0	1	7	3
v New Zealand	South Africa	2007/08	2	2	0	44	43	22.00	42.71	0	0	1	0
v West Indies	South Africa	2007/08	3	3	0	92	59	30.66	45.77	0	1	10	0
v Bangladesh	Bangladesh	2007/08	2	3	1	34	21	17.00	29.56	0	0	12	0
v India	India	2007/08	3	5	1	136	70	34.00	43.87	0	1	5	1
v England	England	2008	4	6	1	138	45*	27.60	47.58	0	0	18	0
v Bangladesh	South Africa	2008/09	2	2	0	132	117	66.00	58.92	1	0	8	0
v Australia	Australia	2008/09	3	4	0	122	89	30.50	44.20	0	1	8	1
v Australia	South Africa	2008/09	3	5	0	62	25	12.40	24.80	0	0	8	1
v England	South Africa	2009/10	4	7	1	341	95	56.83	67.92	0	3	16	0
v India	India	2009/10	1	1	0	39	39	39.00	52.00	0	0	3	0
v West Indies	West Indies	2010	3	3	0	103	69	34.33	43.27	0	1	10	0
v Pakistan	UAE	2010/11	2	3	0	69	45	23.00	44.80	0	0	3	0
v India	South Africa	2010/11	3	4	1	72	55	24.00	63.71	0	1	14	0
v Australia	South Africa	2011/12	2	3	0	20	13	6.66	58.82	0	0	5	0
v Sri Lanka	South Africa	2011/12	3	3	0	75	65	25.00	50.33	0	1	17	1
v New Zealand	New Zealand	2011/12	3	4	1	108	46	36.00	47.78	0	0	11	0
TOTALS													
For SA			146	204	24	5498	125	30.54	50.18	5	35	530	23
For World			1	2	0	17	17	8.50	37.77	0	0	2	0
All			147	206	24	5515	125	30.30	50.13	5	35	532	23

He hit 657 fours and 20 sixes in his Test career.
As a wicket-keeper he was involved in executing 20 run outs.

Against each opponent

Against	M	Inns	NO	Runs	HS	Avg	SR	100	50	Ct	St
Australia	21	38	3	779	89	22.25	46.17	0	5	66	2
Bangladesh	8	7	2	251	117	50.20	51.22	1	1	38	2
England	25	37	4	1141	108	34.57	53.71	1	6	103	2
India	14	20	4	546	70	34.12	54.87	0	5	58	2
New Zealand	17	19	2	372	76	21.88	46.09	0	1	49	1
Pakistan	15	22	1	646	78	30.76	51.72	0	6	48	7
Sri Lanka	17	26	2	775	92	32.29	51.12	0	7	70	5
West Indies	24	33	5	793	122*	28.32	45.34	2	3	77	0
Zimbabwe	6	4	1	212	125	70.66	55.20	1	1	23	2

In each country

Country	M	Inns	NO	Runs	HS	Avg	SR	100	50	Ct	St
Australia	10	18	1	427	89	25.11	50.17	0	3	29	1
Bangladesh	4	4	1	105	71	35.00	42.16	0	1	21	2
England	14	20	2	493	68	27.38	51.30	0	2	60	2
India	6	9	2	220	70	31.42	46.21	0	1	18	1
New Zealand	9	9	1	152	46	19.00	41.53	0	0	28	1
Pakistan	5	8	0	204	72	25.50	52.84	0	2	10	4
South Africa	75	103	14	3001	122*	33.71	52.73	4	20	301	8
Sri Lanka	7	13	1	364	85	30.33	51.05	0	4	16	3
United Arab Emirates	2	3	0	69	45	23.00	44.80	0	0	3	0
West Indies	12	17	2	341	69	22.73	37.93	0	2	40	0
Zimbabwe	3	2	0	139	125	69.50	54.50	1	0	6	1
Home	75	103	14	3001	122*	33.71	52.73	4	20	301	8
Away	70	100	10	2445	125	27.16	47.42	1	15	228	15
Neutral	2	3	0	69	45	23.00	44.80	0	0	3	0

At specific venues (minimum 3 matches)

Venue	M	Inns	NO	Runs	HS	Avg	SR	100	50	Ct	St
Cape Town	18	22	3	737*	122	38.78	54.55	1	5	60	5
Centurion	15	18	2	656	117	41.00	52.52	2	3	67	0
Johannesburg	15	23	2	565	95	26.90	55.50	0	4	57	1
Durban	14	23	3	516	108	25.80	45.46	1	4	63	1
Port Elizabeth	7	11	1	298*	68	29.80	52.09	0	2	24	1
Sydney	4	8	0	188	89	23.50	50.00	0	1	9	0
Bloemfontein	4	5	2	215	76	71.66	61.60	0	2	21	0
Bridgetown	3	4	0	48	28	12.00	30.18	0	0	13	0
Birmingham	3	4	2	100*	45	50.00	56.49	0	0	9	1
Leeds	3	5	0	99	39	19.80	49.74	0	0	21	0
Lord's	3	3	0	107	68	35.66	80.45	0	1	10	1
Melbourne	3	5	0	74	43	14.80	52.48	0	0	7	0
Colombo-SSC	3	6	1	179	85	35.80	44.86	0	2	6	3
Port-of-Spain	3	4	0	151	69	37.75	42.77	0	1	9	0
Wellington	3	3	0	54	46	18.00	40.00	0	0	11	1

Test batting

Test centuries

Start Date	Against	Venue	Runs	Mins	Balls	Fours	Sixes
15/01/1999	West Indies	Centurion	100	209	183	16	0
11/11/1999	Zimbabwe	Harare	125	322	236	18	0
26/12/1999	England	Durban	108	290	220	14	1
02/01/2004	West Indies	Cape Town	122*	247	173	21	0
26/11/2008	Bangladesh	Centurion	117	275	190	16	0

Scores of 25 or more
Coming in with the total < 150 with 5 or more wickets down or < 100 with 4 wickets down

Match

Start Date	Inns	Against	Venue	Score	Start	End
14/02/1998	1	Pakistan	Johannesburg	78	149-6	364-10
26/02/1998	4	Pakistan	Durban	52	114-6	219-9
23/07/1998	3	England	Nottingham	35	136-6	193-8
15/01/1999	1	West Indies	Centurion	100	123-6	302-9
24/02/2000	4	India	Mumbai	27*	128-6	164-6
30/07/2000	1	Sri Lanka	Kandy	60	34-5	158-6
26/12/2001	1	Australia	Melbourne	43	131-5	198-6
02/01/2002	2	Australia	Sydney	35	93-5	148-9
08/03/2002	1	Australia	Cape Town	26	73-5	147-7
01/05/2003	1	Bangladesh	Dhaka	71	63-4	219-6
14/08/2003	2	England	Nottingham	48	132-5	284-7
14/08/2003	4	England	Nottingham	52	50-5	131-10
04/09/2003	3	England	The Oval	25	118-5	193-7
11/08/2004	4	Sri Lanka	Colombo-SSC	51	36-5	137-6
31/03/2005	2	West Indies	Georgetown	41	30-4	172-9
24/03/2006	4	Australia	Durban	51*	146-5	297-10
31/03/2006	3	Australia	Johannesburg	63	140-6	258-9
19/01/2007	1	Pakistan	Port Elizabeth	35	58-5	120-8
26/01/2007	2	Pakistan	Cape Town	40*	133-6	183-10
01/10/2007	3	Pakistan	Karachi	29	132-5	188-6
08/11/2007	1	New Zealand	Johannesburg	43	141-5	219-9
02/01/2008	2	West Indies	Cape Town	59	131-5	260-6
26/11/2008	2	Bangladesh	Centurion	117	134-5	405-6
26/12/2009	3	England	Durban	29	44-5	108-8
03/01/2010	1	England	Cape Town	51	127-5	216-6
02/01/2011	3	India	Cape Town	55	130-6	233-7

Century partnerships

Wkt	Part	With	Against	Venue	Season
9	195	PL Symcox	Pakistan	Johannesburg	1997/98#
8	148	SM Pollock	Zimbabwe	Harare	1999/00
8	119	L Klusener	England	Port Elizabeth	1999/00
5	192	G Kirsten	England	Durban	1999/00
6	124	L Klusener	Sri Lanka	Kandy	2000
7	121	L Klusener	India	Bloemfontein	2001/02
7	141	ND McKenzie	Australia	Adelaide	2001/02
7	132	SM Pollock	Sri Lanka	Centurion	2002/03
5	107	JA Rudolph	Bangladesh	Dhaka	2002/03
6	129	ND McKenzie	England	Nottingham	2003
8	146	JH Kallis	West Indies	Cape Town	2003/04
6	101	HH Dippenaar	Sri Lanka	Colombo-SSC	2004
6	120	HH Gibbs	England	Johannesburg	2004/05
5	100	AG Prince	India	Durban	2006/07
6	129	AG Prince	West Indies	Cape Town	2007/08
6	112*	GC Smith	England	Birmingham	2008
6	271	AG Prince	Bangladesh	Centurion	2008/09##
6	115	M Morkel	Australia	Sydney	2008/09
6	120	AB de Villiers	England	Johannesburg	2009/10
7	103	JH Kallis	India	Cape Town	2010/11

World record ## South African record
He and SM Pollock hold the world record for most runs added for the 7th wicket in Tests: 908 in 28 partnerships (one unbroken) at an average of 33.62 with one century and four 50 partnerships.

Bowlers dismissed by

Bowler	Times	M
M Muralitharan	12	12
SK Warne	9	13
JM Anderson	6	14
Danish Kaneria	5	7
GP Swann	4	4
Z Khan	4	7
PM Siddle	4	8
CA Walsh	4	9
CS Martin	4	13
B Lee	4	15

Bowlers not dismissed by

Bowler	Times	M
CL Hooper	0	10
Harbhajan Singh	0	8
FH Edwards	0	8
CRD Fernando	0	8
AF Giles	0	7
SJ Harmison	0	7

Most Test runs for South Africa

Name	M	Inns	NO	Runs	HS	Avg	SR	100	50
JH Kallis	161	272	39	13045	224	55.98	46.09	44	58
GC Smith	109	190	12	8741	277	49.10	59.64	26	37
G Kirsten	101	176	15	7289	275	45.27	43.46	21	34
AB de Villiers	85	142	16	6364	278*	50.50	54.66	16	32
HH Gibbs	90	154	7	6167	228	41.95	50.25	14	26
HM Amla	70	121	10	5785	311*	52.11	52.60	19	27
MV Boucher	146	204	24	5498	125	30.54	50.18	5	35
DJ Cullinan	70	115	12	4554	275*	44.21	48.98	14	20
SM Pollock	108	156	39	3781	111	32.31	52.55	2	16
WJ Cronje	68	111	9	3714	135	36.41	44.48	6	23

Test wicket-keeping

Milestone Test dismissals

Dis	Test	Details	Year
1st	2nd	Aamir Sohail ct off SM Pollock at Johannesburg	1998
50th	10th	D Gough ct off AA Donald at Nottingham	1998
100th	23rd	A Flintoff ct off JH Kallis at Port Elizabeth	1999
150th	38th	CH Gayle ct off JH Kallis at Georgetown	2001
153rd	39th	WW Hinds ct off AA Donald at Port-of-Spain	2001
		This took him past DJ Richardson as the leading wicket-keeper for South Africa.	
200th	52nd	DR Martyn ct off JH Kallis at Durban	2002
250th	63rd	AF Giles ct off SM Pollock at Nottingham	2003
300th	79th	BRM Taylor ct off M Ntini at Cape Town	2005
350th	92nd	NJ Astle ct off DW Steyn at Centurion	2006
396th	103rd	Umar Gul st off PL Harris at Karachi	2007
		This took him past IA Healy as the leading wicket-keeper in Tests.	
400th	104th	Danish Kaneria ct off M Ntini at Lahore	2007
		He was the first wicket-keeper to reach this milestone.	
417th	110th	Mushfiqur Rahim ct off JH Kallis at Mirpur	2008
450th	119th	Mehrab Hossain ct off M Ntini at Bloemfontein	2008
		This took him past AC Gilchrist as the leading wicket-keeper in Tests; Gilchrist had passed him earlier.	
500th	133rd	R Rampaul ct off M Morkel at Basseterre	2010
550th	146th	KS Williamson ct off VD Philander at Hamilton	2012
555th	147th	DR Flynn ct off M Morkel at Wellington	2012

Most dismissals in Tests

Name	M	Cts	Sts	Dis	Dis/M
MV Boucher (SA)	147	532	23	555	3.77
AC Gilchrist (Aus)	96	379	37	416	4.33
IA Healy (Aus)	119	366	29	395	3.31
RW Marsh (Aus)	96	343	12	355	3.69

Most Tests as wicket-keeper

Name	M
MV Boucher (SA)	147
IA Healy (Aus)	119
AC Gilchrist (Aus)	96
RW Marsh (Aus)	96
APE Knott (Eng)	95

Bowlers he took most dismissals off in Tests

Bowler	M	Cts	Sts	Dis
M Ntini	96	84	0	84
SM Pollock	88	79	0	79
JH Kallis	137	69	0	69
DW Steyn	51	58	0	58
AA Donald	35	53	0	53
A Nel	36	32	0	32
M Morkel	38	30	0	30
VD Philander	7	16	0	16
PR Adams	34	11	5	16
PL Harris	36	6	8	14
N Boje	41	7	7	14

Batsmen he dismissed most often in Tests

Batsman	M	Cts	Sts	Dis
MP Vaughan	14	9	0	9
KC Sangakkara	15	8	1	9
A Flintoff	16	8	1	9
CH Gayle	16	9	0	9
RT Ponting	21	9	0	9
RS Dravid	13	8	0	8
DPMD Jayawardene	15	8	0	8
MS Dhoni	9	6	1	7
Inzamam-ul-Haq	10	4	3	7
WW Hinds	11	7	0	7
N Hussain	14	6	0	6

Most dismissals by a wicket-keeper/bowler combination in Tests

Keeper	Bowler	Team	M	Cts	Sts	Dis
RW Marsh	DK Lillee	Aus	69	95	0	95
AC Gilchrist	GD McGrath	Aus	71	90	0	90
MV Boucher	M Ntini	SA	96	84	0	84
AC Gilchrist	B Lee	Aus	65	81	0	81
MV Boucher	SM Pollock	SA	88	79	0	79
PJL Dujon	MD Marshall	WI	68	71	0	71
MV Boucher	JH Kallis	SA	137	69	0	69
RW Taylor	IT Botham	Eng	51	60	0	60
AC Gilchrist	SK Warne	Aus	70	39	20	59
MV Boucher	DW Steyn	SA	51	58	0	58

Five dismissals in a Test innings

Dis	Cts	Sts	Against	Venue	Season
6	6	0	Pakistan	Port Elizabeth	1997/98
6	6	0	Sri Lanka	Cape Town	1997/98
6	6	0	Zimbabwe	Centurion	2004/05
6	6	0	Sri Lanka	Centurion	2011/12
5	5	0	England	Lord's	1998
5	5	0	England	Johannesburg	1999/00
5	5	0	India	Mumbai	1999/00
5	5	0	West Indies	Kingston	2000/01
5	5	0	Sri Lanka	Centurion	2002/03
5	5	0	Australia	Johannesburg	2005/06
5	5	0	Bangladesh	Chittagong-D	2007/08
5	5	0	England	Leeds	2008
5	5	0	England	Centurion	2009/10
5	5	0	India	Durban	2010/11

Five dismissals in an innings most often in Tests

14	MV Boucher (SA)
12	RW Marsh (Aus)
11	IA Healy (Aus)
8	AC Gilchrist (Aus)
6	MS Dhoni (Ind)
6	ATW Grout (Aus)

Most dismissals in a Test innings for South Africa

Name	Dis	Cts	Sts	Against	Venue	Season
DT Lindsay	6	6	0	Australia	Johannesburg	1966/67
MV Boucher	6	6	0	Pakistan	Port Elizabeth	1997/98
MV Boucher	6	6	0	Sri Lanka	Cape Town	1997/98
MV Boucher	6	6	0	Zimbabwe	Centurion	2004/05
MV Boucher	6	6	0	Sri Lanka	Centurion	2011/12
AB de Villiers	6	6	0	Pakistan	Johannesburg	2012/13

Most dismissals in a Test match for South Africa

Name	Dis	Cts	Sts	Against	Venue	Season
AB de Villiers	11	11	0	Pakistan	Johannesburg	2012/13
DJ Richardson	9	9	0	India	Port Elizabeth	1992/93
MV Boucher	9	8	1	Pakistan	Port Elizabeth	1997/98
MV Boucher	9	9	0	England	Leeds	2008
MV Boucher	9	9	0	India	Durban	2010/11

Byes

Boucher conceded 966 byes in 147 Tests. This is the most by any wicket-keeper.
Second is PJL Dujon with 767 in 79 Tests as wicket-keeper.
Boucher's 6.57 byes per match is 13th lowest out of the 26 players who have kept wicket in 50 or more Tests.
Boucher is the only wicket-keeper to keep for a 5-match Test series without conceding a bye: 1998/99 vs West Indies in SA.

Longest innings without conceding a bye

Score	Overs	Against	Venue	Season
419-9*	178	Zimbabwe	Bulawayo	2001/02
574-9*	170	England	Durban	2009/10
352	160.4	New Zealand	Auckland	1998/99
543-5*	152.1	West Indies	Georgetown	2004/05

Most dismissals in a Test series for South Africa

26 (ct 23, st 3)	JHB Waite	v New Zealand in South Africa	1961/62
26 (ct 25, st 1)	MV Boucher	v England in England	1998

Fifty and five dismissals in an innings in the same Test

Batting	Dismissals	Against	Venue	Season
52 & 4	6 cts & 2cts, 1 st	Pakistan	Port Elizabeth	1997/98
63 & 22*	3 cts & 5 cts	Sri Lanka	Centurion	2002/03
24 & 63	0 & 5 cts	Australia	Johannesburg	2005/06
49 & 63*	1 ct & 5 cts	England	Centurion	2009/10
65	2 cts & 6 cts	Sri Lanka	Centurion	2011/12

Limited Overs International career

Competition	M	Inns	NO	Runs	HS	Avg	SR	100	50	Ct	St
World Cup	25	19	5	381	75*	27.21	94.07	0	2	31	0
ICC Champions Trophy	17	13	0	288	69	22.15	77.62	0	2	17	2
Other matches	253	189	52	4017	147*	29.32	84.51	1	22	355	20
Totals											
For South Africa	290	216	57	4523	147*	28.44	84.65	1	25	395	21
For Africa	5	5	0	163	73	32.6	87.63	0	1	8	1
All	295	221	57	4686	147*	28.57	84.75	1	26	403	22

*He hit 356 fours and 83 sixes in his Limited Overs International career.
As a wicket-keeper he was involved in executing 78 run outs.*

Against each opponent

Against	M	Inns	NO	Runs	HS	Avg	SR	100	50	Ct	St
Asia	5	5	0	163	73	32.60	87.63	0	1	8	1
Australia	40	37	10	676	76	25.03	79.81	0	5	49	5
Bangladesh	9	4	0	38	12	9.50	61.29	0	0	19	0
Canada	1	1	0	21	21	21.00	58.33	0	0	2	0
England	32	26	6	460	55	23.00	74.91	0	1	38	1
India	33	22	5	558	68	32.82	73.80	0	3	40	2
Ireland	2	1	1	2	2*	–	66.66	0	0	5	0
Kenya	9	4	3	139	57	139.00	149.46	0	2	17	1
Netherlands	1	1	1	75	75	–	241.93	0	1	0	0
New Zealand	39	28	8	709	58	35.45	89.74	0	3	48	1
Pakistan	33	22	3	477	78	25.10	80.03	0	4	58	1
Scotland	1	0	0	0	0	–	–	0	0	1	0
Sri Lanka	35	31	5	598	70	23.00	80.81	0	4	51	4
West Indies	36	25	7	425	52	23.61	88.54	0	2	43	4
Zimbabwe	19	14	8	345	147	57.50	116.94	1	0	24	2

In each country

Country	M	Inns	NO	Runs	HS	Avg	SR	100	50	Ct	St
Australia	24	21	7	631	76	45.07	90.66	0	7	25	2
Bangladesh	8	5	1	108	48	27.00	81.81	0	0	11	1
England	27	22	8	286	55	20.42	67.93	0	1	34	2
India	19	15	2	396	73	30.46	72.39	0	3	23	1
Ireland	4	4	3	91	55*	91.00	93.81	0	1	6	0
Kenya	6	4	1	98	60	32.66	72.05	0	1	9	1
Morocco	4	4	0	139	70	34.75	74.33	0	2	2	0
Netherlands	1	1	0	3	3	3.00	50.00	0	0	1	0
New Zealand	13	10	1	143	48*	15.88	102.87	0	0	17	0
Pakistan	10	8	1	84	24	12.00	67.20	0	0	18	0
South Africa	135	97	26	2160	147	30.42	90.45	1	7	204	8
Sri Lanka	13	11	1	166	58	16.60	71.24	0	1	20	2
United Arab Emirates	5	3	0	98	57	32.66	77.77	0	1	7	1
West Indies	23	14	4	264	75	26.40	97.77	0	2	24	3
Zimbabwe	3	2	2	19	15	–	73.07	0	0	2	1
Home	135	97	26	2160	147	30.42	90.45	1	7	204	8
Away	94	75	19	1322	76	23.60	77.17	0	8	118	8
Neutral	66	49	12	1204	75	32.54	84.31	0	11	81	6

At specific venues (minimum 5 matches)

Venue	M	Inns	NO	Runs	HS	Avg	SR	100	50	Ct	St
Centurion	21	16	4	395	78	32.91	89.56	0	1	34	1
Durban	21	15	5	269	45*	26.90	89.36	0	0	30	1
Cape Town	20	16	4	431	51*	35.91	98.62	0	1	43	2
Port Elizabeth	18	15	5	250	48	25.00	74.18	0	0	16	2
Johannesburg	17	13	4	304	55*	33.77	79.58	0	2	27	1
Bloemfontein	11	9	2	148	57*	21.14	94.26	0	1	17	0
East London	9	6	0	147	55	24.50	82.12	0	2	10	1
Dhaka	8	5	1	108	48	27.00	81.81	0	0	11	1
Nairobi	6	4	1	98	60	32.66	72.05	0	1	9	1
Benoni	6	3	0	38	18	12.66	62.29	0	0	8	0
Colombo-RPS	6	5	1	75	58	18.75	86.20	0	1	9	1
Potchefstroom	5	3	1	160	147*	80.00	195.12	1	0	9	0
Kimberley	5	1	1	18	18*	–	163.63	0	0	9	0
Sharjah	5	3	0	98	57	32.66	77.77	0	1	7	1
The Oval	5	5	2	99	55	33.00	76.74	0	1	7	0
Lahore	5	5	0	39	14	7.80	72.22	0	0	9	0
Birmingham	5	3	1	21	13	10.50	55.26	0	0	6	0

Limited Overs International batting

Limited Overs International century

Date	Against	Venue	Runs	Mins	Balls	Fours	Sixes
20/09/2006	Zimbabwe	Potchefstroom	147*	91	68	8	10

Fastest Limited Overs International centuries

Name	Balls	For	Against	Venue	Season
Shahid Afridi	37	Pakistan	Sri Lanka	Nairobi	1996/97
MV Boucher	44	South Africa	Zimbabwe	Potchefstroom	2006/07
BC Lara	45	West Indies	Bangladesh	Dhaka	1999/00
Shahid Afridi	45	Pakistan	India	Kanpur	2004/05

Fastest Limited Overs International fifties for South Africa

Name	Balls	Against	Venue	Season
MV Boucher	19	Kenya	Cape Town	2001/02
JM Kemp	19	Zimbabwe	Durban	2004/05

Century partnerships

Wkt	Part	With	Against	Venue	Season
7	114	L Klusener	India	Nagpur	1999/00#
5	106	JN Rhodes	New Zealand	Cape Town	2000/01
5	100	ND McKenzie	Sri Lanka	East London	2000/01
5	138	JN Rhodes	New Zealand	Perth	2001/02
7	101	HH Dippenaar	Sri Lanka	Tangier	2002
5	107	ND McKenzie	India	Dhaka	2002/03
4	111	JH Kallis	England	The Oval	2003
6	131	JM Kemp	Pakistan	Mohali	2006/07
5	128	JH Kallis	Pakistan	Centurion	2006/07
4	134*	JH Kallis	Netherlands	Basseterre	2006/07

South African record

Bowlers dismissed by

Bowler	Times	M
V Sehwag	6	22
Shoaib Akhtar	5	12
UDU Chandana	5	17
B Lee	5	19
Shahid Afridi	4	21
DL Vettori	4	32

Best strike-rates in Limited Overs Internationals for South Africa

Name	M	Inns	NO	Runs	HS	Avg	SR	100	50
AB de Villiers	143	137	23	5667	146	49.71	93.03	14	33
HM Amla	76	73	6	3675	150	54.85	91.19	11	21
L Klusener	171	137	50	3576	103*	41.10	89.89	2	19
SM Pollock	294	196	70	3193	90	25.34	85.67	0	13
MV Boucher	290	216	57	4523	147*	28.44	84.65	1	25

Batsmen he dismissed most often in Limited Overs Internationals

Batsman	M	Cts	Sts	Dis
DPMD Jayawardene	35	9	1	10
Mohammad Yousuf	36	9	0	9
SC Ganguly	24	8	0	8
Younis Khan	28	8	0	8
N Hussain	10	7	0	7
MS Atapattu	31	6	1	7

Five dismissals in a Limited Overs International

Dis	Cts	Sts	Against	Venue	Season
6	6	0	Pakistan	Cape Town	2006/07
5	5	0	England	Johannesburg	1999/00
5	5	0	Australia	Durban	1999/00
5	5	0	Pakistan	Colombo-SSC	2000
5	5	0	Bangladesh	Dhaka	2002/03
5	5	0	New Zealand	Centurion	2005/06
5	5	0	Pakistan	Johannesburg	2006/07
5	4	1	India	Ahmedabad	2009/10

Byes

Boucher conceded 218 byes in 295 Limited Overs Internationals. His 0.74 byes per match is 8th lowest out of the 21 players who have kept wicket in 100 or more Limited Overs Internationals.

Limited Overs International wicket-keeping

Milestone Limited Overs International dismissals

Dis	LOI	Details	Year
1st	1st	SP Fleming ct off M Ntini at Perth	1998
50th	36th	Wajahatullah Wasti ct off AA Donald at Nottingham	1999
100th	65th	Inzamam-ul-Haq ct off L Klusener at Colombo-RPS	2000
150th	100th	CO Obuya ct off CK Langeveldt at Cape Town	2001
166th	113th	DR Martyn ct off R Telemachus at Centurion	2002
		This took him past DJ Richardson as the leading wicket-keeper for South Africa.	
200th	136th	Younis Khan ct off M Ntini at Paarl	2002
250th	166th	MHW Papps ct off M Ntini at Auckland	2004
300th	201st	G Gambhir ct off M Ntini at Hyderabad-RG	2005
350th	233rd	Abdul Razzaq ct off AJ Hall at Johannesburg	2007
400th	275th	SE Marsh st off J Botha at Sydney	2009
425th	295th	MG Johnson ct off JH Kallis at Durban	2011

Most dismissals in a Limited Overs International for South Africa

Name	Dis	Cts	Sts	Against	Venue	Season
MV Boucher	6	6	0	Pakistan	Cape Town	2006/07

Most dismissals in Limited Overs Internationals

Name	M	Cts	Sts	Dis	Dis/M
AC Gilchrist (Aus)	287	417	55	472	1.64
KC Sangakkara (SL)	354	353	85	438	1.23
MV Boucher (SA)	295	403	22	425	1.44
Moin Khan (Pak)	219	214	73	287	1.31
MS Dhoni (Ind)	226	212	75	287	1.26

Bowlers he took most dismissals off in Limited Overs Internationals

Bowler	M	Cts	Sts	Dis
M Ntini	164	75	0	75
SM Pollock	243	61	1	62
JH Kallis	256	47	0	47
AA Donald	64	26	0	26
L Klusener	136	23	0	23

Most dismissals by a wicket-keeper/bowler combination in Limited Overs Internationals

Keeper	Bowler	Team	M	Cts	Sts	Dis
MV Boucher	M Ntini	SA	164	75	0	75
AC Gilchrist	GD McGrath	Aus	167	72	1	73
MV Boucher	SM Pollock	SA	243	61	1	62
AC Gilchrist	B Lee	Aus	151	57	0	57
Moin Khan	Saqlain Mushtaq	Pak	119	16	31	47
KC Sangakkara	M Muralitharan	SL	205	22	25	47
MV Boucher	JH Kallis	SA	256	47	0	47

Twenty20 International career

Competition	M	Inns	NO	Runs	HS	Avg	SR	100	50	Ct	St
ICC World Twenty20	16	13	4	153	36	17.00	93.86	0	0	15	1
Other matches	9	8	2	115*	36	19.16	102.67	0	0	3	0
Totals	25	21	6	268*	36	17.86	97.45	0	0	18	1

He hit 22 fours and 2 sixes in his Twenty20 International career.
As a wicket-keeper he was involved in executing 3 run outs.

Against each opponent

Against	M	Inns	NO	Runs	HS	Avg	SR	100	50	Ct	St
Afghanistan	1	1	0	4	4	4.00	66.66	0	0	3	0
Australia	5	5	2	98*	36	32.66	127.27	0	0	1	0
Bangladesh	1	0	0	0	0	–	–	0	0	0	0
England	4	2	0	38	29	19.00	95.00	0	0	3	0
India	3	3	1	51	36	25.50	87.93	0	0	3	0
New Zealand	5	5	1	40	23	10.00	83.33	0	0	4	1
Pakistan	2	2	1	12	12	12.00	85.71	0	0	0	0
Scotland	1	1	0	2	2	2.00	66.66	0	0	0	0
West Indies	3	2	1	23*	17	23.00	79.31	0	0	4	0

In each country

Country	M	Inns	NO	Runs	HS	Avg	SR	100	50	Ct	St
Australia	3	3	0	53	29	17.66	112.76	0	0	0	0
England	6	5	2	36*	17	12.00	100.00	0	0	3	1
South Africa	11	8	2	150*	36	25.00	94.93	0	0	10	0
West Indies	5	5	2	29	12	9.66	85.29	0	0	5	0
Home	11	8	2	150*	36	25.00	94.93	0	0	10	0
Away	4	3	0	53	29	17.66	112.76	0	0	2	0
Neutral	10	10	4	65*	17	10.83	92.85	0	0	6	1

Boucher took 999 dismissals in all internationals. This includes 1 catch taken as a fielder (DM Bravo off RE van der Merwe at Port-of-Spain in a Limited Overs International in 2010). This is the most in all internationals. AC Gilchrist (Aus) is second with 905.

Career summary

Career record

Competition	M	Inns	NO	Runs	HS	Avg	SR	100	50	Ct	St
Tests	147	206	24	5515	125	30.30	50.13	5	35	532	23
First-class	212	306	42	8803	134	33.34	51.80	10	53	712	37
LO Internationals	295	221	57	4686	147*	28.57	84.75	1	26	403	22
List A Limited Overs	365	287	70	6219	147*	28.65	84.33	2	35	485	31
T20 Internationals	25	21	6	268	36*	17.86	97.45	0	0	18	1
Twenty20	90	76	27	1378	60	28.12	115.50	0	4	48	16

Highest scores

Tests	125	South Africa v Zimbabwe (Harare)	1999/00
First-class	134	South Africans vs Western Australia (Perth)	2001/02
LO Internationals	147*	South Africa vs Zimbabwe (Potchefstroom)	2006/07
List A Limited Overs	147*	South Africa vs Zimbabwe (Potchefstroom)	2006/07
T20 Internationals	36*	South Africa vs Australia (Johannesburg)	2008/09
Twenty20	60*	Warriors vs Titans (East London)	2010/11

First-class record for each team

Team	M	Inns	NO	Runs	HS	Avg	SR	100	50	Ct	St
Border	26	49	9	1684	112	42.10	54.49	3	10	101	9
Border B	4	5	1	70	47	17.50	38.37	0	0	1	1
Cape Cobras	3	4	0	180	131	45.00	64.05	1	0	2	0
South Africa	169	229	29	6302	134	31.51	51.19	6	39	578	26
South Africa A	1	1	1	26	26	–	35.13	0	0	5	0
Warriors	8	16	2	524	65	37.42	52.55	0	4	23	1
World XI	1	2	0	17	17	8.50	37.77	0	0	2	0

First-class record in each competition

Competition	M	Inns	NO	Runs	HS	Avg	SR	100	50	Ct	St
Test	147	206	24	5515	125	30.30	50.13	5	35	532	23
SuperSport Series	34	63	11	2166	131	41.65	53.20	4	12	119	8
UCB Bowl	4	5	1	70	47	17.50	38.37	0	0	1	1
Other First-class	27	32	6	1052	134	40.46	60.95	1	6	60	5

First-class centuries (outside of Tests)

Start Date	For	Against	Venue	Runs	Mins	Balls	Fours	Sixes
06/11/1998	Border	Northerns	Centurion	100*	158	102	10	4
28/01/2000	Border	Gauteng	Johannesburg	112	270	189	16	0
07/12/2001	South Africans	Western Australia	Perth	134	184	150	21	0
11/10/2002	Border	Boland	Paarl	112	257	215	11	0
02/02/2012	Cape Cobras	Knights	Cape Town	131	354	208	17	0

List A limited overs centuries (outside of internationals)

Date	For	Against	Venue	Runs	Balls	Fours	Sixes
16/10/2007	South Africans	Pakistan Cricket Board XI	Lahore-B	103	106	14	

Bowling

Boucher took one wicket in the 5.2 overs he bowled in first-class cricket and conceded 28 runs.

He bowled 1.2 overs and took 1 for 6 in Test cricket.

His only wicket in Test (and first-class cricket) was DJ Bravo, whom he dismissed ct AG Prince at St John's in 2005.

He did not bowl in List A limited overs or Twenty20.

Captaincies

Boucher captained South Africa in 4 Tests. South Africa won 2 and lost 2 of these Tests:

Start Date	Against	Venue	Toss	Decision	Result
22/02/2002	Australia	Johannesburg	Lost	Bat	Lost
08/03/2002	Australia	Cape Town	Won	Bat	Lost
15/03/2002	Australia	Durban	Won	Bowl	Won
18/10/2002	Bangladesh	East London	Lost	Bowl	Won

He captained South Africa once in a Limited Overs International: vs Pak Rawalpindi on 21/10/2003 and won.
In all first-class cricket he was captain 10 times, winning 4, losing 3 and drawing 3 of these matches.
In all List A limited overs matches he was captain twice and won both.
He captained Eastern Cape 7 times in Twenty20 matches, winning 3 and losing 4.

Appearances

Most Tests for South Africa

Name	Start	End	Tests
JH Kallis	1995/96	2012/13	161
MV Boucher	1997/98	2011/12	146
GC Smith	2001/02	2012/13	109
SM Pollock	1995/96	2007/08	108
G Kirsten	1993/94	2003/04	101
M Ntini	1997/98	2009/10	101

Boucher missed only 6 Tests in his career.

Most consecutive Test appearances for South Africa

Name	From	Until	Tests
AB de Villiers	17/12/2004	22/02/2013	85
MV Boucher	14/02/1998	11/08/2004	75
HM Amla	27/04/2006	22/02/2013	67
JH Kallis	26/12/1997	02/01/2003	60
MV Boucher	13/01/2005	06/02/2010	54
G Kirsten	26/12/1993	18/03/1999	53

Boucher, IA Healy and Kapil Dev are the only players to have two separate sequences of 50 consecutive appearances for their country in Test cricket.

Most consecutive Limited Overs International appearances for South Africa

Name	From	Until	Tests
SM Pollock	28/03/2000	13/02/2005	133
WJ Cronje	21/12/1994	27/03/2000	125
MV Boucher	06/10/2002	01/07/2007	120

Most Limited Overs Internationals for South Africa

Name	Start	End	LOIs
JH Kallis	1995/96	2011/12	316
SM Pollock	1995/96	2007/08	294
MV Boucher	1997/98	2011/12	290
HH Gibbs	1996/97	2009/10	248
JN Rhodes	1991/92	2002/03	245

Team-mates appearing in 100 or more Tests together

Players	Team	Tests
RS Dravid and SR Tendulkar	India	146
MV Boucher and JH Kallis	South Africa	137
RS Dravid and VVS Laxman	India	132
A Kumble and SR Tendulkar	India	122
VVS Laxman and SR Tendulkar	India	120
DPMD Jayawardene and KC Sangakkara	Sri Lanka	115
RS Dravid and SC Ganguly	India	113
ME Waugh and SR Waugh	Australia	108
RS Dravid and A Kumble	India	107
Kapil Dev and DB Vengsarkar	India	104
GD McGrath and SK Warne	Australia	104
SK Warne and ME Waugh	Australia	103
IA Healy and MA Taylor	Australia	103
SC Ganguly and SR Tendulkar	India	103
JH Kallis and GC Smith	South Africa	102
IA Healy and SR Waugh	Australia	101